W9-CEH-006

THE AMERICA OF JOSÉ MARTÍ

THE AMERICA

OF JOSÉ MARTÍ

Selected writings of José Martí

translated from the Spanish

by JUAN DE ONÍS

with an introduction

by FEDERICO DE ONÍS

MINERVA PRESS

Copyright 1954 by The Noonday Press, Inc.
Library of Congress Catalog Card No.: 68-23105

First paperbound edition published in 1968
by arrangement with Farrar, Straus &
Giroux, Inc.

Printed in the United States of America

Funk & Wagnalls, *A Division of* Reader's
Digest Books, Inc.

CONTENTS

José Martí

When the news reached New York of the death of José Martí in action on the 19th of May, 1895, Charles A. Dana wrote an editorial for *The Sun* on May 23 which might have served as Martí's epitaph. Today, fifty-eight years later, no better introduction could be found for this selection of his writings here presented to North American readers for the first time:

"We learn with poignant sorrow of the death of José Martí, the well-known leader of Cuban revolution. We knew him long and well, and esteemed him profoundly. For a protracted period, beginning twenty-odd years ago, he was employed as a contributor to *The Sun*, writing on subjects and questions of the fine arts. In these things his learning was solid and extensive, and his ideas and conclusions were original and brilliant. He was a man of genius, of imagination, of hope, and of courage, one of those descendants of the Spanish race whose American birth and instincts seem to have added to the revolutionary tincture which all modern Spaniards inherit. His heart was warm and affectionate, his opinions ardent and aspiring, and he died as such a man might wish to die, battling for liberty and democracy. Of such heroes there are not too many in the world, and his warlike grave testified that, even in a positive and material age, there are spirits that can give all for their principles without thinking of any selfish return for themselves.

"Honor to the memory of José Martí, and peace to his manly and generous soul!"

It is good to know that there was at least one outstanding North American, during Martí's life-time, who was aware of the calibre of this Spanish-American who created a body of writing which, in the opinion of his contemporaries and posterity, makes him one of the pinnacles of the Hispanic literary world. He was not merely one of the many great writers Spanish America has produced since the literary revolution known as *Modernismo* at the turn of the century. Martí represents something of a far higher and more enduring import: a man who alone and by the sole virtue of his creative power converted his human and literary personality into the purest and most intemporal expression of his race, and who, for this reason, stands out above all the others of his epoch.

When Dana said that "he was a man of genius," without knowing it he, the North American, was saying what the Spanish Americans who were reading what Martí was writing in New York had been saying. His articles in the newspapers of Argentina, Mexico, Venezuela and other countries brought to those distant and separated points of the broad Hispanic world that new voice with new ideas and a new style which aroused an immediate response in the greatest men of the period. The greatest of them all, the old Argentinian Domingo Faustino Sarmiento, shortly before his death in 1889, wrote to Paul Groussac, an Argentinian of French birth, and the mentor of the new generation, urging him to translate into French the articles Martí was writing for *La Nación* of Buenos Aires, because there was nothing in Spanish comparable to him, nor in French after Victor Hugo, and he likened his literary style to that of Goya's painting. About the same time a young Nicaraguan, Rubén Darío, who was just beginning his glorious literary career, and who was to become the greatest poet of the Spanish language since the Golden Age, and one of the greatest of any language, stated as his literary goal: "If only I could put into verse the luminosities of Martí!" And after Martí's death the evaluation he passed on him has been confirmed by all succeeding critics: "What is known as genius has raised its head twice in Spanish America; the first time in an illustrious son of this land, Sarmiento, the second, in Martí." These judgments were confirmed in Spain by the greatest writer of the period, Miguel de Unamuno, in whose opinion there had been three culminating moments of the Spanish spirit in America in three moments of its history: Bolívar, at the time of its independence; Sarmiento, at the time of the nations' formation; and Martí, creator and leader of the contemporary epoch.

This unanimous opinion on the part of men so different from each other cannot be mistaken, nor the fact that Martí has been steadily growing until today he is the most vibrant and living of Spanish-American writers and the one who exercises the strongest influence on the new generations. When the centenary of Martí's birth was observed in Havana this year, at the congress of writers devoted to the study of Martí there were men and women from every country of the Hispanic community. All of them look upon Martí as their own. For the Cubans he is, naturally, their national hero; he was a Cuban, and he lived and died for Cuba. The others regard him as theirs, for in his incredibly active, incredibly fecund, brief, exemplary and dolorous life, one of the purest that has ever been lived on this earth, he identified himself with every Spanish country as though it were his own, thus living his concept of Spanish America as a *magna patria*. His greatness does not come from the events in which he participated, which, in the last analysis, were episodic and limited even in the framework of America's history, but resides in him, in the universality and eternal quality he breathed into everything he touched. The political and revolutionary labor to which he sacrificed his life, was the work of his spirit expressed through the medium of words. His action and his example live on for us in his writings. Everything he wrote reveals the same powerful originality, and makes us realize that we are in the presence of a writer of unique, unmistakable accent.

This was the impression he produced during his lifetime on all who heard him speak or read his articles. The opinions quoted from Sarmiento, Rubén Darío and Charles Dana are outstanding examples of the reaction of all who knew him. A humble Cuban cigar maker spoke for all of them who listened rapt to his speeches in New York and Tampa when he said: "At times we don't understand him well, but we would die for him."

His wandering, tormented existence denied him the concentration and repose he would have needed to produce more ambitious works, and his writing for the most part was of the moment; but every word he wrote has enduring vitality. He began writing as a youth in Cuba—the deep root of his childhood, always alive in him, as is the case with every man of genius—until in 1871 he was exiled to Spain. From 1871 to 1874 he wrote in Spain, the Spain of his parents, while he was a student in Madrid and Zaragoza; it was there "the slight flower of my life" came into bloom, and his spirit was formed in the fervor of the new ideas brought by the revolution of 1868. But America was his destiny, and after a brief stay in France in 1874 he came to Mexico in 1875. There and in Guatemala he lived until 1879, forming part of the literary and intellectual life of those countries, until on January 3, 1880, he came to New York where, except for several months in Venezuela in 1881, he lived until January 31, 1895. This was the date on which he set out with the expedition of liberation for Cuba where he met his glorious death on May 19. Up to the day before his death he wrote his diary and his letters. All this literary output, so varied, so haphazard, much of it unpublished or buried in publications of local circulation and in limited private editions printed in New York, was inaccessible to Hispanic readers until it was collected years after his death. Acquaintance with the work of Martí has consequently been slow and difficult even in Spanish, and much more so in other languages. Aside from a contemporary translation of several of his poems by the North American poetess, Celia Charles, in 1898, only a few of his poems and articles have appeared in English.

Martí's literary life was bounded by the triangle—Spanish America, Spain, the United States—symbolic of the new epoch which began with him, of which he had a clearer awareness than anyone else, and which we can comprehend only through him. This is the essential theme of Martí's work: the search for the originality of Spanish America—which he and all the Spanish Americans who followed him were to call "Our America"—with Spain as its past and unity, and the United States as its common destiny, for better or worse.

The fifteen years Martí lived in New York represent the peak of his literary activity. He wrote occasionally on Spanish themes for North American publications like *The Sun* and *The Hour,* and abundantly for Spanish-American newspapers on all manner of themes. In these articles, as in his prologues and speeches, he reveals an ideology pregnant with flashes of genius and expressed in one of the most personal styles in Spanish literature. In his poems, he gives the purest and noblest of himself, with supreme power and originality. In his work is to be found the origins of *Modernismo* and the literature which has developed from it down to this day. The style of his prose and his poetry comes from a deep, highly personal assimilation of Spanish classics and the cosmopolitan literature of the end of the nineteenth century, especially the English and North American. His style is difficult in Spanish and almost defies translation into a foreign language, as Dana remarked in a letter telling Martí how much he admired the prose of the articles he contributed to *The Sun*, and how difficult it was for him to do them justice in translation.

Many of the articles he wrote in New York dealt with North American subjects. These comprise the many volumes of his completed works entitled *North American Men* and *North American Scenes*. Martí was the interpreter to South Americans of the culture of the United States, of its writers, politicians, its good and its bad men, as well as of the most diverse aspects of the life and customs of this country. It is a searching moral interpretation of the United States of the Eighties, from the pen of a foreigner, European in his culture and formation, but an American from the other America, who understood and loved what was American as opposed to European, and was able to perceive the original values of the United States, and, at the same time, to see the difference between the two Americas.

By way of the United States and Europe, Martí arrived at a new interpretation of Spanish America, more comprehensive than that of the nineteenth century, and which is still valid and effective today. The North American reader will find in the examples of Martí's work presented here much to remember and much to learn about his own country at a moment that was decisive in its history, though not too well known. But, above all, he will learn to understand the other America by understanding the man who was not only its finest interpreter, but the most eminent product of its spirit in modern times.

Federico de Onís

THE AMERICA OF JOSÉ MARTÍ

I: THE OTHER

AMERICA

GENERAL GRANT

September 1885

He came into the world poor; as a boy he took more pleasure in horses than in books, and he hauled cord wood; at the Military Academy he distinguished himself by his fine horsemanship; he reached the rank of captain in the Mexican War, but either because of lack of sobriety or some question of debts, he was asked to resign from the Army; his fortieth year overtook him setting up billiards, tanning hides, and collecting rents; four years later he was commander-in-chief of a standing army of 250,000 soldiers fighting for the liberty of man; another four years and he was presiding chaotically over the destiny of his republic.

Later he toured the world in triumph, received the keys to the first cities, and accepted the greetings of presidents and kings on behalf of their nations; then he fell into the toils of shady finance from a vulgar craving for wealth; now he has died, ennobled by his sufferings. The generals he conquered in battle have accompanied him to his tomb at the head of 50,000 soldiers. These are men of a new cast, living in radiant times, who, in twenty years, have learned to sincerely love the one who frustrated their hopes, laid waste their dominions, and conquered them on the battle-field. These are true men, who do not mortgage the lives of generations and the peace of their homeland to avenge defeats and settle old scores!

One fights the good fight. Nature has placed the need to see justice done in some souls, and the need to flout and affront it in others. But once justice has been at-tained, men who are worthy of peace bury enmity in a superior brotherhood that springs from common con-tact with death, and devote themselves to the accus-tomed tasks of life, enriched by the national bounty that falls to nations whose sons have stood the acid test. The brave forget. It is those who fought less bravely, or those who fought without justice and live in fear of their victory, who forget the least. There are nations and men that present a golden surface beneath which is a cave of ghosts that will not be laid. Only petty nations perpetuate civil strife. Conflicts in which man's reason is supplanted by his ferocity are resolved man to man, horse against horse; afterward, like Washing-ton's militiamen when they emerged victorious, like the Confederates at Appomattox where they conceded de-feat, soldiers bid their generals farewell, and return to the free pursuits that preserve the strength and majesty of men, enriched by their new stature and that of their adversaries, without subjecting their country to the crushing burden of idle arms, or demanding com-pensation, like crass mercenaries, for simply having done their duty.

Ulysses Grant was the one born poor, in a squat

wooden cabin in an out-of-the-way corner of Ohio; velvet and black crepe hung from the marble buildings and stone mansions when, to the tolling of bells across the nation, his coffin was followed through the streets of New York by Johnston, routed from Atlanta by Sherman, Grant's lieutenant; by Buckner, from whom Grant himself took 7,000 prisoners at Fort Donelson; by Fitzhugh Lee, nephew and lieutenant of the brilliant and kind man whom Grant alone forced to surrender. Mountains culminate in peaks and nations in men. Let us see how a great captain is formed in a modern nation.

His birthplace was a typical settler's home: one story, wooden walls, a ridgepole roof with an inside chimney, a door set between two windows, a board fence, a shrub-filled backyard hard against the forest, and beside the door, a tree. There, in the affection of his good wife, Grant's father would rest from his work as a tanner, relate the exploits of his forebears, who were brave, resolute Scots, or dash off a newspaper article with an experienced hand. Grant was the product of eight American generations of farmers and soldiers. Are the qualities of parents intensified as they are handed down to their children? Can it be that men are simply embodiments of concentrated and accentuated spiritual forces? "Steadfast! Steadfast!," read the mottoes of Grant's lineage: they are blazoned on a smoking mountain and four burning heights. "Steadfast, Craig Ellachiel!" An English regiment that was of the bravest to serve in India mingled its blood in Grant's veins. Burning mountain, regiment, steadfast: all are found in Grant, all go forward with him, mauling, crushing, grinding, punishing. On the Chickahominy, where in one quarter of an hour he had just lost 11,000 men, he ordered the attack renewed without moving from his camp chair. At Vicksburg, he said to an old lady who gave him water: "I will stay here until I take Vicksburg if it takes me thirty years!" At Chattanooga: "Upward! Upward!," up the mountain, through the clouds, over the clouds; those below see what seem ribbons of fire and hear the rattle of gunfire; the flag comes up among the flashing muskets; from the crest, the shot rains down the far slope in pursuit of the Confederates; the burning mountain!

He was a dull student as a boy. Books irked him, as they always would. They say he heard a shot at the age of two without flinching: "Again! Again!" By the time he was eight, he was clambering atop every horse at hand. He appeared slight, but actually he was strong. He was educated in the manner of all poor country children of his day: school in the winter, work in the summer.

When he was twelve, he drove the buggy of some ladies on an outing. As they forded a stream, the ladies noticed in shrill alarm that the horses had lost their footing. "Keep quiet, and I will get you through safely." They reached the far bank unharmed.

He asked his father to buy him a horse to make a team with one he owned, and repaid his father by hauling logs cut from the forest by the hired hand. He hauled wood for eight months. One day he could not find the hand. He unhitched the horse from the wagon and made it drag the logs piled on a felled tree, from which he rolled them on to the wagon and drew them home. "What has become of the hand?" "I do not know, and care less. I loaded the wagon by myself."

And so he grew, beside a plain and loyal mother, and an intelligent, if unsuccessful, father.

Through the good offices of his congressman, he entered the Military Academy at West Point, at seventeen. He excelled in riding; his studies went badly. He was the best rider in his class; but at the end of the course of study, of thirty-nine graduates, he ranked twenty-first in his class. He had been quiet, little given to games, obedient and courteous: "a good cadet." Mathematics were not distasteful to him. He learned more of military discipline, tactics, ordnance and ballistics than of mineralogy, geology, chemistry, engineering and mechanics. He fell deeply in love, which is a sign of personality. He married young, which is a sign of nobility. He went, as a second lieutenant, to the frontier, like all young officers.

In those years, ambitious men and slave-state advocates had joined forces in the United States to wrest from Mexico a portion of its territory. American settlers poured into Texas, and soon raised the territory in rebellion as a state rightfully belonging to the United States by will of its inhabitants. Mexico protested. The Southern slaveholders, who had been struggling since the turn of the century to introduce slavery into the free states, or increase the number of slave states, favored the annexation of Texas on that basis. Van Buren, aspiring to the Democratic presidential nomination, criticized the proposed annexation on the grounds that it would lead to an unjust war with Mexico; but Polk, his opponent and the embodiment of the annexationist principle, was nominated and elected. American troops entered Texas on the pretext of protecting their fellow citizens and presently advanced beyond the southernmost borders of the state. Arita's troops opposed them, which Polk seized on as an excuse to officially declare war. Taylor marched on Mexico with Grant among his officers. He made headway, as injustice generally does. Grant fought against the downy-cheeked cadets who fell smiling side by side on the lava bluffs of Chapultepec in the shadow of the last Mexican flag. Grant was cited for bravery in one engagement. But he distinguished himself in no other way, although he was now twenty-five years old. However, he served creditably as paymaster, which taught him how to care for soldiers on campaign, and how to handle transportation and supplies. The knowledge of details is indispensable to greatness; impetus must be sustained by experience.

+

It seems that on his return from Mexico, where he was breveted captain, he did not maintain the sobriety that decorum counsels. It is generally thought that the sad habit became so manifest in him that if he had not acceded to a request by his superiors that he resign his commission, he would have faced court martial; but it must be added, in all fairness, that it does not appear that he persisted in the habit during the dark and bitter years spent in drab employments until the Civil War burst upon the country, although some of his biographers insist that he continued in it even during the glorious years and that it accounts for some of the

errors and blunders of his command. Grant knocked
about on farms and in small villages. He set up a bil-
liard parlor in California, but the venture failed. He
went to live on a farm belonging to his wife where he
would cut fire wood, haul it to town, and sell it for a pit-
tance. He was not much good at making money, for he
was openhanded, and could not close his eyes to misery.
He hungered for wealth; yet he was not grasping or
bullying by nature. So when he began collecting rents,
as he made his rounds selling wood, heavy shouldered
and deliberate in his walk, his face hidden by the
slouching brim of his felt hat, in shirt-sleeves, with his
trousers tucked into high boots, there were more accounts that mounted in arrears than those he collected,
although he always remembered those labors with some
pride. "Those were good days, friend," he once said in
the White House to a former customer, since elected to
Congress, who timidly paid him a visit when he was
President Grant: "Those were good days, because I was
doing everything I could to support my family." He continued the conversation with the wife of the old customer, recalling how he would come with the wood on
the chill mornings, piling and measuring it with his
own hands, and go around later to her husband's office
to collect payment. But things went badly, and he
finally had to take a job at $600 a year in Galena where
his father and brother had a tannery; by then Grant
was pushing forty.

He was a better listener than a talker, and seemed an
ordinary sort to the townspeople. He aspired to an appointment as county engineer, but he was disappointed.
He walked; he listened; he smoked. He never showed

impatience. Yet he harbored deep-seated envies, dating
from the war, of others, who by fortune's whim, or the
influence of powerful friends, attained prominent posts,
without the qualifications, perhaps, which he thought
to see in himself. These resentments barely suggest
themselves, even to the most discerning eye, in his intimate confidences, few and far between to be sure, as it
should always be with confidences, with a brother officer who felt a sympathy toward Grant that bordered
on veneration: Sherman, who looked after Grant's interests as though he were a child in his trust, and his
reputation even more than to his own.

Sherman, tall, eloquent, fiery, tense, stimulating,
restless, outspoken, formidable; Grant, short, heavy-
shouldered, slow, colorless in speech, of impassive eye,
who took in all he heard, but kept his own counsel.
Grant, who conceived laboriously, and turned over what
he had heard slowly in his mind; Sherman, who erupted
in ideas and plans, like a shower of sparks, before his
silent friend. Sometimes a whole speech by Sherman
would go unanswered by Grant. He would retire within
himself, and although he was always quick to praise
merit in his subordinates, and spontaneously recognize
the part they played in his triumphs, with a singular
and absolute generosity, if he felt their influence, he
never showed it, and would worry at another's plan and
reflect on it so long that by the time he put it in action
it was virtually his own. And his person attained such
exaggerated dimensions in the eyes of others, that it
took on the highest importance to him, and clouded his
judgement.

But in those dark days in Galena in the obscurity of

the tannery, he gave no evidence of remarkable qualities. Perhaps the cloud that hung over his departure
from the Army, and the failure that dogged his humble
enterprises, had undermined his self-confidence and
discouraged him; perhaps, with that impatience that is
characteristic of all original, forceful characters, he
chafed constantly in mute outrage at the disharmony
between the meanness of his reality and the boldness of
his aspirations. Silence is the modesty of men of great
character; complaint is a prostitution of character.
Whoever is capable of greatness and dies without being
summoned to fulfill his promise, dies in peace, for he
knows that somewhere his hour will come. And if it
does not come, well and good; there is greatness enough
in the capacity for greatness.

Grant was not of an amiable nature, and while he did
not reject the infrequent affections he inspired, he
never sought friendship, even in his darkest hours. He
lived and journeyed within himself. He came from the
country, always original and renewed, and from himself. He was little alloyed by the stuff of the human
average, and he always felt strange and uneasy among
the worldly, sometimes like a man overwhelmed, habit-
uated to defeat at every turn, sometimes rebellious, like
one who heeds the call of a superior voice. The first
mood, nurtured by his painful memories of military life,
and his unsuccessful bid for the engineer's post, caused
him to shun politics, that complex art, even in villages,
of allaying fears and inspiring confidence in simple
souls. Yet it was not that he disliked artifice in itself; it
simply was not his way. His martial calling predisposed
him to attack and seize rather than lay plans and wait,

and he lacked the subtlety and pliability which assure success in politics. His domineering nature recoiled from the trying, constant servitude that is nearly always the price of political pre-eminence. Entrance into politics would have appealed to him, but only as one enters an enemy garrison: laying down terms. His understanding of politics sometimes seemed uncertain; but in his country, politics was the only form of authority. He was a Democrat, because in those days the Democratic party stood for state's rights and the rights of individuals, which appealed to Grant for he was always jealous of his own. But at the age of forty Grant had voted in only one election. A citizen who fails to vote is to a republic what a soldier who deserts is to an army.

An irresistible sympathy draws original spirits together. Looking closely, one can discern two types of men in constant struggle: those who spring from Nature, vigorous and genuine, active and solitary, recognized and acclaimed only in the moments of grave crisis when they are needed; and those who are molded by conventions, who hide their spirit as though it were a sin, who defend and maintain the established, who live in comfort and happiness, and in the social movement are only useful as a healthy resisting force in those cases in which a natural character, drunk with power, takes the bit between his teeth and exceeds his function.

There was another natural character in Galena: the lawyer Rawlins, a tree of virtue, wholly compounded of valor and justice. He spoke in explosions. He gave birth to ideas, and emitted them directly, like rays of light.

He spoke with biblical conciseness and grandeur and the
supreme eloquence that springs from life itself, beside
which the eloquence of the academies pales, as a painted
coquette beside the bloom of a maiden of natural
beauty. Rawlins made his living as a charcoal burner
until he was twenty-three. The same Rawlins would die
later while serving as Secretary of War: self-educated;
self-taught in the law; self-established in the esteem
of his fellow attorneys; and self-reliant in thought and
deed. He could think and act on his own without fear,
for he was dominated by only one passion—justice. But
he had that superior prudence which prolonged suffering engenders in men of true strength, the fortunate
quality which in the scale of natural characters dis-
tinguishes the disinterested from the egotistical; but
only in the disinterested is there real greatness. Rawlins was well endowed with powers of expression, with
intuition, staunchness, honesty, judgement. He crushed
intrigues as he might have crushed vipers. He could
not tolerate an arbitrary act or an injury committed,
even against a turtledove. He wanted truth to triumph,
even when his role in the triumph went unsuspected.
Back in the days when he sold leather, Grant drew close
to that man, little by little. He learned by listening to
his pleadings; in his counsel, he found a master; from
Rawlin's lips, Grant heard the ideas that in their rudimentary, instinctive form taxed his brain, delivered
in their finished and perfect form. The lawyer and the
tanner discussed at length the mounting quarrel with
the South, whose growing recklessness caused amazement in the townspeople of Galena, as throughout the
Union.

Those were the days of the noblest crusade that has ever been seen on earth. From ocean to ocean the northern states rallied to one cry: "There shall be no more slaves."

From the day Garrison founded *The Liberator* there was no peace in the Union. How ideas prosper! *The Liberator* was an insignificant sheet when it appeared in 1831, the first vehicle of the abolitionist idea; by 1840, it had produced divisions within the major parties contending for power, and given rise to the Liberty party composed of abolitionists who insisted on the preservation of the Union against the fulminations of their own apostle, Garrison, who described the Constitution, which sanctioned slavery in the South, as a "covenant with death and an agreement with hell." The 7,000 voters who gave their support to the Liberty party in 1840 had grown to 62,500 four years later. In 1848, an impressive anti-slavery front made up of dissidents from all parties, carried 300,000 votes under the standard of "free soil for a free country." By 1856, they were 1,341,000 and in 1860 they were the presidency: they were Lincoln. Where has such greatness been seen before, such generous motives, such burning words, such disinterested leadership, such fruitful, militant virtue? Crusaders of other ages have fought in time of war from a desire for heavenly rewards and a love of adventure; but these American crusaders sacrificed the tranquility of their homes in a period of peace and prosperity to free the most wretched race on earth. Theirs were the purses, and the sacrifice; theirs the raised voices, and the passion; theirs the families, the anchor of life, the endearing bond in a free and prosperous country. The South, accustomed to having its way, looked with rage on the opponents of its will, and rampant upon its slaves, defied the freemen of the North.

Slow, like all that are strong, cautious, like all workers, the North looked, first with fear and always with sorrow, on the dangers of the rupture which the South was provoking. There was no peace after *The Liberator* appeared in 1831. The South pursued Garrison's newspaper with every weapon at its command; through President Jackson it asked Congress to enforce strict measures against abolitionist propaganda.

The South asked for new lands in which to breed slavery; the North, obligated by the Constitution to recognize slavery in states where it already existed, fell back on the Constitution to combat its introduction into new states. If a territory came up for statehood, the South would claim it for itself in order to extend slavery and gain a voting advantage over the North in the Senate. The North, weary of the inhumanity and arrogance of the South, would demand free statehood for the territory, already teeming with Southern marauders challenging abolitionist settlers for possession of the land with nocturnal raids and rural forays. When Wilmott proposed that any states that might enter the Union as a result of the Mexican War be allowed to determine freely whether they wanted to be slave or free, the South rose up as though a blow had been struck at its vitals. It countered the energetic stand of the North, the policies of the Free Soil party, and the words of Wendell Phillips with this brazen proposal put forward through the person of Calhoun when the question arose of admitting California to the Union: legal formalization of an equal balance of power in Congress between the North and South. Henry Clay's powerful speeches obtained the famous compromise, that put off the conflict already impending in 1850, by which the South agreed to recognize California and the District of Columbia as free and the right of New Mexico and Utah to declare themselves free or slave, in exchange for the North's acceptance of Texas as slave, and return of runaway slaves under a fugitive slave law. The South, victorious again, felt itself secure. The North fumed in shame and frustration against the fugitive law. Diplomatic envoys, who were adherents to the Southern cause, met in Europe and put forward a project for the territorial extension of slavery; and in 1856, against the Republican party, which came into being with 1,500,000 votes against the extension of slavery into the free states and territories, Buchanan, one of the three European ministers, was elected to the presidency. The North picked up the gauntlet. The North was now one party and the South another.

Who in the North will return a runaway slave? The legislatures of the free states passed laws which ran counter to the provisions of the fugitive slave law. The fires of martyrs and apostles burned bright again. John Brown offered himself as a sacrifice, and transformed idea into action. From the scaffold on which he died, because he violated the written law, an army arose, swarming in search of leaders and a field of battle. When the new elections approached and the Republican party, in a glorious stroke, elected Lincoln without a single vote from the routed Southern states, the omi-

nous war was now on every tongue. The legislature of
South Carolina called a popular convention to discuss
the right of a state to leave the Union; whereupon, she
and eleven other states seceded and, in congress united,
formed the Confederacy of America and elected Jefferson Davis president. Arsenals, customs, forts, all the
installations and property of the government fell without opposition into hands of the Confederates, who
finally fired on Fort Sumter. A rail-splitter was in the
White House; a tanner was in Galena!

Grant heard the news. "Feeling it the duty of everyone who has been educated at Government expense to
offer their services for the support of that Government,
I have the honor, very respectfully, to tender my services. . . ." Rawlins, in a fiery speech, broke with his
party and backed the Union, in whose defense he en-
listed immediately. Lincoln had called for 75,000 volunteers. Since Grant was the only soldier in Galena, he
was assigned the task of training the company from
Galena and delivering it to the Governor. It is painful
to recall that in those days the crestfallen soldier had
to go from door to door like a beggar seeking a command that was everywhere denied him. He, who five
years later would lead four armies with sure tread on
the path to victory, could not find at first the meanest
place in the armies of his country. He applied to the
Adjutant General, who gave him no reply. Twice he
tried for an appointment under McClellan, who knew
him; twice he was ignored. For lack of qualified in-
structors, they finally made him colonel of a regiment,
which he trained and organized with such ability, that
when he was made brigadier general, thanks to a state

official who was always friendly to him, it came as no surprise to those who had seen him among his soldiers. Rawlins, who rarely erred, was already at his side as his secretary and aide, preparing his victory; Rawlins, the veiled suggestion, the shrewd yet self-effacing counsel, the prudence that restrains, the exact word. Then was seen again the power of man to rise to the level of his difficulties.

Sixteen thousand men comprised the army of the United States at the beginning of the war, which ended five years later under Grant's command with 1,000,561 soldiers in active service and 2,254,000 reservists under arms; sixteen thousand men, scattered about the country in distant posts by Buchanan's Secretary of War so they might not impede the organization under arms of the Confederacy which vied with the North in a race to see who could cover its territories with soldiers first. The North had an army of volunteers in a matter of days. The states and cities organized troops in competition. The Government offered from $100 to $400 to each volunteer. In an instant there were 750,000; then another 450,000; then 300,000 more. One can expect these sudden surges of deep-seated vigor in the United States, which assume a special greatness in the moments of their appearance because of the indecision and reluctance that have preceded them. Superficial observers take this for indifference, when it is actually the natural caution of a marvelously prosperous country that looks at its problems long and hard before deciding on a course of action that might prove dangerous. The elephant is slower in rising than the deer.

Almost no one foresaw the magnitude of the war at its start. One general laughed at another's request for 200,000 to defend a position in the West. But in a later campaign, 100,000 Federals died in one winter between the Rapidan and the James, which run close by and almost side by side. There was hardly an engagement in which casualties did not run into the thousands. Shiloh, Gettysburg, Antietam, Chattanooga, Wilderness, Chickahominy, which of these did not see at least 20,000 dead?

When Grant advanced against Lee, powerful and impenetrable as a mobile mountain, the Federals died at the rate of 1000 a day from May to June in one sector of the front. Forward, ranks! A nation forged from men of all nations must remain free for all men! Free! said Lincoln, and the shackles fell from four million slaves when he fulfilled his promise to himself and to his Maker to issue the Emanicipation Proclamation if the Confederates were driven from Maryland. Those who oppose the freedom of four million souls must finally surrender, broken forever!

There is no political juggling that can give their cause the slightest semblance of justice. Wars should be seen from the clouds. It is well that a half-million human beings should have died if by so doing they preserved for Humanity the only free home it has in the universe. Seething, working, clasped in an embrace, even to fight, mankind must seem like those great banks of living tubers, slowly, incessantly moving to break the roots of the trees that perhaps become tubers themselves in a freer, more active form of life. Mankind is a clenched fist straining to break out from the bowels of the earth. Who does not glimpse in the immensity of man's tribulations in his rudimentary state, the joyous glory that awaits him after his purifying and dolorous passage through the world? What peace must crown such a beginning! Thoughts of a happiness so supreme carry one away, yet how few discern it, smug in their own small machine, their shell of bones!

The war bursts into flame; the South throws itself against the North; it holds the Southern coast; it establishes the Confederate capital in Richmond, thirty leagues from Washington, the seat of the Union. It controls the Southwest; its tents are pitched along the Potomac and the James. It ascends and dominates the Mississippi in the West, and the ports at the junction with the Ohio, swollen not far upstream by the Tennessee and the Cumberland. Victory falls to the master of the rivers, for rivers are the veins of war. With them go all the lands they drain. With control of the Mississippi, the Confederacy cannot be hedged in between the river and the ocean in its eastern states, nor divided from the rebel territories to the West where it wants to breed slavery. How do the rivers give their waters to such men?

By occupying the mouths of the Ohio, the Tennessee and the Cumberland, the South assures itself of the central states which become the northern and western fronts of the war. The mouth of the Ohio acts as a hub for Illinois, Missouri, Tennessee, and Kentucky, which converge on that point like spokes. The master of the Tennessee has an open road on its waters to the heart of the rebel state of Alabama. The master of the Cumberland controls Tennessee and Kentucky. Galena is in Illinois, whose southern limit is the mouth of the Ohio. Grant of Galena is in command in that sector! The Confederates move up toward that hub to forestall a Federal advance and extend northward, with a buffer zone of defense, the territory covered by their railroad system, which is indispensable to the movement of troops and supplies. The railroads of Mississippi, Alabama, Georgia, South Carolina, and Virginia converge on Chattanooga, on the Tennessee. The Confederates fortify their rivers. They seal themselves within their bastion between the river and the sea.

To the West they have the Mississippi; to the North, the Ohio, Tennessee, and Cumberland; their eastern flank is covered by the Atlantic, and their southern, by the Gulf of Mexico.

Vicksburg defends the Mississippi against the Federals; Fort Henry defends the Tennessee; Fort Donelson defends the Cumberland. Charleston is the bulwark in the east, and New Orleans in the south. One need not occupy all points in war, only the principal ones. In the interior, the Potomac and the James, mushroomed with campaign tents, defend Richmond. From the very beginning, then, the war will be a struggle for control of the rivers; the coastal cities are less important. The armies will take their names from the rivers. Their routes are already laid out for them. If New Orleans and Charleston must be taken by sea, Fort Henry and Fort Donelson must be taken by land to control the Tennessee and strike into Alabama; Vicksburg must be taken to control the Mississippi and divide the Confederacy; the Potomac and the James must be crossed to take Richmond.

Now comes the protracted planning, the paralysis of the Northern armies, the surprise, and the jealousy between generals. Only the genius is unruffled by the unexpected, because that is the province of genius. It is not seen that this is a war of size and numbers, and can be won only in those terms. There is one who sees this, but as yet he holds his peace; there is one who is advised by an inspired, energetic man. It is a question of conquering not a skilled, but a daring enemy. Daring must be met with daring. The South advances; there is not time to train a perfect army. Perfect armies are not improvised. The South attacks with its brilliant, disordered masses; they must be opposed, if it is possible, with larger numbers. If the North delays to make preparations, the South will also prepare; at the end of long preparation both will remain equal in strength. "The one who attacks first now will be victorious." This was the case in Fort Donelson, where Grant said it, as in the whole course of the war. With barely enough troops to launch an attack, Grant goes forward, with his high-crowned hat and the cigar in his lips, to "attack first," while the academic generals wander in the proximity of the defiant Potomac with their courage mired in a bog of theories.

Paducah is in Kentucky on the Ohio near the mouth of the Tennessee; Cairo is on the junction of the Ohio and the Mississippi, and is the key to the West. The rebel marauders are already abroad in the loyal state of Kentucky. Grant must secure the mouth of the Ohio before he can attack Fort Henry for control of the Tennessee, and Fort Donelson for control of the

Cumberland. He occupies Paducah without violence. "I
am not concerned," he said in his proclamation, "with
opinions, only with the armed rebels and those who aid
and conceal them." Grant's good judgement always per-
ceived the utility and high purpose of Rawlins' plans,
who, in turn, put into lucid and memorable expression
the confused inspirations of his chief. Grant moves on
Cairo, which has 7,000 men, with only 3,000 raw, un-
disciplined Federals. The enemy comes out to meet
him; the day ends in hard fighting and he appears to
have won; in that night of waiting "my heart was in
my throat." The dawn finds him on the road to Cairo,
abandoned by the Confederates: "From that day, I
never hesitated in attacking the enemy."

+

Grant now commands the Cairo district. His horse,
wounded at Belmont, is sound again and he is "impatient" to move on Fort Henry and Fort Donelson. He
sends his gunboats against Fort Henry, and the Confederates withdraw. Grant, master of the Tennessee,
leaves 2,500 men to garrison the fort, and advances on
Fort Donelson with his remaining force of 15,000.
The fort stands on an elevation between two creeks that
flow into the river and its cannon enjoy great range.
The enemy feints at Grant's center, but really throws
his strength against the extended right flank. Grant
concedes the enemy the maneuver, and attacks with his
left after a shattering bombardment of the fort, which
is now at his mercy. The command is passed down by
the rebel officers and devolves on Buckner who sues for
terms. "Unconditional surrender," Grant insists. "I

propose to move immediately upon your works." Fifteen thousand prisoners surrender with Buckner; the Cumberland and the first great victory of the war belong to Grant. He may take an idea or two from his staff, and even a whole plan of battle, such as Chattanooga from General Thomas, or Vicksburg, from Rawlins; but the attack, the unexpected maneuver, the disaster averted, the original deployment of troops, the lightning perception of the momentary advantage, are Grant's own contribution for which he need not turn to others. Quaver? The rocks over which the battle rages may quaver; not Grant. It was not courage with him, but an insensibility toward fear. It never occurred to him that he could be beaten. Checked, yes; but never beaten. The charge splinters the enemy's first defenses; but tenacity wins battles. Where all other generals withdraw, Grant hangs on and triumphs. Now they have him by the throat; now the dead are strewn so thick his horse can not put one foot before the other; now his back is to the river; he masses his forces, smokes his cigar, and calmly awaits the arrival of the reinforcements that should be on the way; he gathers his men at the foot of his cannon. "I will still beat them," he says, and makes good his words.

That was Shiloh, which left the South amazed at such fortitude, and the North appalled at such slaughter. Despite the victory at Fort Donelson, the general of the department, a strait-laced man, relieved him of his command because he had returned "to his old bad habits," the general said, referring to his drinking. But Rawlins denies it, and he is reinstated. The Confederates do not want Grant, supported by reinforce-

ments that are on the way, to drive down the Tennessee
and threaten one of their railroads. At an hour when
he is away from camp and his officers are off guard,
they attack the Northern forces, which here resist, there
fall in droves, turn tail elsewhere, and Shiloh was
"terrible." But Grant arrives in time. Steadied by his
calm and courage, the Federals manage to keep their
lines unbroken until nightfall. He pulls back the remains of his army, inflicting heavy bombardment on
the enemy in preparation for the attack he will launch
as soon as reinforcements arrive. They appear at an
opportune moment, and with their aid he scatters the
Confederates. But the victory is shocking. The surprise is attributed to carelessness, or something worse.
His commander's confidence in him is shaken; the armchair strategists in Washington, where he never sought
friends, hold him in low regard; the few who suspect
his strength attack him. Washington was a hotbed of
intrigue throughout the war.

Jealousy puts on the garb of patriotism. The incom-
petents band together to bar the way to the gifted.
What do they care about the welfare of their country?
The only thing they care about is if someone is pro-
moted over them. Men whose aspirations exceed
their qualifications, and whose ambition outstrips their
patriotism, place greater importance on preserving
their jobs than in saving their country. These setbacks,
added to the resentments he still harbored from the
Mexican War, produced in Grant a justified hatred of
the appointments by crony that paralyzed the prosecution of the war and deprived him of his best troops.
Lincoln, with his greatness and tact, finally managed

to temper that hatred of Washington, composed of
fear and scorn; yet Grant was not able, or was not in-
clined, to forget, which is perhaps explained by his
psychology of a conqueror, in which his personal desires were interpenetrated by a certain rough principle
of honesty. It was not until he came to enjoy an excessive authority, which his people never really be-
grudged him, that he acquired that fondness for
Washington that made him the maximum personifica-
tion of the dangers and vices of the capital. But his
command was restored after Shiloh through the inter-
cession of the old friend who had first had him commissioned brigadier. His grey eyes would dampen in
those days when he saw himself being cast aside and put
off, perhaps forever, from the road to victory. Men who
concentrate everything in themselves suffer greatly.

He was at the head of his army again, and he was
not to relinquish his command until he surrendered
it, with his native magnanimity, at the doors of humbled Richmond so as not to enter as a victor. He was
the commander of his army. The Tennessee was his.
The generals of the Potomac and the James vanquished
or were vanquished, but they did not cross the rivers.
Not he; he would cross all the rivers! On to Vicksburg,
the key to the Mississippi!

The Federal generals had been making the mistake
of dividing the Union army into small bodies, whose
movements were exposed and difficult, to accomplish
the rooting out of an enemy concentrated in formidable
positions. The general who concentrates his forces
gains the advantage of forcing his opponent to give or
receive battle on the ground of his choosing. There is a

great difference between engaging the enemy where
he has made preparations to resist and where he must
take hasty, improvised measures. That is what Grant
pressed for continuously: to force the enemy to give
battle. There is no danger in concentrating; the enemy
must also concentrate, and can no longer make ma-
rauder strikes when his own vital points are in jeopardy.

Grant turns his forces toward Vicksburg: his own
troops, Sherman's and the reinforcements from Washington.

He goes by land, and the enemy cavalry harasses his
rear. He moves down the river, with the nation hanging
breathlessly on the outcome of the campaign. Vicksburg is surrounded on every side by marshlands. Where
can one force the enemy to join battle? Where can one
establish a camp where high water will not reach the
soldier's knees? An attempt to open a canal to by-pass
Vicksburg to the south falls through.

The North becomes impatient with the delays. In
Washington there is talk of changing the command.
"God bless him," Lincoln says to Dana, the present
editor of *The Sun* in New York, when he leaves Washington for Vicksburg, traveling through enemy territory, for there is no other road, to see what is happening. He arrives. He sees that what should be done is
being done. Rawlins proposes that they run the Confederate batteries downstream, for there is no other
alternative. "Madness!" say the other chiefs; in the
end, madness must be attempted. The Army passes
down the Mississippi under the cannon at Vicksburg
and another fort downstream, and disembarks. Grant

strikes at Jackson to the east where there is a strong enemy force, and routs the rebels. He throws their forces back in confusion when they come out to do battle from behind the impregnable works at Vicksburg. He invests the city, and the starving garrison surrenders.

+

The Mississippi falls to the Union with 27,000 rebel prisoners and 120 cannon. The skies over the Northern states are red from the victory bonfires. A committee of "Christian gentlemen" choose that moment to approach Lincoln and inquire if it is true—oh, puerility of fanatics!—that Grant is given to drinking. "I don't rightly know," said Lincoln, stroking his beard, "but if he is, I would surely like to know what brand of liquor he uses so I could send a barrel to all his generals." The Christian gentlemen pull long faces and withdraw, while Grant, now commander of all the West, rushes to the aid of the Federal army besieged in Chattanooga. Chattanooga, the coveted keystone on the banks of the Tennessee, which gathers into one fist all the railroads that transport the Southern armies, and carry the grain and meat of the fertile valleys to the army of Virginia; Chattanooga, where the South mercilessly persecutes the brave mountain folk who are loyal to the Union. Chattanooga lies between two crests bristling with Confederates calmly awaiting its fall. The river, dominated by the enemy heights, is the only escape route left the famished Federals. The road by which they receive reinforcements and supplies is at the mercy of Confederate raiders. Lookout

Mountain and Missionary Ridge look down from their
heights on Chattanooga like two giants regarding a
child. Grant arrives in a tremendous downpour under
cover of night. His soldiers must carry him in their
arms from time to time, for he is lame from a riding
fall. How shall one describe those glorious events?
Grant deploys his forces without overlooking a single
detail, without relinquishing an inch of valuable
ground, without exposing the road to Chattanooga's
rear, without arousing the suspicions of the enemy,
who with consummate stupidity, and confident of re-
pulsing any assault on his lofty citadels, sallies forth
to block the advance of a supporting column moving
on Chattanooga. Thomas's plan will be carried out by
the troops that Grant directs with such skill and foresight; Thomas, who replied to an order from Grant
that he hold Chattanooga "at all hazards" saying: "I
will hold the town until we starve." The day comes, a
beautiful morning that augurs well for victory. But
the crest of the highest citadel is wrapped in fog.
Without the enemy being aware of their movements,
the Federals have crossed the river on pontoons and
taken possession of a string of foothills below the
mountain from which the attack jumps off. Thomas
moves out from the city and makes a successful frontal
assault on a nearby position. Up the mountain go the
Federals with fixed bayonets flashing under the blazing
sun. To those below, it seems that a great serpent
with silver bands is snaking upward on its belly! The
assault is irresistible. A cannon ball splits the ranks, as
lightning divides the clouds; the ranks close together,
like clouds after a thunderbolt. The attackers pene-

trate the clouds and almost disappear from sight of those below. They cut down the terrified gunners at their stations. Whole regiments surrender. The Confederates tumble down the far slope under fire from their own batteries turned against them by the Federals, who win "the battle over the clouds." The other height is still in rebel hands and they storm it at bayonet point. The steep face of the bluff is a maze of redoubts, trenches, rifle pits and works. Sherman's troops, storming the slope, shatter the Confederate ranks. Red, white and blue flags flutter in a hundred different places. Trench by trench, ridge by ridge, they advance. The assault is hurled against the entire Confederate line at the same instant. Missionary Ridge, overwhelmed at its crest, surrenders to the Federals. They count their dead: 7,000 killed!

The rivers of the West are won; now to the rivers of the East. Congress, applauded by the nation, revives the rank of Lieutenant General in Grant's honor and bestows on him the distinction which only Washington had held before in the United States. Lincoln, who promises him full support, "as God is my witness," places Grant in command of all the Union forces, dispersed at that moment by the bad tactics of former commanders into isolated armies that harry the enemy and hold him at bay, but neither invade his territories, reduce the war to a limited field of operations, disrupt his lines of communication, divide his forces, prevent him from defending more than one position with the same force, nor break his will to fight, which as long as it continues will leave the Union cause in doubt.

The Mississippi and the Tennessee are open; but the

banks of the James and Potomac are still covered with rebel tents; Richmond still stands defiant ninety miles from Washington; Lee's unvanquished army still operates between the two capitals; Johnston still commands a formidable army in defense of Atlanta, the heart of the railroad system still moving the soldiers and supplies of the Confederacy; there are still 9,000,-000 persons obedient to the laws of Richmond, defended, in an area of 800,000 square miles, by more than a half-million soldiers. The roads of the war converge on Virginia and on Georgia, protecting Atlanta in the West. The land between is filled with Southern raiders and the detached columns that pursue them.

+

Grant ignores Sherman's entreaties that he return to the West, "for the love of God," lest the intriguers in Washington strip him of his fame. He does not tarry in Washington where the battlefield is distant and he fears he may be defeated by those "in my own house." No: he goes forth to "water my horse in the Potomac and the James." Lee's army on the Potomac has never been defeated; he sets out to defeat it. No more separate and independent campaigns; no more periods of rest during which the enemy can lick his wounds and help the plantation Negroes sow in summer the provisions for the coming winter; no more useless attacks on cities, not even Richmond. It is necessary to "crush the military strength of the South once and for all"; to pursue the enemy, bottle him up, trap, deplete and exhaust him. The Union forces must attack in a body, from all sides at once, and destroy the Confederate

armies, still redoubtable in courage and numbers;
march against them incessantly, in all seasons; keep
constant pressure on them from all sides, so that one
force cannot be shifted from the defense of one quarter
to meet a threat in another. Not one day without battle;
not one day without some advance. Sherman moves
against the Confederate nucleus in Georgia, but in
such a way that when he triumphs he will be able to
join forces with the Federal armies facing Lee in the
East, who must contend with a force that attacks him
from the north, and another force that cuts off his retreat in the south. Grant has the plan worked out
completely, and he makes it fully understood and re-
spected by the Secretary of War before he leaves
Washington. Against Lee, then, from every quarter,
with the road to Washington well protected during the
march on Richmond! His prime purpose was to obliter-
ate the power of Lee's army, exerting unrelenting
pressure at all points, while wearing him into submission with repeated sledge hammer blows. With this
plan, he attacks Lee with 30,000 men from May of one
year to June of the next. Grant drafts the order to
advance, while seated on a log, and despatches it to all
the Union armies as the first battle gets underway;
in the pitch of the fighting in the battle of the Wilderness, where the Union generals, disconcerted in the
heart of a strange forest, suffered casualties of 2,261
dead and 8,758 wounded, the news arrives from the
generals of all divisions: the march has begun which
will carry Sherman from triumph to triumph to the
sea, and Grant to the doors of Richmond! No general
ever moved the army that Grant commanded at that

moment. Rawlins is no longer at his side, and Grant's attacks seem to lack their former luster; but not his order, his inexhaustible patience, nor his capacity to dictate each night from his tent, not always visited by victory, the order of the following day for four armies.

Grant does not fight against Lee like a general that plans, but like a mole that advances. Lee may come out to meet him, as he does, and baffle Grant's effort to force his hand. Grant cannot make a move that Lee does not anticipate, and when he thinks he has outwitted him, there is Lee waiting; but each time more exhausted. That campaign is without precedent! What manner of waging war is this? What Grant purposes, he accomplishes. One time, ten times Lee's spirited and courageous troops repulse him; Grant turns his horse and tries again a little further downstream, never looking back on the 50,000 dead lost in little more than a month; and in the end he can say, "What I set out to do, I accomplished."

That is Grant's campaign of the Potomac that ended the war, from start to finish. Forward, forward: not brilliant tactics, but numbing blows. One river today, tomorrow another; one trench today, tomorrow another. Lee gradually falls back on Richmond protected by the works he improvises wherever he makes camp. But how can the South, demoralized now and disheartened, with enemies closing in on every side, with Atlanta and the four railroads that lead to Richmond in Federal hands, give its leader, anxious to avoid useless bloodshed, regiments of fresh, robust soldiers to match the unlimited number that the North, now as determined as Grant to bring the war to a speedy conclusion, places at the disposal of its commander? Grant is arrayed before Pittsburgh, which is Richmond's bulwark. He has lost 100,000 men, it is true, in less than a year; but Lee's forces are so reduced that "he can barely man the pickets." Grant assaults the last bastions of the Confederacy outside Pittsburgh in hopes of forcing Lee's surrender before he can join forces with Johnston, who is leading his defeated army north from Georgia. Lee makes one last thrust against Washington to break the strangling ring that encircles him, and Sheridan, who sleeps with a map in his hand, flies on horseback to where his troops are on the run. "It is nothing! It is nothing!" he tells a soldier bleeding from a head wound; and the dying man replies: "No, general; it is nothing," and follows his leader. Lee's cavalry falls back in defeat; Five Forks is the battle that ends the war. Jefferson Davis is at a church service in Richmond when he receives the news from Lee that Richmond and Pittsburgh are to be evacuated that night. A few days later, on April 9, Lee marches sadly at the head of his generals to surrender his sword, so many times victorious, to Grant, who treats him like a friend, and will not accept it.

Grant was impatient of the arts of war, nor would it seem that he had many at his disposal when it came to attacks requiring brilliant conception; but he had not set out to fight the war "by the book." His objectives were to spare men; to finish quickly; to destroy the military strength of the South. "Butcher," they said, because he watched his men fall by the hundreds without withdrawing from his positions; to which he replied that to prolong the war because of such considerations would only bring about greater future losses. He saw that by bringing to bear his greater weight of numbers against a debilitated enemy, he would eventually bring him to his knees; and he did just that. What is the objective of war, to fight brilliantly, or to defeat the enemy? He was wanting in instruction, short on imagination, and slow in conception; yet it was he who saw the overall strategy, the great mass outline, the innovations demanded by an unprecedented war, and the sources of the enemy's strength, which he destroyed by his method, with no thought but to deliver the rebels, forever vanquished, back to the Union in a triumph unsullied by vindictiveness or injustice. It seemed at Appomattox, by the modesty of his dress and bearing, and the humility of his words and gestures, that he, and not Lee, was the defeated. He closed the peace in the same spirit with which he waged the war: with neither enthusiasm nor rancor. He sensed his achievement; his arrogance as yet unfolded, he saw only that he had "accomplished what I set out to do."

+

It is true that at the beginning of the war he had Rawlins to advise him, ponder issues, put down intrigues, propose plans of action and direct battles; thanks to Rawlins' good advice, or his own good sense, he no sooner took command than he surrounded himself with men of natural character like himself, who owed nothing to intrigue and hated it as he did, which, together with his merits, drew them to him. It is true that in Washington he had Lincoln, more than any other a child of Nature, who said "I cannot spare that man," and knew how to distinguish between him and the conniving generals and politicians who would have had Grant removed from command without a thought to the good of the country had it not been for Lincoln. It is true that behind him stood a people sharing his origins and inclinations, who filled his ranks with a generosity and determination equal to the scope of the struggle, and recognized with satisfaction their own spirit in that man who advanced and conquered. Not even his most sympathetic biographers deny that fortune was kind to Grant, who did not always show the foresight that might have been expected, avoid the bloodshed he might have in some cases, nor hesitate to compensate for his blunders and oversights with victories gained, at times, at a shocking human sacrifice. Yet, viewed from the higher plane of understanding that comes with intimate knowledge, that amazing war discloses nothing of the supernatural, and emerges as one of the most complete and spontaneous manifestations of the purely human, perhaps the most achieved, with the consummate artistry of the universal, that man has yet seen by virtue of the perfect harmony, arrived at in the heat of untrammeled freedom, between the elements of the struggle, and its agents and methods.

Truly historical facts are those which not only reflect all of human nature, but most particularly, the characteristics of the epoch and nation in which they occur. Remove the fact from its nation or epoch, and it ceases to be revealing or grand.

Neither men nor deeds derive permanent greatness other than in their assimilation of an epoch or a nation.

In its cautious and prudent determination; in the sudden and amazing creation of its armies; in the hard-headed trust in facts and mistrust of theory which characterized those who distinguished themselves; in the initially disorganized, almost unprofessional, and later blind and brutal manner in which the war was prosecuted; in the very magnanimity of its leader, in the harshest of the fighting and in the hour of bloody defeat of the enemy, there never ceased to be an absolute analogy between the formation, the spirit, and the methods of the war, and the formation, the spirit, and the methods of the North. All efforts to introduce extraneous or unnatural elements were completely eclipsed by this vital relationship. A meteoric nation of commercial and tolerant customs and immense size naturally produced a meteoric war, brought on more by humanitarian convictions than by the undeniably powerful internal political differences, regarded throughout its course and in its conclusion in terms of public interest, and prosecuted with all the resources consistent with the magnitude of the combatants and the struggle, yet without the cruelty still found in more cultured and artistic nations which have not been shaped by the general, continuous exercise of free will, which dignifies and strengthens character.

The North waged a war that was enormous, improvised, unschooled, original and noble, which were the very qualities of the nation that carried it forward at that time. The leader who gave the war its natural,

ingenuous spirit, and kept it free of the academic, exotic spirit, sprang, just as his nation, from poverty and
privation; like his nation, he devoted more time and
interest to direct, fruitful endeavors than to the weak,
second-hand endeavor of books. He replaced conventional, imported ideas with new ideas that Nature suggested to him in local conditions and virgin fields; and
always, like his nation, he put all his strength into
the pursuit of his objectives until they were attained,
steadfast and irreducible as the mountains.

Like his country, too, he compromised his glory by
base politics, and in this he outdid his country. He
had risen on his merits from the chores of the tannery
to such heights, that to fittingly recognize them, Congress created the title of general, which even Washington never enjoyed, despite all he signified in the United
States.

This was not love, but a form of frenzied worship.
The spectacle emerged of a man regarded by his fellow citizens as the master of their home by virtue of
being its savior, for which he was made the object
of such devotion that his gravest errors were forgiven,
and it was almost as if his country encouraged his
errors so it might have the pleasure of forgiving him.
He did not have that aloofness which is a desirable
quality in public figures, although he would have been
hard pressed to maintain it, for wherever he went he
was greeted with open arms. Citizens and cities vied
in gifts and presents for the savior of the Union:
New York gave him $100,000; Philadelphia $30,000;
Galena presented him with a beautifully furnished
home; Boston filled it with books; no matter where

he went, his path was strewn with roses. During the war, when he was sought as a political candidate against Lincoln, he said that the only political office that interested him was to be mayor of his city so he could repair the sidewalk that ran from the railroad station to his home. When he arrived at the station in Galena, the whole town was out to meet him and he was escorted to his new home amidst the greatest enthusiasm along the newly repaired sidewalk.

+

Whoever imagined that the silent walker of five years before would be satisfied with those tranquil honors did not know him well. Peace puts character to greater tests than the fortunes of war. The pent-up power, the stifled energy, the conflicting personality, and the unpurged rancor against fortune's neglect and those who were conscious or unwitting parties to fortune's design, had discovered ample outlets now, and natural employments. Repose did not suit that violent and expansive nature which required constant expression in attack and conquest, never in speech, to be sure—for he was as tight-lipped in peace as in war with all but his closest intimates—but in action. Politics was no longer disagreeable to him as he no longer had to woo it, contrary to his nature. Now it came knocking at his door. President Johnson asked him to restore to order the war machine he had carried in his hands. Democrats and Republicans alike proposed to use his prestige in winning the impending presidential elections. He served in Johnson's cabinet after the assassination of the one whose name will always be spoken with reverent praise, until the Senate, feuding with the president, refused to confirm the appointment. He withdrew, and by this token of respect toward the governing body, enhanced his glory. By bowing to the expression of the public will through its legitimate organ, his candidacy and election were assured. The Democratic nomination was his for the asking, but the shrewd politician Thurlow Weed unexpectedly proposed to him at a luncheon that he be the Republican standard bearer, for with Lincoln dead, the only way "to forever stamp out the spirit of secession is to place at the head of the Union the man who has saved it with his sword." President he became, as the Republican candidate, although in the election that precipitated the war, he had voted for Buchanan, the most uncompromising Democrat.

Who is that strange, moody man, ignorant of the most elemental laws of the Republic, and the courtesies and graces of government; oblivious to the difference between the personal rights and the public authority of the president of a nation; incapable of perceiving the indispensable relation in which national officers must stand to their positions of high trust; high-handed and defiant, who brings to the administration of a country—jealous of its liberty and self-respect— all the garb and testy frankness that the practices of war permit, and even demand, by their peculiar objectives and constitution? It is Grant, who wears his campaign boots in the White House, and does wrong. There is no more complicated and subtle task than government, nor one that requires greater practice in worldly affairs, willingness to learn, and skill. Instinct alone falls short if the knowledge, or genius, of details is lacking; genius is accumulated knowledge.

Awareness of one's own rights and respect for the rights of others must be present in equal degree, with a livelier and more delicate sense of the second than of the first; abuse of the first can lead to weakness, but abuse of the second can lead to despotism.

It goes without saying that the president does not assume office to employ the national funds for the benefit of his family and friends, nor to reshape the nation to suit his way of thinking, nor by neglect or misapplication to stultify the spirit of the laws. He must govern, guided by virtue, with the laws his people give him, and without taking for himself or for his friends that which the nation gives him in custody and trust. Government is obedience.

Everything that lives expresses itself. Whatever is repressed eventually overflows. Let us look more closely into that character. That he had a personality of his own was demonstrated clearly by the war. He complemented his own qualities with the judgement, prudence, and eloquence of others; but he always acted independently and in his own right, accepting or rejecting the proposals of his inferiors as he saw fit. No sooner was he somewhat free of the excellent Rawlins, than his personality became more marked. As early as Chattanooga he was beginning to chafe at the inescapable contrast between his aide's noble and courteous qualities and his own lack of them. He issued commands incessantly, without show or effort, as though they came naturally to him; he did not seek advice, or listen if it was volunteered, as if to prove

that he had no need of others. Since he had hit on the
simple, effective idea of conquering by weight of numbers, and was supplied with the numbers he needed to
conquer, he regarded himself with satisfaction and admiration, and he did not find it strange to be numbered
among the great captains of all time, and sometimes
placed at their head. Who had commanded more soldiers? Who had conquered a greater enemy with fewer
ideas from others? Who, by his wars, had produced a
greater number of freedmen on one side and a more
prosperous country on the other? Throughout the war,
he feared, with some basis in fact, and spoke ill, with
sufficient cause but without complete fairness, of
"those in Washington," of those who did not do justice to the fighting soldier, of the armchair generals
who connived with the politicians, and of "the politicians." He did not see that Lincoln was a "politician";
"politicians" to him were only those who wanted to
put Rosencrans or McClellan over him. Sherman, who
loved justice with a passion, and like Grant, also had
his roots in Nature, fanned his hatred of those who
gave preferential positions to those who did not deserve them. When they passed through Washington
during the war, he came away like a live ember: "No;
this time the Commander-in-chief is going to direct
the war: Washington has done nothing,"—and it was
true—"but delay and hamper its prosecution at every
turn."

He commanded during the war without brooking contradiction. He had to be very fond of whoever contradicted him to tolerate it. Little by little, the members of his staff, anxious to stay in his good graces, made it a rule never to contradict; Rawlins did, and it came to irritate him. After the peace, the greatest country in peace, and the noblest in war that the universe contained at that time, sang his praises without rest as they have never been sung of any man before, and he listened with the feeling that they were well deserved.

He entered the presidency, the highest political office in his nation, with these qualities: abomination of politics and a reservoir of hatred for all who represented it; self-complacency and the habit and desire for expansion, conquest, and march; a pampered practice of commanding without opposition and an absolute lack of the habit of obedience; an utter contempt for the observance of careful, progressive laws and a meteoric career outside the natural and ordered province of the laws; and a way of seeing all things as if they originated in him and were realized through, and in accordance with, his will.

This is the man of instinct, who, by reason of an uncontrolled personality or an excessive attachment to Nature, which may stem from either sincerity or crudity, refused to benefit from the civilizing instruction in man's record of achievement. Carried upward by his natural strength, and opportune strokes of luck, to the complex functions of government, which include the employment of the most perfect discoveries and fruits of human civilization, he dashed himself to pieces against the stern exigencies of his office, since he could not shatter a nation practiced in defending its interests, and stronger than he.

There are other primary and natural characters sprung directly from Nature, or not far removed, who have something more than just strength, as in the case of Grant, and that certain generosity that always accompanies true strength. Lincoln, Garfield, even Rawlins, were of a superior order among primary characters, for they had intellect and beauty, which gave them the capacity and active need to assimilate the whole of human achievement. The ultimate greatness in these superior characters is the inevitable result of a union between these qualities and an extraordinary will, whereas, in characters of strength alone, it is simply an accident and as blind as strength itself, requiring adventitious circumstances outside the character of the individual for its realization.

It is natural for man to think of himself; his existence inexorably and pitilessly forces him to do so. But there are those who, at fortune's smile, develop a self-centeredness that is odious in its tenacity and scope, for it engenders egotists in private life, and despots in government. Yet there are others who see themselves as a word to be communicated, an indignation to be vented, or a charitable act that must be done. They make human benefit the first and dominant thought in their lives, with self secondary; and suffer sharply—as if conscience-stricken—until they have delivered themselves of the word, the wrath, or the kindness that is their reason for being.

But even when primary characters are not disin-

terested, a kind of common originality attracts and
draws them closer to those who are disinterested than
to the common run of men. Although they tend to hate
and combat those whose strength is graced by intellect
and beauty, who in turn abominate and censure those
who have strength alone as monstrosities, these nevertheless have a capacity for moments of personal, conscious greatness, which seems to escape them through
most of their lives. But no sooner are they stimulated
by contact with disinterested characters or some for-
tuitous circumstance, than an intellectual and spiritual
greatness blossoms from its opaque and rudimentary
state, as if simple energy were the raw stuff from
which intelligence and beauty evolve. Then careers of
strength are bathed in the fresh, soft, penetrating light
that men of good will and purpose spread in their wake.

What a nation Grant sought to govern with the scorn
for others, self-indulgence, and willful thinking to
which he had become accustomed by the simple, rough-
hewn realities of the war! A nation in danger, to be
sure, where the consciousness of power, and appetite
for wealth, imperil the national decorum, the independence of neighbor countries, and perhaps of the
human spirit itself. But a great country nonetheless,
where man realizes and fulfills himself with no let or
hindrance beyond the natural limitations imposed by
co-existence with fellow beings; where the sublime
spectacle had just been witnessed of a peaceful nation
embarking upon a tremendous war for the sake of a
human principle; where, under Grant's very eyes,
250,000 men paraded homeward bound through the
streets of Washington, with their flags in tatters,

their uniforms patched, maimed in limb, yet resplendent with victory. A nation where questions are asked
and answers given, where no man is above public
scrutiny, and woe to him who falls under suspicion,
for every act is probed to its core. A nation of prayer
meetings, where, before the congregation, men and
women alike learn the use of the spoken word, confess-
ing their sins aloud, denouncing those of their neighbor, and asking the pastor to clarify their doubts on
points of dogma. A nation where newspapers are living
things, and no sooner does a cause emerge than
it has its organ to which all who are interested have
equal access, so that there is no injustice or suspicion
that lacks a voice, or a newspaper to air it, or a bar
of opinion disposed to censure wrongdoing. A nation
infatuated, it is true, with a man as martial, stubborn,
and aggressive as itself, which had broken its rivals
and opened the way to the greatest prosperity the
world has ever seen; but above all, a nation that de-
nounces and overthrows whoever curtails or threatens
its rights.

The political career with which Grant tarnished the
memory of his magnanimous deeds during the war was
painful to witness, from its violent beginning, through
the weakness and crimes that followed.

+

He acted from the very first in keeping with his loath-
ing for politics, and rancor toward those who represented it, thinking all the while that he was doing the
right thing; yet, by the manner in which he proceeded,
he gave childish proof of his ignorance of the laws and

the sense of fitness that inspires them. He chose as
his advisers men who were not professional politicians.
He named an important, and still active, businessman
as Secretary of the Treasury. The old friend who
brought about his commission as brigadier and who
had him restored to command of his army became Secretary of State. He appointed an obscure businessman to
be Secretary of the Navy, and a certain Williams, who
rose by dubious means from village justice to senator,
became Attorney General. But in that terrible, track-
less wilderness of supreme authority, in which Grant
felt himself both ignorant and under scrutiny, he
turned to the old friend whose counsel he knew to be
always sound, to Rawlins, who went to his friend's
side without a murmur, although he felt death approaching, and served Grant while he lived as Secretary of War and intimate adviser. While Rawlins was
in the cabinet, the thieves and wicked counselors did
not cross the threshold, although they did work their
depredations further off. But once Rawlins was gone,
how were those complex matters to be dealt with by
one who deliberately scorned them and was ignorant in
the bargain? He was like a rudderless ship driven before the storm. He frowned upon any who sought to
give him advice, and rejected their proposals; but despite himself he had to seek the advice of others in
matters outside his ken which he had to know. The
result was, that without realizing it, he became the
tool of those who counseled him adroitly, by always
making it appear that it was he, and not they, who
proposed the ideas.

Vanity is susceptible by nature, and flattery has

endless arts. Grant kept those who flattered him at his side; he could not suffer those who did not. He gave everything that was asked to those who seemed to place their faith in him, and being a man guided by instinct, his loyalty went with everything he gave, even to the jeopardy of his honor. What can an ignorant man in government be but the natural prey of those who know his defects and play on them?

His self-complacency exposed him to the persuasion that the government was his personal belonging, like the nation itself, which could not reasonably refuse to be guided by its savior. He saw all his assistants as projections of himself, and all who defended his person and carried out his wishes. As if complying with a national mandate, he proceeded to appoint every relative, and every relative's friend, to comfortable government jobs, to such a point that his government came to be known as the "in-laws government." Some from admiration too freely given, others from a desire to curry favor, followed his wishes without contradiction, and carried out his singular and autocratic, when not unlawful, demands with undue zeal. There were also ready hands to do the work of his powerful sycophants, who used him to destroy their political enemies in the North, or to raise the specter of Southern secession in the North as the basis for their perpetuation in power through every election. Even his natural magnanimity toward the rebels, which could not have been greater, was poisoned by those who presented the legitimate resistance of the defeated states to the abuses in the Federal policies as ingratitude. They so stirred up his habit of command, and his reluctance to heed advice

or duty, that he went so far as to sponsor an iniquitous
plan, discovered in time and spiked, to muzzle the free
press that criticized him by establishing a special court
of venal judges in Washington to pass upon cases of
"crimes" by the political press throughout the nation.

Urged on by his thirst for expansion and advance,
and in keeping with his ignorance of the spirit and
form of the laws, he sent his private secretary, on the
pretext of studying the bay of Samana, to sign a treaty
of annexation with the government of Santo Domingo,
circumventing the legitimate diplomatic channels. Sum-
ner protested indignantly before the Senate against
both the violence of such a plan, which would make it
appear that a weak country had been subjected to the
ambitions of a powerful expansionist, and the danger to
a government of republican institutions when the executive usurps authority that rightfully rests only with
the nation. To gain support for this plan of usurpation,
Grant entered into secret agreements with members of
both houses of Congress and promised to support certain reprehensible projects in exchange for the votes
he needed in favor of annexation and his method of
carrying it through. It was a miserable affair in more
ways than one. Not only was there the spectacle of the
nation that stands for freedom in this world being prepared to violate—as in fact it did violate—the freedom
of a small, but gallant, country—but there was the
well-founded suspicion that a ring of speculators, familiar with Grant's spirit of conquest and expansion,
inspired the idea of annexation with the intention of
reaping the profits for themselves while leaving him
out of account.

Thus the government drifted without compass or reckoning through Grant's first administration and through his second. He was re-elected because of his personal candor, which made him appear innocent of the crimes of his underlings, as in fact he was, and the unique place he held in the hearts of his people. His candor was apparent in the advantage his associates took of the blind support he gave to those who showed him loyalty, and the people, who loved him deeply as their most prized hero, felt secure in the face of an apparently smoldering South while he was in the White House. But for all that, when there was talk of a third term after his re-election, such a clamor of fear and anger arose that even his most ambitious supporters were cowed into silence.

The public refused with unswerving tenacity to blame Grant for the scandalous frauds of his secretaries, in which his brother and closest relatives were involved on occasion; for the tax swindle by the major corporations, with the connivance of the treasury employes, who stood to gain by the scheme; for the crime, later revealed by the swindlers themselves, who insisted that their tax payments had not gone to the Treasury because they had been applied to Grant's campaign expenses for a third term. The public demonstrated an unwavering determination while Grant lived, even in more deplorable instances, to justify Grant in honorable fashion, by his candor as a soldier and by his loyalty as a friend. The subservience of public trust to his private interests did not matter; nor the defilement of national offices by unworthy supporters and objectionable cronies; nor the incredible stupidity shown in the appointment of tainted, obscure and incompetent individuals to positions of the highest trust and responsibility; nor the reckless plan, more substantiated than offset by a letter he wrote in explanation, for consolidation of power on a perpetuating basis, which by every indication, is what the intimate counselors of the discredited president had in mind. His discourteous silence was excused by the austere politeness that was apparent in his manner and bearing; his manifest disregard for the personal opinions of his cabinet was softened by pointing out his humble way with subordinates; and his determination to have all around him bow to his wishes in public affairs, whether of his own design or of others, was countered by calling attention to his outer modesty, which in him, as in so many others, was a blind for the dangerous immodesty within. But despite this, all the brilliance of his ostentatious trip around the world, in which the greatness of his country was recognized and celebrated in his person, could not move his people to elect him president a third time. He lost his majesty by endangering the majesty of the laws.

Alas, his final years! His desire for power unabated, he turned now to the needless pursuit of wealth, despite the guarantee by his friends of the income from a fortune of $250,000. With no slackening in his urge to conquer and march, his mysterious quality of hero-merchant led him to nose around Cuba and Mexico, and recommend a project, with himself at the head, for the extension of North America's railway network into Mexico. His countrymen did not hesitate in shouldering his associates with the blame for his business fiasco, although it was apparent that he was equally responsible. But those who knew him best kept a close watch on his public utterances, as if they knew that a powerful group gravitated around him, ready, at the first opportunity or unguarded moment, to raise itself above the laws of the republic with the support of the enormous monopolies that must protect themselves against the lower classes, whose well-being and future they oppose.

This North American public, which seems selfish and indifferent, is profoundly generous, or decorous, or discreet. If not, how then explain the persistent good will it showed in refusing to blame Grant for the scandalous manipulations, the colossal fraud, of the commercial firm that misused his name, secured his signature on seriously compromising documents, and was conducted in the same calamitous fashion as the government during his years in office? Would it not have been natural for people, noting the repetition of similar circumstances in Grant's career in government and in business, to suppose that the fault might lie with him? But no; the fault was not his. He may have sanctioned some half-understood scheme that seemed useful to him, but he never knowingly sullied his hands with tainted profits. His blame, if any, was in his overweening desire for visible pre-eminence; in his perpetual inner urge for leadership and command; in his lack of intellect and beauty which would have embellished the strength of his primary character; and from that lack, his deplorable inability to recognize the sweet majesty of modesty and the greater influence exercised even in the practical matters of a true republic by those who do not use the trust placed in them to set themselves above the law.

In the end, it was sickness that brought a luminous and memorable conclusion to that life that was pure strength. It was brilliant in some respects, and sordid in others, yet the magnitude of the services he rendered made it definitively, undeniably great. To some it will seem appropriate that an existence, whose great merit was to have preserved without cruelty the greatest political system yet devised by man's imagination, ended with a spectacular funeral in which the entire nation accompanied the bier from the mortuary to the tomb on Riverside, covered now by the clinging branches of what was once a shoot from a vine on Napoleon's tomb on St. Helena. They will see a fit ending to that fruitful life in the funeral train that came down from the lofty mountain with its black curtains whipped by the rain and the wind; in the ranks of New York militiamen who accompanied the corpse through the still wet streets from the railroad station to City Hall, where the vestibule had been converted into a funeral crypt; in the tireless homage of men and women, black and white, workers on their way home, soldiers who had fought in his armies, and the curious, who for two days and nights formed a line that stretched unbroken for the distance of a mile from City Hall; in the day of the solemn burial, decreed a day of mourning throughout the land, on which the enormous hearse drawn by twenty-four black horses bore the remains to the tomb through streets hung with crepe and crowded with people, many of whom had been waiting since the previous morning, huddled on corners, clinging to the rooftops, perched on telephone poles, packed on balconies at stations dearly bought, to see General Hancock pass by with the general staff, which included one Southerner; the ranks on ranks of splendid militia; the battalion from Virginia that Grant drove before him, and another battalion of those who drove them under Grant's command; the deceased, at whose passing all heads were bared; the President, in a coach drawn by black horses, and two ex-presidents; five hundred carriages filled with notables, secretaries of state, governors, bishops, and generals; and the daughter and daughters-in-law of the great man, wrapped in their long veils.

But it was not this that brought Grant's life to a luminous conclusion. It was his superior spirit that waxed bright in the last, long days before his death, endured with great fortitude by that wasted old man, in which he revealed the best of his natural energies, long obscured by the passions and vulgarities of existence, through words and acts of great tenderness. A profound self-examination put him in clear possession of the true greatness of his life. The vanities, which he once prized so high, fell from him like dust from an old statue when he came to write his personal memoirs of the war, which was all the fortune he had to leave his children, and whose final pages he wrote with trembling hand and with the sweat of death's agony on his brow. He rose to an awareness of the greatness of the spirit, with the capacity for elevation that is given primary characters by their genuine grace, and he saw, prized, and recorded only the essential acts of his achievement, in which he was great in combat only to be greater in the manner of his triumph.

His deep-set eyes, softened by the gratitude he felt toward his good-hearted countrymen for their forgiveness of his errors and vigil at his death, turned with dignified and elevated kindness toward the mistaken heroes it was his lot to combat without rest, and subdue without anger. The fleshless hand he extended in good will from the border of the grave has been clasped with loving admiration by his gallant former enemies who count that gesture a national treasure. A nation of men has appeared on this earth, and this man, for all his grave errors, helped clear the way.

ROSCOE CONKLING

April 1888

Never has there been a more patent example of the sterility of selfish genius than the magnificent orator who died yesterday—Grant's lord regent, Blaine's implacable enemy, the maverick in Garfield's presidency, of all the orators in the United States the most dashing and literary: Roscoe Conkling.

His person was majestic, and his walk so arrogant, that Blaine, finding the comparison with a peacock inept because his feet showed the same preening care he gave the rest of his dress, called Conkling a turkey, "a majestic, supereminent, overpowering turkey-gobbler" in a puerile debate in which the smoldering rivalry between these two Republican leaders in the House of Representatives burst into flame.

The personal rivalry between these two men, more than the political differences in which they dressed it, caused such a cleavage in Republican ranks that even the death of one probably will not suffice to reconcile the rival elements whose overriding preoccupation, year in, year out, has been to publicize whatever might offend or damage the reputation of the other.

But then, alas, what is practical politics but the struggle for the enjoyment of power?

Did not Conkling, after thirty years of high-handed and absolute political authority, find himself abandoned by his friends, almost to a man, when he resigned his seat in the Senate? He was certain that his state legislature would return him triumphantly to Congress as a rebuff to Garfield and Blaine, who, he felt, had flouted his senatorial prerogatives when they laid before the Senate the appointment of a port collector hostile to Conkling without consulting the Senator, violating the practice in all important appointments in the United States. But no sooner was he in conflict with the source of patronage than those who were most weary of his authority, and those basest by nature, turned against their leader and representative of thirty years standing, and voted in favor of the candidate endorsed by the White House!

Conkling's enmities are embedded in the history of the United States like battle monuments. His support was tantamount to victory; his silence, to defeat. His oratory was as elegant and sinuous as his hair, sometimes sonorous, flashing crimson and gold like heraldic trumpets with scarlet pennants, sometimes swift and piercing like a winged dirk.

He opposed Washburne and blocked his bid for the presidency. He opposed Blaine, and twice by attacks in the conventions, and once by abstaining from the campaign against Cleveland, thwarted his election. He opposed Garfield, and Garfield died.

How did he rise, what were the sources of his power, how did he direct politics, how did he pass untarnished through a corrupt administration, how is it that despite his faults this extraordinary man died secure in the general esteem? His life is a thoughtful lesson and provides a supremely interesting chapter in practical politics.

+

From earliest youth in his father's house, where judges, lawyers and politicians came and went, the handsome son of Utica revealed the extraordinary qualities that would set him apart from mediocrity, and the determination to demonstrate to men his capacity and will to rule.

It was not wealth, but pre-eminence, he sought. But for all his vainly dissembled ability, if he had not joined forces with the side that was in power and distributed the benefits that derive therefrom, neither the force of his mind nor the prestige of his oratory would have made it possible for men to endure so long in power one who constantly offended them with the display of his superiority, the involuntary crime of those who possess it, but which men rarely forgive even in those who know how to employ it self-effacingly for the general good.

Virtue is not necessarily excluded from the province of government, although those generous spirits who seek the ideal good on earth are more at ease, and burn with a brighter light, where the compromises and silences essential to politics do not hamper the defense of the ideas which save and alleviate suffering. But Conkling, who was born with his eyes fixed on the White House and found proof in his own bright and

ambitious spirit of that natural aristocracy which
he thought violated by the democratic constitution,
Conkling was not won, as was the generous Wendell
Phillips, by the inner delights and secret rewards which
fall to the champion of the humble. He was drawn to
the pomp of ostentatious combat in the public assem-
blies where power is the reward of those who employ
their talents in the defense of interests, for such cham-
pions never lack a following.

History balances these accounts by lifting up those
who fought for man and forgetting those who fought
for power.

He received Nature's gift of thought, not as a trust
to be employed in the service of his fellow men, but as
a title to the right to make himself served. He traversed
the republic with imperial tread. He was indifferent to
public opinion, but made the weight of his opinion felt
among the public. The prime objective of his politics
was to vanquish, not so much his enemies, as his rivals.

His was not the world of thought, but of action.
Apart from those rare instances when all who contain
a measure of greatness rise to the challenge of grave
national problems, the arts, lightning flashes, and
pounding surf of Conkling's grandiloquent oratory
found themselves pressed into service on behalf of personal quarrels, or low, trivial party issues, sputtering
and strutting in the void like Rabelais' chimera, or
cloaking scarecrows in imperial robes.

Language is smoke when it does not serve as raiment
for the generous sentiment or the eternal idea.

The notable thing about this man was to have won
pre-eminence in a democracy without wooing it. He was

an applauded orator at nineteen; a district attorney at twenty; and at twenty-one, a lawyer so feared that the shrewdest lawyers of Utica advised their clients to retain him to prevent their opponents from engaging him.

His love of duty, his zeal in fulfilling the obligations of office, his constant study, his mastery of detail, his oratory, devastating in a formal address, and picturesque and lively in debate, his very person, proud, athletic, and handsome, made him the cynosure of the city, which no sooner elected him mayor, than it took him from that post and sent him to Congress as a representative. He was everything, congressman, senator, state Republican leader, the power behind the throne during Grant's administration, and he might even have been president because political parties, scornful of those who seek them, seek those who scorn them. But it was not this brilliant career, not the personal majesty and rectitude with which he created the illusion of greatness, and even bestowed true greatness on conflicts of no moment, that was the most original thing about him, but a wise combination of dissembled ability and outward haughtiness that introduced a new method of flattering without appearing to flatter, of serving the interests and even the vices of those whose company he shunned, and the frenetic and theatrical arrogance with which he made himself admired and followed by a public to whom he was only superior in singleness of purpose, and an eloquence with which he manipulated public passions toward the achievement of his objectives. As though one who veils the entrance to the den of thieves were not their accomplice!

He believed in display and reserve, for he avoided
contact with the public except when he could appear in
all the trappings of his senatorial dignity. He did not
control the masses directly, but through intermediaries,
who served him out of sincere admiration, and because
"the Senator never forgets a friend." He served his followers in their enmities as well as in their needs.
"Never," he once said with accuracy, "have I asked
anyone to vote for me."

Why, then, did they vote for him?

Because by his counsel he taught them how to win;
because by continually serving others he made himself
served; because through the influence he acquired as
party leader of the state, he was able to lead the state,
to its benefit, into a position of great influence in the
councils of the national party and government; because
that proud man, with eyes for the presidency alone,
who declined appointments as Chief Justice of the Supreme Court and Ambassador to England "because I
want no offices but those the nation gives me at the
polls," knew how to menace the president so effectively
with his hostility when the distribution of jobs in the
state was left to the senior senator, that the White
House lost no time in violating the standing rule and
placed all patronage in the hands of the rebel.

He kept the rank and file of his party in his pocket
by catering to their interests, and by that charm that
one who holds sway by the force of his character,
speech and appearance exercises over men, especially,
as in Conkling's case, when these qualities are united
in a remarkable degree. He was a skillful boxer, and
peerless commander; he knew how to wed passion and

judgement and was no run-of-the-mine orator, but a
Hercules in frock coat and white gloves, whose bludg-
eon remained unsuspected by the enemy, until, with
an enormous rhetorical flourish, he brandished it over
his head. All his runners and delegates, the ward-heelers
and lieutenants to whom he entrusted the dirtier jobs
of political direction, as well as the authority in which
they reveled, stayed at his side not so much because of
those great qualities which his impertinent arrogance
cheapened, but because he provided them with comfortable jobs, thanks to his almost unerringly successful
strategy and the influence built on their support which
he had acquired in the politics of the nation. His touch-
stone in granting or withholding his support in political issues was whether they served his interests and
those of his backers in the state.

He had another way of dominating, more certain
than the charm of his conversation and the memorable
power of his addresses, which was a superior knowledge of political affairs and techniques. No one could
outdo him in a political debate, and those who withstood his domineering character were forced to bow to
his reason. Like all strong men, he knew how to wait.
Only the fool puts his trust in raw power alone.

When he was elected district attorney, he waited a
full year until he had learned his job, statute by statute,
and case by case, before making his first public appearance. When he was elected representative, it was not as
an orator that he sought to make a name for himself,
as well he might have, but, securing a position on one
of the committees, he applied himself with such intensity
to a study of its workings, that by the end of the term

he was chairman. When he lost so many friends, as a result of his arrogance, that he was not returned to the House, he devoted himself with such vigor to a study of public issues—the abolition of slavery, the secession of the South, the formation of the Republican party—that his re-election finally proved inevitable. The prestige he gained in the House through his political acumen was so well-founded and unbroken that he finally attained the national platform he desired when he made a famous speech in the name of the "Committee of Thirty-Three," appointed to advise Congress in the development of a policy toward the rebel states.

At the same time, he steeped himself in literature with which he embellished his high-flown speeches, and whatever laws, dates and events might have even the slightest bearing on matters under debate. As a result, his impromptu remarks and rebuttals came to be as polished, meaty and trenchant as his prepared speeches —replete with quotations and as colorful as caparisoned horses—which he would commit to memory in full.

He was able to recall his major speeches, word for word, until the day he died, which suggests that such powers of memory were founded on an excess of self-esteem. What are a few clusters of words measured against the important things of this world? He carried entire plays in his memory, and the best of the ancient and modern orators, which is apparent in the weight of his spoken or written word, and in the fact that even when improvising, he never loosed disordered legions or makeshift images or a babble of words, but rather each word incorporated an idea, and was a position, rebuke, and demolishing thrust. He used to entertain his friends reciting passages from the English masters and he never traveled without a book of verse. On his desk in the Senate there was always a volume of poetry.

But that command of his subject and sense of delivery, to which he adhered as an actor to his cues, was often tarnished by his arrogant propensity to feel that any and all who opposed him were wrong and basely motivated, even when they had more unassailable reputations than his own in their favor.

One day, for example, he said to the honest reformer George William Curtis, who spoke words of pure gold and whose writing was drawn silver: "Johnson put it well when he said that patriotism is the final refuge of knaves, but he did not know at the time everything that can hide behind the word *reform*!" Driven by his personal passion, his sarcasm became unworthy of the admirable language with which he invested it, and arrogance, envy and hatred frequently deprived his oratory of that high art of making the form fit the thought, that glorious and transcendental beauty which only justice can give to human endeavor.

Every manner of being, just as all things material and spiritual, carries within it an equal measure of life and death. So in Conkling, the aristocratic spirit, of which he thought himself the living embodiment, was as much the source of his weakness and fall as of his strength and buoyancy.

He felt a greater responsibility to himself than to mankind, and he made a cult of his person, both physically and mentally. His devotion to friendship was such that whoever had shown him loyalty could be assured of his gratitude, as surely as of his hatred, if he had succeeded in offending his great vanity and touchy pride. If his friend was poor he would lower himself to his poverty to serve him; but as one who does a favor, not as equal to equal. He thought the republic an error, that the people should not rule, and that those of greater intellect and strength should exercise their natural right to govern. Was he not the living proof, with the excellent qualities with which life had endowed his strong and handsome person, of a natural aristocracy?

For that reason, as much as to maintain the spell of distance, he refused to rub elbows with the political rank and file; with an artist's independence he studiously avoided those barren social gatherings where vulgar and insignificant people conducted conversations bereft of wit; he counted for little during the time of Lincoln, the great Commoner, and he reached his full power with Grant, who saw only grounds for contempt in the blind devotion of his countrymen. Conkling waxed with Grant, and with him he waned. He turned against Grant when as president he gave the other Senator from New York the right to dispense federal jobs in the state; but once the cowed president had capitulated to his demands, he never abandoned him. One was the power behind the scenes, the other the visible power. Grant had need of Conkling's energetic mind, which he would turn darkly on his inferiors, but which he made silky and pliant toward the restive general in such a way as to influence him without Grant being aware of how or to what purpose. Ambitious men endure such indignities, for power must nearly always be reached on bended knee. Those who attain it erect are its natural heirs.

Conkling's hand escaped detection where his hand was known to be; he came away without a personal smirch, like Grant himself, from that heyday of barefaced corruption and plunder, when the Secretary of the Navy made himself millions and the Secretary of War sold jobs, when public indignation forced the removal of the Secretary of the Interior, and the presidential secretary reaped the profits of the Treasury fraud, when the President's family concocted for their benefit the panic of "Black Friday" that cost the country so dear. But if Conkling came away from this corruption with clean hands, not so his tongue, which persistently defended the party to which he had linked his fortunes and the man in whose shadow he hoped to attain his goal.

He was the aggressive leader of Grant's bid for a third term in the convention where 93 delegates backed Conkling; under Grant's wing he would have continued to prosper; Grant also wanted a strong government; he could use Grant as a powerful weapon with which to destroy Blaine, already so firmly entrenched that he weathered the famous, epic, flaming tempestuous speech, introduced by four lines of verse and followed by 306 loyal delegates, with which Conkling proclaimed Grant's candidacy against Blaine's, and with fewer delegates than he was to command in the following convention, still managed to muster enough votes to block Grant and throw the nomination to Garfield. And Garfield was killed by the ambitious idiot who took counsel for his crime in the poisonous quarrel that capped the rivalry between Blaine and Conkling. Conkling thought himself badly repaid for the services he and Grant had lent Garfield toward the end of the campaign, services which, in the uncertain nature of the campaign, perhaps assured Garfield's election. For the President-elect failed to carry out his end of the bargain by not giving Conkling, as he had apparently promised, the right to distribute patronage in his state, but instead, counseled by Blaine's hatred, appointed to posts in New York, without prior notice or consultation, the very people who, on Blaine's behalf, had most strongly combated Grant and Conkling.

Such abject dealings are hidden behind the pomp of politics!

Conkling angrily resigned, certain that the New York legislature would return him to the Senate in protest against the violation of senatorial prerogatives; but in politics, everything that is not pure virtue in the long run proves to be shifting sands. Those who had supported him out of self-interest, out of self-interest abandoned him.

His sincere admirers—and no one in this country has had more—fought unsuccessfully to block the triumph of the candidate hand-picked by Blaine, who was grinding his own axe and preparing his later candidacy, while Garfield thought in all good faith that he was fighting the first battle in the honorable campaign to lift national politics out of the mire and straits into which it had fallen.

Garfield died; and Arthur, who owed the vice-presidency to Conkling's efforts alone, thought it imprudent on succeeding to the presidency to summon Conkling immediately, as if to glory in such a dismal victory. For it was not a struggle between two political systems that had agitated the country and ended in death, but the clash between the ambitions of two rival pretenders. Nor was the selection of Garfield and Arthur the spontaneous agreement of a party seeking worthy standard-bearers, but a hasty compromise between the friends of Blaine, who found themselves impotent to triumph in his name and threw their strength behind Garfield, while allowing Conkling's friends, as a means of closing the party ranks for the campaign, to select the vice-presidential candidate, Arthur.

Conkling would never accept from the man he had raised to office a position inferior to that on which he had set his sights since youth! He would never solicit from the legislature the election that his jackal friends had denied him! He folded his arms and watched the party that had dared to disdain him fall to pieces without him. He gave Arthur no assistance and Arthur was not re-elected, from the sorrow of which, more than from illness, he died a few months later. He gave Blaine no assistance when he was the presidential candidate, and by the invisible strength of that fallen hand, Blaine was defeated.

And it was then, free of political ambition, that Conkling revealed in full measure the virtues that made him a representative and extraordinary man. In the sadness of defeat he had acquired that wisdom that mellows genius. His silence was more eloquent than his most impassioned speeches. Politics, accustomed to the flattery of the ambitious, recognized a noble temper in that man who knew how to scorn her. As one might draw the steel from the wound, so, perhaps, certain of his final victory, he dislodged that disenchanted ambition. With the greatness of those friends Euripides drew, he honored without a murmur all the notes, amounting to $100,000, which he had endorsed for an unfortunate friend who proved unable to make them good. With the self-confidence that had raised him so high among men, he returned with notable success to the practice of the law, to the discussions at the club, where he was the object of endless admiration by reason of the picturesqueness and magnificence of his language and his unerring political judgement, and to the noble obscurity of one who believes that no crown in the world is worth kneeling before other men to attain.

The nation has honored him like a hero and the city has mourned him like a son. His defeat was his glory. He began to be great when he ceased to be ambitious.

PETER COOPER

April 1883

Flags are at half-staff today, hearts also: Peter Cooper is dead. He leaves behind him a nation of sons. I was not born in this land, nor did he ever know of me, yet I loved him like a father. If our paths had ever crossed, I would have kissed his hand. And when the flowers of spring sway on their graceful stems in the breeze and sun of May, I shall gather an armful of wild flowers, not the pale, languid flowers of winter that bloom under glass, and lay them on the tomb where the great-hearted old man's body lies, like the robe cast off by an angel before winging heavenward. Those who knew him well placed a lily on his breast as he was lowered to his grave; the whole city shared in that gesture. Oh, marvelous breast, on which, after ninety-three years of earthly life, a lily unfolds its petals. Living today is like a battle waged by a youth in white raiment who struggles with feverish hands to preserve his purity from defilement by packs of sly, satanic beasts, who leap out at him under the cover of night from every turn of the road, dragging their bloated bellies, their human faces lighted up by the sinister gleam of their eyes, their sharp fangs, avid of purity, oozing a slimy poison. It is fitting that the earth should kneel in homage at the death of a man who has passed through the ranks of the beasts with tunic undefiled.

He loved, he created, he comforted. He lived the Sermon on the Mount. He put peace into resentful hearts, bread into outstretched hands, sustenance into hungry minds, dignity into life, and brought happiness to himself, and glory to his country. He leaves behind a school bearing his name where two thousand workers study, and thousands of men read and find repose. What saint has a finer altar in his cathedral than Peter Cooper has in this school? In his lifetime, he dug the earth, felled forests, stitched cloth, invented machines to cut it, devised mechanisms to lull the sleep of children, to empty the mines, to navigate canals, and to harness steam, which had not responded to other hands, as though furious at finding itself confined. The earth, like a bountiful mother, bared her breast to him. He smelted ore, which is an occupation that breeds singular strength; new worlds seem to bubble in the blast furnaces; men take on the appearance of gods in the glow of the hearths.

He lived serenely because he lived without sin. His wife was not like other wives, willful Amazons who ride their horses with a hard bit, but a sheltering wing. He was so gentle that he seemed weak; but he had the amazing strength of gentle men. The weeping of a child would bring tears to his eyes, but he sent the first successful locomotive in America hurtling through the woodlands. He fashioned a cap for an old neighbor

woman with his hatter's skill, and then went to his desk
to design with the same hands a machine to harness
and employ the tides.

He attended school fifty-two times, and not one day
more. Each year from the school he founded, hundreds
of men and women go forth to do battle with life,
armed with the buckler of the arts and crafts. His
parents were miserably poor. At the age of five, Peter
Cooper was helping his father sell beer. At ten, he was
already making hats; at fifteen when he needed shoes,
he shaped the last with his own hands, and then the
shoes; soon, he was making carriages, and saving money,
which he gave to his needy father. The country was
short of clothing and of machines for cutting garments
during the War of 1812, and the lowly beer peddler de-
signed them. With the profits from the machines, and
despite all he gave away, because he lived giving, he
came to New York to sell spices—across from the spot
where today, with his generous institute, he redeems
souls. He constructed houses; he bought factories; invented marketable products; drained swamps; moved
sand-banks; tunneled mountains, gave livelihood to
thousands of men, discovered all he needed, triumphed
over every obstacle, erected colossal steel mills, made
his inventions available for the benefit of everyone,
gave his fortune to his children, and rose again like
the tide with new fortunes. And always, his patriarchal
hands extended over the tormented heads of his fellow
men.

In Peter Cooper's eyes it was not a virtue to be good,
but a crime not to be. He would have trembled, as
though fearing the wrath of some gigantic, irate hand,

the day he neglected to do a good deed. He regarded human existence as a divine calling and selfish comfort an act of apostasy. He did not challenge God in anger because he felt his presence but could not see him, nor did he shake his fist at the inscrutable sky; instead, he lived meekly, as one who glimpses a vision of indescribable delight, and he was happy, because he understood the object of life. There is but one key to the door of happiness: Love. He who loves does not suffer even when he suffers, because a heady perfume rises from the soul of one who burns with love for his fellow men, like incense from a censer. He saw that the greatest pleasure comes from doing good, and the deepest suffering from not being able to accomplish it; that sorrow which is pure gives sustenance, but that which is ignoble or base, as are the majority of human sorrows, rowels the soul, like the barbed scourges with which the Roman charioteers drove the maddened horses in the savage races of the circus.

And he saw that whoever locks himself within the confines of self lives among lions, and that whoever emerges from self, and gives of himself to others, lives among doves. If the wicked sink their poisonous fangs in his flesh, he does not suffer from the wound, but from the fact that there are still fangs that wound. He lays his hand on the brow of the biter, and looks into his eyes so tenderly, that the vanquished biter finally draws his fangs from the wound.

In a word, Peter Cooper lived with assurance in another life, a life whose rays already bathed him in light. No mortal pleasure, no music played by any orchestra, seemed to him comparable to the music and delights of his spirit. "Why do you confer on me the degree of Doctor of Laws?" he once asked the university president who handed him the scroll inscribed in Latin by which the university conferred its title on one who already held his title from Nature's university. "If you give it to me because I have spread the tidings of how to be happy, which is to be good; because my years prove that to give strength to others fortifies one's own; because my shining gray hair and my still rosy cheeks teach that he who feeds on young ideas will always be young; because I hold the idea that science is not the wizard mantle of the teacher, nor a mystery to be reserved for the select few, nor the prerogative of the aristocrats of the mind, but man's only means of explaining to himself the laws of life, then give me your generous diploma, even though I am not a knight of the halls of learning, and all this Latin is Greek to me." And the man who talked in this fashion was already ninety years of age.

He was never physically strong, nor did he need to be, with his strength of spirit. He never gave up anything he attempted until he had found the answer, and then, on to a new venture. He matched every marvel of nature's power with a similar marvel of ingenuity to harness that power. As the sun's warmth incubates the spawn of fish, so his hand hatched inventions. Whatever he turned his hand to was bettered by his touch. During his years of dry bread at a pine table, he had to rock the baby's cradle while his wife did the cooking. His fertile mind hit upon a device which, as it rocked the cradle, shooed away the flies and wound a music box. He was induced to invest in a long stretch of coastal land, and everyone said it would be his ruination; but he turned the property to profitable account. A railroad was needed to transport ore, but the terrain demanded a roadbed with many curves, and the engines of those days, like iron crocodiles, were clumsy on the curves. He crawled inside the engine, redesigned the vitals, thereby inventing the tubular steam engine, and sent the first locomotive racing across America. Railway charges raised the price to the consumer of products that could be shipped more cheaply by canal; but the horses pulling the barges from the bank made slow progress upstream. He devised a mammoth system of cogwheels along the canal banks that moved the vessels at the rate of a mile every six minutes. It was necessary to transfer ore from a high mine down a rough mountain to a far off dump; nobody could figure out how to lower the filled ore receptacles and return them empty. So he invented the endless conveyor, which he suspended high above the slope over a distance of three miles. The ore buckets were loaded at the mine, and their own weight carried them down the hill on the belt, while the momentum of the descending receptacles sent the empty ones back uphill to the mine. The news reached him that the Turks were drowning Greece in blood; what magic power does a nation fighting for its independence possess that it transforms the criminal into an apostle, and the dove into a raging lion? Peter Cooper went to work on a device of death, a torpedo to be guided from the shore by long wires, like a horse's reins, that would blow the Mohammedan ships sky high on contact. It occurred to him that it would be a good thing—so that the fire of the wood should not destroy the altar where the flame of the spirit burns—to make the Institute of Arts and Science fireproof, and he spent $75,000 tooling machinery to manufacture iron girders.

At times he seems like a Satan of Good. When he overcomes a harmful force of Nature, a smile of angelic malice spreads across his wide lips. He loves to shut himself away with retorts and test tubes. He does not seek gold, which lies within him; he seeks means of surprising Nature in one of her secrets, and when he succeeds, he laughs triumphantly, like a player who has won a difficult match, or a child who finally finds the toy his mother hid from him. His constant goal is to produce expensive materials at low cost, so the poor man, who is his friend, may enjoy them. He can always be found seated among his workers, asking them if they want more wages, or if the work is too tiring, or if they have any suggestions of things he can do to improve their lot, although there is nobody around him who is not contented. All that his genius produces, his hand lavishes on the unfortunate. He feels himself under obligation to spend every cent he earns. He regards himself as the steward of his wealth, not its owner. With each new business success, he added another room to his Institute. His industry brought him millions, which his charity distributed—silently, without any ostentation, and with no desire for formal recognition or public praise. He was at the head of every great enterprise; thanks to him, the trans-Atlantic cable became a reality; although the cable broke again and again, he never gave up, and advanced great sums until it was finally laid. He looked after his business ventures, had a hand in public affairs, and personally supervised his school, day by day. Do not ask him if he has children, for he will tell you that all workers are his children. He carries his wounds in his heart, and he pleads with the rich to be merciful; he pleads with the discontented to be patient, and he sets them an example, showing them all the treasures that, like ribbons from a magician's hat, have come from that simple cap he made in his youth for the old neighbor woman. He does not believe in the power of wrath, but in the power of science. He preaches the doctrine that ignorance at times can make even justice hateful. He proclaims that there is no force that will not eventually succumb to trained human intelligence. From the harmony that exists between all known physical laws, and the imperfection and brutal harshness of human life at present, it may be inferred that man does not yet see the gentle, generous rules of life, and that the earth contains in lavish abundance enough to satisfy the desires of all its dwellers. To study the forces of Nature, and learn to direct them is the best way to solve the social problem. Intellectual exchange ennobles men. The ignorant man has not yet begun to be a man. The quiver of man's arrows and all his lances lie behind his brow.

But Peter Cooper was not satisfied to alleviate; his purpose was to redeem. Charity is a narcotic, not a cure. It dries the tears on the cheek, but not the source of the tears. And Peter Cooper, who had started life's rough journey barefoot, wished to strengthen men's feet for the journey. What good does it do a man to learn words by rote; numerals, whose capricious combinations are as superfluous to the mind as cold, un-

fleshed bones in a doctor's cabinet; or the boundaries
of the Holy Roman Empire, which enters the mind
by one ear and goes out by the other? Take the unhappy souls out of the cloistered schools, and see if they
can fight the battle of life with such weapons. Men live
by chance, and thanks to the kindness of others, and by
acquiring when they are grown, at a great effort,
what they should have learned in their apprentice
years with no effort at all. Since living is man's purpose, education should be a preparation for life. Men
should be taught in schools those skills with which they
can master life; they should not be called schools, but
workshops. The use of the pen should be taught in
school in the afternoon; but in the morning, the spade.

It was thus that Peter Cooper, who had longed to
learn but had no school to go to, conceived the idea, in
the sixty-fourth year of his exemplary life, of opening
a training center of industry, arts, and sciences, for
those who must earn their living in trades that require
them. Are not the children of the desert taught to ride?
Then teach the living, palpitating, multiple Earth to
those who must live on it and from it. Solemnly, the
arches were raised; the broad floors were laid, and the
shelves were filled with thousands of books; eminent
teachers were appointed; the doors were opened wide,
and the untutored workers poured in, as if mingling in
a river of redemption. Some to the chemistry section,
others to lithography, photography, applied and indus-
trial design, or mechanics. Men and women go side by
side in the teeming crowd to learn in that noble house
the arts of life and receive a degree at the end of the
year, with which they fare forth, the reins of Fortune

in their hands, to employments which the school itself has often secured for them. Enter. What silence! Two thousand men reading. Here is another room. What a beautiful sight! Three hundred young women studying! Look about these vast halls and spacious rooms; everywhere, eager groups await their teachers! They will instruct them in the use of tools and instruments; they will explain how electricity is harnessed and put to work; they will lay bare the play of social forces; or, as Peter Cooper wants it said, they will teach that the only religion worthy of man is that which bars no man.

And now he is dead! He will no longer come, as was his habit each Saturday, on the arm of his daughter, to visit his beloved Union. His eyes will no longer see the grateful crowd of young people that waited for him at the foot of the stairs, or stopped him on the street, and filled the air with cheers and waving hats. The strong, rude carters and teamsters will no longer draw to one side to allow his carriage to pass, and greet him with profound respect. Groups of poor people will no longer await him, certain of his generosity, to hold the door of his carriage. No longer will he descend from his old, battered carriage to help his coachman, with those ninety-three-year-old hands that had amassed millions, mend a broken trace with a wooden needle and a piece of twine, nor will he ever talk again, as he did that day, when the crowd gathered spontaneously at the sight of him, and broke into prolonged, thunderous acclaim of its modest benefactor.

The whole city has followed his coffin. The crowd that gathered in the rain at the church where his body lay was so vast that it seemed that it might have borne the whole church upon its shoulders. In six hours, 150,-000 New Yorkers filed past the body of the dead man.

The church was a basket of flowers, and the street, a carpet of bared heads. Congress, entire cities, business organizations have proclaimed him a national father, and put on mourning bands.

In the homes, men, women, children, and servants rise to their feet at the mention of his name. And as his coffin passes the windows, the women remove their gay, feathered hats in a delicate and unprecedented act of tribute.

NEW YORK

UNDER THE SNOW

March 1888

The first oriole had already been spied hanging
its nest from a cedar in Central Park; the bare poplars
were putting forth their plush of spring; and the leaves
of the chestnut were burgeoning, like chattering women
poking their heads out of their hoods after a storm.
Notified by the cheeping of the birds, the brooks were
coming out from under their icy covering to see the
sun's return, and winter, defeated by the flowers, had
fled away, covering its retreat with the month of winds.
The first straw hats had made their appearance, and
the streets of New York were gay with Easter attire,
when, on opening its eyes after the hurricane had spent
its force, the city found itself silent, deserted, shrouded,
buried under the snow. Doughty Italians, braving the
icy winds, load their street-cleaning carts with fine,
glittering snow, which they empty into the river to the
accompaniment of neighs, songs, jokes, and oaths. The
elevated train, stranded in a two-day death vigil beside

the body of the engineer who set out to defy the blizzard, is running again, creaking and shivering, over the clogged rails that glitter and flash. Sleigh bells jingle; the newsvendors cry their papers; snowplows, drawn by stout percherons, throw up banks of snow on both sides of the street as they clear the horsecar's path; through the breast-high snow, the city makes its way back to the trains, paralyzed on the white plains; to the rivers, become bridges; to the silent wharfs.

The clash of the combatants echoes through the vault-like streets of the city. For two days the snow has had New York in its power, encircled, terrified, like a prize fighter driven to the canvas by a sneak punch. But the moment the attack of the enemy slackened, as soon as the blizzard had spent its first fury, New York, like the victim of an outrage, goes about freeing itself of its shroud. Through the white hummocks move leagues of men. The snow already runs in dirty rivers in the busiest streets under the onslaught of its assailants. With spades, with shovels, with their own chests and those of the horses, they push back the snow, which retreats to the rivers.

Man's defeat was great, but so was his triumph. The city is still white; the Sound remains white and frozen. There have been deaths, cruelties, kindness, fatigue, and bravery. Man has given a good account of himself in this disaster.

At no time in this century has New York experienced a storm like that of March 13. It had rained the preceding Sunday, and the writer working into the dawn, the newspaper vendor at the railroad station, the milkman on his round of the sleeping houses, could hear the whiplash of the wind that had descended on the city against the chimneys, against walls and roofs, as it vented its fury on slate and mortar, shattered windows, demolished porches, clutched and uprooted trees, and howled, as though ambushed, as it fled down the narrow streets. Electric wires, snapping under its impact, sputtered and died. Telegraph lines, which had withstood so many storms, were wrenched from their posts. And when the sun should have appeared, it could not be seen, for like a shrieking, panic-stricken army, with its broken squadrons, gun carriages and infantry, the snow whirled past the darkened windows, without interruption, day and night. Man refused to be vanquished. He came out to defy the storm.

But by this time the overpowered streetcar lay horseless beneath the storm; the elevated train, which paid in blood for its first attempt to brave the elements, let the steam escape from its helpless engine; the suburban train, halted en route by the tempest or stalled by the drifting snow, higher than the engines, struggled in vain to reach its destination. The streetcars attempted one trip, and the horses plunged and reared, defending themselves with their hoofs from the suffocating storm. The elevated train took on a load of passengers, and ground to a halt half-way through the trip, paralyzed by the snow; after six hours of waiting, the men and women climbed down by ladder from their wind-tossed prison. The wealthy, or those faced with an emergency, paid twenty-five or fifty dollars for carriages drawn by stout horses to carry them a short distance, step by step. The angry wind, heavy with snow, buffeted them, pounded them, hurled them to the ground.

It was impossible to see the sidewalks. Intersections could no longer be distinguished, and one street looked like the next. On Twenty-third Street, one of the busiest thoroughfares, a thoughtful merchant put a sign on a corner-post: "This is 23rd Street." The snow was knee deep, and the drifts, waist-high. The angry wind nipped at the hands of pedestrians, knifed through their clothing, froze their noses and ears, blinded them, hurled them backward into the slippery snow, its fury making it impossible for them to get to their feet, flung them hatless and groping for support against the walls, or left them to sleep, to sleep forever, under the snow. A shopkeeper, a man in the prime of life, was found buried today, with only a hand sticking from the snow to show where he lay. A messenger boy, as blue as his uniform, was dug out of a white, cool tomb, a fit resting place for his innocent soul, and lifted up in the compassionate arms of his comrades. Another, buried to the neck, sleeps with two red patches on his white cheeks, his eyes a filmy blue.

The old, the young, women, children inch along Broadway and the avenues on their way to work. Some fall, and struggle to their feet. Some, exhausted, sink into a doorway, their only desire to struggle no more; others, generous souls, take them by the arm, encouraging them, shouting and singing. An old woman, who had made herself a kind of mask of her handkerchief with two slits for the eyes, leans against a wall and bursts into tears; the president of a neighboring bank, making his way on foot, carries her in his arms to a nearby pharmacy, which can be made out through the driving snow by its yellow and green lights. "I'm not going any further," said one. "I don't care if I lose my job." "I'm going on," says another. "I need my day's pay." The clerk takes the working girl by the arm; she helps her weary friend with an arm around his waist. At the entrance to the Brooklyn Bridge, a new bank clerk pleads with the policeman to let him pass, although at that moment only death can cross the bridge. "I will lose the job it has taken me three years to find," he supplicates. He starts across, and the wind reaches a terrible height, throws him to the ground with one gust, lifts him up again, snatches off his hat, rips open his coat, knocks him down at every step; he falls back, clutches at the railing, drags himself along. Notified by telegraph from Brooklyn, the police on the New York side of the bridge pick him up, utterly spent.

But why all this effort, when hardly a store is open, when the whole city has surrendered, huddled like a mole in its burrow, when if they reach the factory or office they will find the iron doors locked? Only a fellow man's pity, or the power of money, or the happy accident of living beside the only train which is running in one section of the city, valiantly inching along from hour to hour, can give comfort to so many faithful employes, so many courageous old men, so many heroic factory girls on this terrible day. From corner to corner they make their way, sheltering themselves in doorways until one opens to the feeble knocking of their numbed hands, like sparrows tapping against the window panes. Suddenly the fury of the wind mounts;

it hurls the group fleeing for shelter against the wall;
the poor working women cling to one another in the
middle of the street until the snarling, screeching wind
puts them to flight again. Men and women fight their
way uptown, struggling against the gale, clearing the
snow from their eyes, shielding them with their hands
to find their way through the storm. Hotels? The
chairs have been rented out for beds, and the baths
for rooms. Drinks? Not even the men can find anything to drink; the saloons have exhausted their stock;
and the women, dragging their numb feet homeward,
have only their tears to drink.

After the first surprise of the dawn, people find
ways to adjust their clothing so the fury of the tempest
will not do them so much harm. There is an overturned
wagon at every step; a shade, hanging from its spring,
flaps against the wall like the wing of a dying bird;
an awning is torn to ribbons; a cornice dangles from
its wall; an eave lies in the street. Walls, hallways,
windows are all banked with snow. And the blizzard
blows without respite, piling up drifts, scattering destruction, whistling and howling. And men and women
keep walking with the snow to their armpits.

One has made a mask of silk from his umbrella,
with two holes for the eyes, and another for the mouth,
and thus, with his hands behind his back, he cuts his
way through the wind. Others have tied stockings over
their shoes, or bags of salt, or wrapping paper, or strips
of rubber, fastened with twine. Others protect themselves with leggings, with fur caps; another, half
dead, is being carried, wrapped in his buffalo-hide
overcoat. "Sir," pleads the voice of a child, who can-

not be seen for the snow, "help me out of here, I am
dying." It is a messenger boy whom some heartless
employer has sent out in this storm. There are many
on horseback; one, who came out in a sled, is carried
away with it at the first gust, and nearly loses his life.
A determined old lady, who set out to buy a wreath of
orange blossoms for her daughter's marriage, loses the
wreath to the wind. Night fell over the arctic waste of
New York, and terror took over. The postman on his
round fell face down, blinded and benumbed, protecting
his leather bag with his body. Families trapped in the
roofless houses sought madly and in vain to find a way
out through the snow-banked doors. When water hy-
drants lay buried under five feet of snow, a raging
fire broke out, lighting up the snowy landscape like the
Northern Lights, and swiftly burned three apartment
houses to the ground. The fire wagons arrived! The
firemen dug with their hands, and found the hydrant.
The walls and the snowy street were scarlet, and the
sky was blue velvet. Although the water they played
against the flames was hurled back in their faces in
stinging pellets by the fury of the wind, although the
tongues of crimson flame leaped higher than the cross
on the church steeple, although the wind-tossed columns of smoke bearing golden sparks singed their
beards, there, without giving an inch, the firemen
fought the fire with the snow at their breasts, brought
it under control, and vanquished it. And then, with
their arms, they opened a path for the engine through
the snow.

Without milk, without coal, without mail, without
newspapers, without streetcars, without telephone,

without telegraph, the city arose today. What eagerness on the part of those living uptown to read the newspapers, which thanks to the intrepidity of the poor newsboys, finally came up from the downtown presses! There were four theatres open last night, but all the stores and offices are closed, and the elevated struggles in vain to carry the unwitting crowds that gather at its station to their places of work.

The trains and their human cargoes stand snowbound on the tracks. The city is cut off from the rest of the country and no news goes in or out. The rivers are ice, and the courageous cross them on foot; suddenly the ice gives way, and cakes of it float aimlessly with men aboard them; a tug goes out to rescue them, skirting the ice cake, nosing it toward the bank, edging it to a nearby dock. They are saved. What a cheer goes up from both sides of the river! There are also cheers as the fireman passes, the policeman, and the brave postman. What can have happened to the trains that never arrive? The railroad companies, with admirable despatch, send out food and coal, hauled by their most powerful engines. What of those at sea? How many bodies lie buried under the snow?

Like a routed army that unexpectedly turns on its vanquisher, the snow had come in the night and covered the proud city with death.

These unpredictable onslaughts show utilitarian countries to advantage more than any others, for as was amply proven yesterday, in the hour of stress, the virtues that work heightens completely overshadowed those which selfishness withers. How brave the children, how loyal the workers, how uncomplaining and noble the women, how generous the men! The whole city spoke in loud voices today, as though it were afraid of finding itself alone. Those who unfeelingly push and jostle one another all the rest of the year, smile on each other today, tell of the dangers they escaped, exchange addresses, and walk along with new friends. The squares are mountains of snow, over which the icy lacework clinging like filigree to the branches of the trees glitters in the morning sun.

Houses of snow crown the rooftops, where the merry sparrows dig fragile nests. It is amazing and frightening, as though a shroud should suddenly flower in blood, to see the red roofs of the houses reappear in this city of snow. The telegraph poles ruefully contemplate the destruction, their tangled, fallen wires like unkempt heads. The city digs out, buries its dead, and with men, horses, and machines all working together, clears away the snow with streams of boiling water, with shovels, plows, and bonfires. But one is touched by a sense of great humility and a sudden rush of kindness, as though the dread hand had touched the shoulders of all men.

JESSE JAMES, THE GREAT BANDIT

His Crimes, Fame, and Death

April 1882

These Easter days, so festive in New York, have been exciting ones in Missouri where there lived a bandit of noble brow, handsome features, and a hand made for death's work. He robbed banks, not pockets; ransacked towns, not houses; waylaid trains, not travelers. He was a hero of the West. His boldness dazzled his countrymen and drew their eyes from his crimes. He was well-born, the son of a clergyman, looked like a gentleman, not a villain, and married a schoolteacher, not a bawd. And there are those who say that during one of his law-abiding spells he was a political leader and attended the last Democratic Convention under an assumed name, influencing the nomination of the presidential candidate. But the lands of Missouri and Kansas are full of dense woodlands and craggy places. Jesse James and his men knew each nook and cranny of these wilds, every bend in the road, swamp trail, and hollow tree. His house was an armory and his waist became another when he strapped on his two great gunbelts bristling with revolvers. He went to fight in the war as a youth, and before his cheeks lost their down he sent more than one bearded man to his grave. In times of Alba he would have been a captain in Flanders; in times of Pizarro, his able lieutenant; in these times, he was first a soldier and then a bandit. He was not one of Sheridan's magnificent soldiers who fought that slaves might live free in a united land and planted the Union colors atop the embattled breastworks of the Confederacy. Nor one of those hardy soldiers under silent Grant who stalked the bristling Rebels to the final battleground, as the patient hunter stalks the ravenous boar. He was a trooper of the Southern stripe, of those who saw in the battle flag a license for plunder. His hand was an instrument of death. He left his victims unburied, and rode off with the booty he generously shared with his companions in crime, the tiger cubs who licked the hand of the great tiger.

The war ended and a great contest began. On one side were the young bandits. They would appear in the cities on horseback, knock at the doors of the bank, empty the vaults of money in broad daylight, and drunk with danger, which goes to the head like wine, gallop off shouting through the startled communities, aware of the crime only after it was accomplished. There would be a half-hearted chase, and the townsfolk would gather again in front of the empty bank, from where it seemed they could still see the bold horsemen, golden against the horizon with the aura of daring. On the other side were the sheriffs, helpless in those regions of small towns and great distances; the soldiers of the territory, who always returned wounded, or never returned; and the uneasy communities, sometimes dazzled by the trailing splendor of boldness, which transfigured the audacious robber into a prince of plunder, and made hearts beat faster, as hearts heedless of the soul's good counsel ever will in the presence of an extraordinary act, however vile. So it is that in the bloody rings where men kill bulls, the beauties of Spain fling their wide fans in the air, applaud wildly, and shower the matador with silken slippers from their tiny feet, and red roses from their hair, in token of esteem! Once, Missouri was celebrating its state fair, with at least thirty thousand men at the grounds, betting, carousing, gambling and watching the races. Panic suddenly swept through the crowd. Jesse James had appeared, and while all eyes were on the swift race horses, he and his desperadoes burst into the counting room, shot down the guards, and fled with all the receipts. For its magnitude and daring it seemed to many in Missouri that this crime merited pardon. But other times these villains would sink their arms elbow-deep in blood, as when they would tear up the railroad tracks on a curve and lay in wait with their swift horses in the thickets. The train would come and jump the track. Then came the killing of any who resisted the wicked robbery. Then the removal of money by the sackful. Then the loading of horses with bullion. And then the murder of all who could make the train run anew. If there was a wealthy barroom in the territory where a local bully held sway, the bandits went there spoiling for trouble, that no one might say that a man lived who was quicker on the draw and harder in the saddle than Jesse James's boys. If they danced the quadrille at a Texas ranch with all the beauties from near and far, Jesse James would knock at the door with his pistol butts, and as he was the bravest, to him belonged the fairest. A famous agent was commissioned to track him down, and they found the agent's body riddled with bullets and this note pinned to his chest: *Fair warning to all who would hunt Jesse James.*

The strange life men lead in the remote regions of this country exposed to the raw wilderness develops in them all the appetites, magnificence, impulses and elegance of the wild beast! It is fitting that the buffalo hunter, who challenges the powerful beast and sits at ease, as in his own chair, on the flanks of the fallen bull, should let his hair hang to his shoulders, and that his foot should be made to overstep forests, his hand to uproot trees, with his heart tuned to the tempest and his eyes filled with that solemn and melancholy look of one who has looked long on Nature and the unknown.

But where in the life of that bloodier of the highways are those noble deeds of a Don Quixote, which the newspapers insist on finding? It is true he was shot in the back by a friend in the Governor's hire. It is true that the state house should be rid of a Governor who pays an assassin with the hand that should be holding the scales of justice. It is horrifying and shameful that in the dark of night by a side door of the executive mansion, the Governor and a young gunman should settle on the price for a bandit's life.

What respect can a judge command who commits the same crime as the criminal? The shadows that shrouded the thicket where James and his men awaited the train stretched into the Governor's council when the price on his head was fixed. The peacemakers who pursued him in life buried him in a magnificent coffin, which they paid for out of their own pocket, or was it the State's? The body was taken on a special train, for no ordinary train would do, for burial in the earth of his mother's people. The coffin was carried by the lawmakers of the region and thousands of persons turned out, their eyes red from crying, to see the earth thrown over that bandit who shattered so many skulls with the quiet unconcern of a squirrel cracking hazelnuts. The swift mare on which the bandit rode fell into the hands of a turnkey.

WILLIAM F. CODY

"Buffalo Bill"

July 1884

"Buffalo Bill" can now be seen written in huge, colored letters on every street corner, wooden fence, billboard and abandoned building in New York. Along the street go sandwichmen, as they are known here, squeezed between a pair of cardboard signs, which hang from their necks, front and back, like two walls; with every movement of the man who parades them impassively through the laughing crowds, the gaudy, enameled letters flash in the sunlight for all to read: "The Great Buffalo Bill."

Buffalo Bill is the nickname of a hero of the Wild West. He has spent years on the frontier, among buffalo and mining town roughs, who make the buffalo seem tame by comparison. He has chased and run down buffalo, and knows how to encircle, bewilder, outwit, rope and tie them. Ruffians cower in his presence and know their master: let one of them spring at Buffalo Bill with knife drawn, and it is he who falls with Buffalo Bill's blade buried hilt-deep in his chest; or if they shoot at Buffalo Bill, that crack shot shatters the bullet in mid-air and finds a sure target in his adversary's breast, for his marksmanship is such that he can take aim at a bullet in flight, fire, and it vanishes. The Indians hold no secrets for him; he knows their ways and wiles and style of warfare; like them, he sees in the dark, and with ear to the ground, can tell the number of the approaching enemy, how far away they are, and whether they come on foot or on horseback. He is a fighter. He has shot it out in barrooms with quarrelsome cowboys who cannot sleep easy unless they have sent some rival or imprudent traveler, boots and spurs, to the graveyard. He has survived the wild foray of the yelping, agile Indians who attack the white man, hugging the necks of their horses and flourishing their deadly rifles, while he crouches behind his horse's belly or a nearby tree trunk. All these terrors and triumphs are written in the pale, melancholy, yet piercing eyes of Buffalo Bill. The women adore him, and he cuts a fine figure in their eyes. He is never seen alone; wherever he goes there is a beautiful woman on his arm. Children think the sun rises and sets in him; he enchants them with his skill and gentleness. His long, brown hair, touched here and there with silver, hangs to his powerful shoulders. He wears a ten-gallon hat and high-heeled boots.

He has turned his fame to advantage and is traveling around the United States at the head of a troop of cowboys, Indian sharpshooters, horses, antelope, deer and buffalo with which he recreates all the perilous and romantic scenes that have made the West famous.

Sometimes the show goes on under the blazing afternoon sun in a vast enclosure, sometimes in the evening
under electric lights. In a succession of lively and realistic scenes he regales the avid eyes of the city dwellers with all the wonders and dangers of the restless,
primitive life.

First it is the cowboys, with their fringed leather
chaps, short jackets, bandannas, and huge *sombreros*.
In they gallop, more slouched than mounted on their
lively horses, and suddenly they fill the air with the
lariats they carry on the horns of their saddles, or
draw from their holsters the pistols with which they
settle their most trivial differences. These brave rascals,
with neither house nor home, regard death as a glass
of beer; they dispense it or accept it: they bury their
victims, or if they are shot in the breast, they wrap
themselves in a blanket to die.

Having outdone each other in their various skills, the
cowboys ride off, and the Indians appear trailing a
white traveler, who rides along as if unsuspecting.
The Indians advance single file at a slow gallop, holding in check their eager ponies, which, given their
head, will bolt against the white man, as if they had
taken it upon themselves to avenge the race that
mounts them. Men's sorrows seem to penetrate the
Earth and touch whatever she brings forth! For
the pony is as graceful, slender and high-strung as the
Indian; and as cunning and vengeful. He seems a living arrow, as though the arms of a people were no accidental invention, but the expression, realization and
symbol of its physical and spiritual attributes, and the
trials of its history. The Indians sing their slow, mo-

notonous, depressing chant, which makes the heart heavy. It is the lament of a departing spirit that winds painfully into the depths of the Earth. And when the song loses itself in the distance, it still trembles on the ear, like the branch upon which a dove has just expired.

Suddenly the air is filled with smoke and fiendish yells replace the mournful chant; the ponies dart forward with the Indians crouched on their necks; a knife could pass cleanly beneath their flying hooves; shouting, shooting all at once, wrapped in dusty smoke reddened by powder flashes, they whirl about the white man who stands his ground and shoots back, as fast as he can pull the trigger; he holds his pistol in his teeth and reloads with both hands. The Indians fire from between the ears of their horses and under their bellies; they are wraiths through whom bullets seem to pass without effect; the white man, who is Buffalo Bill, is now out of ammunition; he reels, and seems mortally wounded; the Indians close in, like vultures around the dying eagle; he embraces the neck of his horse, whose body has served to protect him, and dies.

The war whoops become ear-splitting shrieks of victory; it is as if the Indians had killed not one, but all white men; they enact the scene in the circus for the entertainment of Easterners; but it is so rooted in their souls that the show takes on the aspect of reality. Now they pick up the corpse; now they sling it across the saddle of a brave who fell in the skirmish; and now they are riding off, happy and shouting, when to the jingle of harness bells, shouts, and the crack of the whip, in comes a stagecoach filled with white men. To the fray! To the fray! The ramshackle vehicle becomes a barricade and the driver's seat a turret; fire spits from every window; the savages defend their prize in vain; once again everything is smoke, flame, powder and dust; the ponies finally flee abandoning the corpse which is carried back to the stagecoach in the arms of its brave avengers. The public breaks into wild applause, for in this they have improved on Rome: the applause was formerly for the gladiator that slew, now it is for the one that rescues. The whip cracks; the band strikes up; music fills the air and the stagecoach disappears in a cloud of dust.

Thus, the troop of Buffalo Bill acts out the scenes that in real life still agitate the Wild West. A horseman appears at a full gallop. A bullet whines through the air; he only spurs on; he unties the saddlebags lashed to the saddle, pulls his heavily spurred boots out of the stirrups, and as he passes a saddled and bridled horse held in waiting, the fantastic rider leaps through the air with his leather pouches, and continues the race on the fresh mount, while his exhausted pony is blanketed and rubbed down. That is how they carried the mail of yesteryear: before there were railroads there were men.

A herd of buffalo now trots in with their great, shaggy heads grazing the ground. In a flash, the cowboys round them up, bewilder them with shouts, drop their unerring lassoes around their horns, rope them by any leg the spectators select, throw them and ride them at will, for all their snorting and bucking. There is generally a skillful cowboy who gallops ahead once his lasso is fast to the buffalo's horns, flicks the slack into a loop around the muzzle of the beast, and pulls the lariat taut into a halter.

The show ends with a fusillade of shots, as sharp-shooters break hundreds of clay pigeons in mid-air, and a chorus of hurrahs, which gradually dies away as the huge crowd makes its way to the railroad cars and heads for home. The electric lights, pouring their brilliance over the empty arena, suggest one of those magnificent scenes that must transpire in the solitude of the wilderness at night.

CONEY ISLAND

December 1881

Human annals record nothing comparable to the marvelous prosperity of the United States. Do its roots go deep? Are the ties of common sacrifice and pain that hold other nations together more enduring than those of common interest? Does that colossal nation contain savage, uncontrollable forces? Does the absence of the feminine spirit, the source of the artistic sense and the complement of the national spirit, harden and corrupt the heart of that astounding country? These are questions which only time will answer.

What is apparent today is that there has never been a happier, more spirited, more comfortable, more integrated, more jovial and light-hearted people engaged in such useful pursuits in any land on earth, nor any that created and enjoyed greater wealth, covering its oceans and rivers with a greater number of gaily decorated steamers, or turning out with more bustling order and ingenuous happiness on sandy beaches, gigantic boardwalks, and brilliant, fantastic midways.

The North American newspapers are filled with ex-

travagant descriptions of the unique beauties and singular attractions of one of these summer resorts,
jammed with people, crowded with sumptuous hotels,
traversed by an elevated railway, brightened by flower
beds, with amusement stands, side shows, cafes, cir-
cuses, tents, legions of carriages, picturesque assem-
blages, portable bathhouses, barkers and splashing
fountains. The echo of this fame is found in French
papers.

From all parts of the United States, legions of intrepid ladies and Sunday-best farmers arrive to admire the splendid sights, the unexampled wealth, the
dizzying variety, the herculean surge, the striking appearance of Coney Island, the now famous island, four
years ago an abandoned sand bank, that today is a
spacious amusement area providing relaxation and
recreation for hundreds of thousands of New Yorkers
who throng to its pleasant beaches every day.

There are four villages joined by drives, trolleys,
and trains. One is called Manhattan Beach, where
there is a hotel whose dining room can accommodate
4,000 persons comfortably at a sitting; another, which
sprang full-blown like Minerva of helmet and lance,
but armed instead with steamships, esplanades, boardwalks, murmuring orchestras, and hotels that are more
akin to nations than to cities, is called Rockaway;
Brighton, the least important, takes its name from an
hotel of extraordinary size and ponderous construction. But what attracts the people from near and far
is not distant Rockaway, monotonous Brighton, or
aristocratic and sober Manhattan Beach. It is Cable
Beach, with its soaring elevated which could overpass

the spire of Trinity Church—twice as high as the spire of our cathedral—and from whose height one cannot look down without feeling dizzy. Cable Beach, with its two boardwalks ribbed with steel girders stretching three-quarters of a mile into the ocean on slender pillars; with its elegant palace at Sea Beach, which is only a hotel now, but was the famed Agricultural Building at the Philadelphia Centennial Exposition, from where it was transported to New York and re-erected as if by magic on the beach at Coney Island in its original form, down to the last board. Cable Beach, with its museums at fifty cents admission, where human freaks are on display, exotic fishes, bearded ladies, melancholy dwarfs, and stunted elephants, blatantly advertised as the biggest elephants in the world. Cable Beach, with its hundred orchestras, gay dancing, endless rides for children, a gigantic cow that never runs dry although endlessly milked, fresh cider at twenty-five cents a glass, and innumerable couples of wandering lovers who bring to one's lip those tender verses of García Gutiérrez:

> *Two and two*
> *In the meadows above*
> *The crested larks woo*
> *And the turtledoves.*

Cable Beach, where entire families come to escape the foul, nauseous vapors of New York and fill their lungs with the healthy, invigorating salt air; where poor mothers, while they empty the contents of the huge hampers that contain the family lunch on the tables that are provided free in the spacious dining halls, press their wretched infants to their breasts. They seem devoured, sucked dry, consumed by the dreadful summer scourge that scythes children like a sickle wheat—infantile cholera. Steamers come and go; whistling, smoking trains, their serpent bellies swollen with families, arrive, disgorge their contents, and depart. The women rent bathing suits of blue flannel and sun hats of rough straw, which they tie with a ribbon under their chins. The men, in less cumbersome apparel, take them by the hand and enter the water. The children wait at the surf's edge for the hissing wave to lave their bare feet. But they scamper back, hiding their terror behind squeals and laughter, when it arrives, only to return in bands, as if better to defy the enemy, when it recedes. It is a game which the innocents, prostrated by the heat an hour before, never tire of playing. Or they flit in and out of the water like marine butterflies, and since each has his little pail and shovel, they amuse themselves by filling each other's bucket with the burning sand. After they have bathed, they throw themselves on the sand in imitation of their seniors of both sexes, who disregard the disapproving looks of those who think as we do in our lands, and allow themselves to be buried, pounded, and rolled in the fiery sand. This is regarded as healthy exercise and a wonderful opportunity to indulge in that superficial, vulgar, and noisy intimacy of which these prosperous people seem so fond.

But the amazing thing there is not this manner of bathing nor the cadaverous faces of the children, nor the whimsical bonnets and incredible attire of those young ladies, famed for the prodigality of their favors,

careless ways, and exaggerated inclination to laughter;
nor the murmurings of lovers, the bathhouses, and the
operas sung from atop tables in the cafes by singers
dressed as *Edgar* and *Romeo, Lucia* and *Juliet;* nor
the grinning and shrieking of the Negro minstrels,
who must be a far cry, alas, from the minstrels of
Scotland, nor even the majestic beach, and the soft,
still sunlight. The amazing thing there is the size, the
quantity, the sudden tangible outcropping of human
activity, that immense valve of pleasure opened to an
immense nation, those dining rooms which, at a distance, seem the pitched camp of an army, those prome-
nades that for a distance of two miles seem like carpets of
heads, that daily overflow of a prodigious nation onto a
prodigious beach, that mobility, that quality of advance,
that purposefulness, constant change, feverish rivalry of
wealth, that monumental aspect of the whole that
makes that land of amusement worthy of measuring
itself against the majesty of the nation which supports
it, the ocean that caresses it and the sky that crowns
it; that flowing tide, that overwhelming and irresistible
expansiveness and the taking for granted of the marvelous: these are the things that amaze.

Other nations—ourselves among them—live devoured by a sublime demon within that drives us to
the tireless pursuit of an ideal of love or glory. No
sooner do we find within our grasp the ideal we pursue, with the pleasure with which one grapples an
eagle, than a new desire seizes us, a new ambition
spurs us on, a new aspiration sends us in pursuit of
a new, burning ideal. From the captive eagle there

emerges a rebellious butterfly, challenging pursuit and summoning us to follow its fitful flight.

Not so with those tranquil souls, stimulated only by a desire for gain. One scans those shimmering beaches; one strolls through these galleries as vast as plains; one ascends to the summit of those colossal structures, tall as mountains; one views the throngs seated in comfortable chairs along the seashore, filling their lungs with the fresh, invigorating air. But it is said that those from our lands who remain here long are overcome with melancholy; they seek and never find themselves. However much the first impressions gratify their senses, enamor their eyes, dazzle and bewitch their reason, the anguish of solitude overtakes them in the end, and a nostalgia for a superior spiritual world invades and oppresses them. They feel like lambs without ewe or shepherd, lost from the fold. Whether or not they rise to their eyes, bitter tears flood their souls because this great nation is void of spirit.

But what coming and going! What torrents of money! What facilities for every pleasure! What absolute absence of any outward sadness or poverty! Everything in the open air: the animated groups, the immense dining rooms, the peculiar courtship of North Americans, which is virtually devoid of the elements that compose the shy, tender, and elevated love in our lands, the theatre, the photographers' booth, the bathhouses! Some weigh themselves, for North Americans are greatly elated, or really concerned, if they find they have gained or lost a pound. Others pay fifty cents to receive their horoscope in an envelope from a robust German girl; others, with inexplicable delight, drink disagreeable mineral waters from long, narrow glasses.

Commodious carriages carry them from Manhattan Beach to Brighton in the soft twilight. One, who has been rowing with his lady friend, beaches the boat, and she places her hand on his shoulder with firm resolve and springs, happy as a little girl, to the shore. A group stands by in open-mouthed admiration while an artist cuts out a silhouette in black paper which he pastes on a white cardboard and presents to whoever asks to be portrayed in such a singular manner. Another group marvels as a lady fashions strange flowers from fish skins in a booth no more than three feet wide. Peals of laughter greet the success of one who has just thrown a ball and scored on the nose of an unfortunate Negro, who day and night sticks his head through a hole in a canvas screen, and in return for a miserable wage, allows the patrons to throw at his head, avoiding the balls with grotesque movements and exaggerated alarm. Others, some bearded and venerable, sit gravely on a wooden tiger, a hippogriff, a mermaid, or a coiled boa, ranged in a circle as if they were horses, which turn for a few minutes around a central stanchion to the accompaniment of off-key sonatas rendered by a group of self-styled musicians. The poor people eat shrimps and oysters on the beach, or pastries, and meats on the free tables provided by some of the big hotels for such meals. The wealthy squander huge sums on purple infusions that pass for wine, and strange, heavy dishes, which our palates, delighted by the artistic and the light, would surely find little to our taste. These people enjoy quantity; we enjoy quality.

This spending, this uproar, these crowds, the activity of this amazing ant hill never slackens from June to October, from morning 'til night, without pause, without interruption, without variation.

What beauty at night! True, the number of married women without their husbands gives pause to a reflective person; or the many mothers strolling along the seashore with their little sons on their shoulders, mindful of their pleasure, but not of the ill effects of the damp night air on the delicate constitution of their child; and so many ladies who leave their child in a hotel in the arms of a rough Irish maid, and when they return from their long walk neither take their whimpering child in their arms, nor kiss his lips, nor satisfy his hunger.

But there is no panorama more splendid in any city than Cable Beach in the evening. Were there many heads by day? There are more bright lights at night. Seen from the ocean, each of the four villages is a separate glowing mass in the distance. It seems that all the stars that populate the sky have fallen suddenly into the ocean in four colossal clusters.

The electric lights flood the verandas of the hotels with a caressing, magic light, the English gardens, the bandstands, the beach itself where one can count the grains of sand by that intense light. From afar, the lights seem restless, disembodied spirits, smiling, diabolical spirits, that mischievously flit through the wan gas lights, the strings of red flares, the Chinese and Venetian lanterns. Newspapers, programs, advertisements, billboards can be read as plain as day. It is a world of stars, with orchestras, dancing, merriment, surf sounds, human sounds, choruses of laughter, gentle breezes, barkers chanting, swift carriages, swifter trains, until the hour comes to go home. Then, like a monster that vomits its content into the hungry maw of another monster, that colossal crowd, that straining, crushing mass, forces its way onto the trains, which speed across the wastes, groaning under their burden, until they surrender it to the tremendous steamers, enlivened by the sound of harps and violins, which take up the holiday throng, convey it to the piers, and debouch the weary merrymakers into the thousand trolleys that pursue the thousand tracks that spread through slumbering New York like veins of steel.

PRIZE FIGHT

February 1882

he pen soars when it has grand things to relate, but it plods, as it does now, when it must give
account of brutal things, devoid of beauty and nobility.
The pen should be spotless like a virgin. It writhes
like a slave, it flees the paper like a fugitive, it swoons
in the hand that holds it as though it shared in the
wrong it describes. There are men here who fight like
bulls, running together, skull against skull. They bite
and claw one another during the fight, and when it is
over, one of the combatants, streaming blood, his gums
depopulated, his forehead bruised and knuckles raw,
staggers through the crowd that swirls around him,
scaling hats in the air and shouting its acclaim, to collect the purse that is his reward for victory. At the
same moment, his opponent lies senseless in the arms
of his handlers, his vertebrae shattered, and women's
hands arrange bouquets of flowers to perfume the
crowded dressing rooms of these base ruffians.

These fights are national holidays, setting trains and
telegraphs in motion, paralyzing business for hours,

and bringing together knots of laborers and bankers in the streets. Bets are laid to the clink of glasses, and the newspapers, which editorialize against the practice, fill their pages with accounts of the comings and goings, the comments, private life, training, feuds, triumphs and defeats of the rivals. Every heartbeat of these low fellows is recorded as though the blood of martyrs flowed in their veins. Their physiques are described minutely, and the whiteness and smoothness of their skin. Their muscles and limbs are measured and compared. Their dress, their meals, their most trivial remarks, their weights, are reported daily. Their battle colors are blazoned. Their footgear for the ring is sketched.

That is a prize fight. With such preparations, the Giant of Troy and the Boston Strong Boy have just fought. In this manner, the Giant was sent reeling to the ground, senseless and gory, while 2,000 spectators roared. That is what has kept New Orleans at carnival pitch, every hamlet in the country on tenterhooks, and Boston, New York, and Philadelphia in visible excitement. I can still see the city urchins, who are like green fruit withered on the vine, clinging to the wheels and sides of the newspaper wagon like an angry swarm of bees. The customers crowd around the wagon, which pulls away, drawn by the dray horse to which it is hitched, leaving behind a welter of newspaper peddlers fighting over the bundles of newspapers dropped off by the wagon. They are miserable little girls, or fierce Irish ragamuffins who get up from the mud cursing the hats they lost in the scuffle. New wagons arrive and the fighting breaks out anew. Those who are fortunate enough to get newspapers cannot sell them fast enough to satisfy the customers who besiege them. Great crowds shiver in the rain and peer up at the bulletin boards the leading newspapers post in front of their offices with the latest particulars on the fight. The children learn from the newspaper their father brings home which blow closed which eye, whose right bloodied whose nose, and how a fighter can kill his opponent by politely pushing back his face with one hand while hitting him on the back of the neck with the other. Pictures of the fighters, drawings of their pennants, and sketches of the fighting are published by the newspapers. The conversation around the family dinner table is of how this friend lost $100, while another won $1,000, and yet another $1,000 more, because some bet on the Giant, and others on the victorious Strong Boy. That was New York the afternoon of the fight.

But what of the fight itself? It was off in the South beside the sea, beneath cedars and live oak. These are not squabbles between knaves, inflamed or cooled by circumstances, and governed by caprice. They are contests between brutes under contract, in which, as in the days of jousting, the field is divided according to the sun, and the weight of the combatants and rules of the contest are formally agreed upon in the greatest detail, as in a horse race. The contestants will fight on foot, without rocks or irons in their hands, and with no more than three cleats, rounded at the ends and not to exceed a half-inch in length, on the soles of their shoes. It is agreed, with an eye to decorum, that this time there will be no biting or scratching, and that no blows are to be struck while an opponent has a knee and a hand touching the ground, nor while he is held by the neck against the ropes or ring posts, which are to mark out an area of level ground no more than twenty-four feet square. Furthermore, the battle colors of the rivals are to be hoisted atop the main post for all to see, in this case, a harp, a sun, a moon, and a shield, with a broad-winged eagle perched on a star-spangled sphere for the Giant of Troy, and an eagle holding an American shield flanked by American and Irish flags aloft in the clouds, for the Boston Strong Boy. For it was from Ireland, with the great migration, that this barbarous sport came to this country.

The ages of man are simply this: a transition from the man-beast to the man-man. There are moments when the beast in man gets the upper hand, and teeth feel a need to bite, a murderous thirst consumes the throat, eyes become flames, and clenched fists must find bodies on which to rain their blows. The human victory consists in restraining the beast and placing over it an angel. But while the industrious Aztecs and cultivated Incas were building roads over the mountains, channeling their rivers through immense conduits, and fashioning delicate rings for the fingers of their women, the men of those northern lands, like the Cain of Cormon, who opposed their hairy chests and hide-covered backs to the spears of Caesar's legions, pitched their nomad tents in the craggy highlands, and tore the half-cooked flesh from the steer roasted in the hide, which they had throttled in their arms of steel. Their arms seemed mountain sides, their legs tree trunks, their hands maces, and their heads forests.

Living was once a struggle with the beasts for control of the forests. Life is no longer a wild mountain, but a statue carved out of the mountain.

So it is, that one's eyes start, as if one saw Cain lumbering through the streets of a modern city, to see how the arts of illustration and printing abjectly lick the horned feet of these human beasts, represent and celebrate the magnificent brutes, and breathlessly seize on the instant in which, naked to the waist and flexing his trunk-like arm, he propels a leather ball toward the ceiling from which it hangs with the same blows he will later loose, to the sound of hurrahs and cheers, against the creaking skull, the swollen lips, and the trembling body of his terrified opponent. They train for the fight, build up their strength, work off the superfluous flesh that burdens and does not withstand assault; they retire with a camp retinue to isolated training sites where their coaches teach them excellent blows, forbid them excesses of the flesh, and show them off to the professional gamblers, who demand to see the fighter in action before betting because "this is strictly business," and they want to bet on "the best man." It is strictly business with the fighters, too, who often have never laid eyes on each other before meeting face to face in the ring. A promoter, with $2,000 backing one fighter, and a newspaperman, with $2,000 on the other, have arranged the match for the "heavyweight championship of America." The fighters are delighted, for the winner of the bloody fight stands to gain fame and fortune by shattering the bones and rattling the brains of his opponent. There are 130-pound runts who battle for the honor of being the wealthiest fighter among the lightweights, and there are 200-pounders who fight for the title of heavyweight champion.

As soon as the match is set, those who train the boxer, his "seconds," take charge, making sure that the "fighting man" does not jeopardize the investment of his "backer" by drinking and wenching. The nation becomes the pit for a cockfight. The two men tour the country and box with gloves, naked to the waist, in theatres, squares, and casinos, where their colors are displayed. The managers mingle with the crowds, boast of their fighter's accomplishments, let the spectators feel their muscles, argue the odds, and take bets from the local gamblers. Factions develop in every town, and often as not, the exhibition ends in a riot with the rival gangs leaping onto the ring or the stage with pistols and knives drawn. Troy loves its Giant, who is the owner of a theatre, a family man, and a prodigy of the ring; it burns with envy of Boston, which boasts that no man ever measured himself against the Strong Boy without being carried all bloody from the ring. Do not ask who halts this barbarous practice, for it occurs in public places month after month, and no one lifts a finger. There are laws to be sure, but it is the same as in Mexico with the bullfights, which serve to make bulls out of men. Bullfighting is prohibited in Tenochtitlan, but it is permitted in nearby Tlalnepantla, where Netzahualcoyotl, the poet king, once prayed in his tower, and now men born to better things because of the greatness of the land that bred them, affect the costume of the bullfighter and slaughter beasts in the ring.

As the day of the fight draws near, the fighters keep
one jump ahead of the law, for each state has different
statutes, and there are many distinguished lawmakers
who are strongly opposed to prize fighting. But there
are states that will take them in, and their arrival
touches off a general celebration. The trains come
from every direction loaded with bettors, who have
closed down their businesses, widowed their wives,
orphaned their children, and come thousands of miles
to stand in the midst of the turbulent multitude that
will crowd around the ring with burning faces, flailing
arms, and hats pushed back on their heads, the morning
of the long-awaited fight. It is not only riffraff and touts
who attend these fights; there are bankers, judges, men
of position, pillars of the church in their communities,
and young bucks, whose money should be cast into a
yoke to bow their brazen necks. Every city has a boxing
club, and some cities have many. Every club sends a
representative; every bettor commissions an observer;
every enthusiast goes to experience the thrills of the
encounter. The doors of the hotels and saloons never
stop swinging. The free-spending gamblers with their
extravagant ways, and the boxers with their bulging
muscles, have the ladies and girls of the city agog.
They do not shun them as abhorrent beings, but watch
them with curiosity and delight, as if they were great
men and privileged beings.

In New Orleans, near the scene of the fight, the old
families unearthed their savings, hidden away since
the days of the terrible war, and staked the tarnished
coins on the courage of one or the other of the brutes.
The streets were filled day and night, and it was like a

family affair. Everywhere one heard the clink of glasses, boisterous talking, heated discussions in stores and on street corners of the respective merits of the fighters, and the rush of feet as droves of people hurried to satisfy their hungry eyes with a glimpse of the broad back, sloping shoulders, and whipcord thighs of the athletes. Some came away crestfallen because their idol seemed fleshy about the ribs, and others came away elated because their man was all muscle and bone. Physicians went in groups to examine these rare physical specimens. Ladies went to touch the gnarled fists of the heroes with their slender fingers.

The whole city seemed in preparation for a journey during the night that preceded the dawn excursion. People slept in chairs, in sofas, and elbow to elbow in balconies, fearful that the train might leave without them and render useless the $10 they had paid for a place from which to watch the fight. They emptied their pockets of valuables and stripped the rings from their fingers and had them deposited in hotel safes so they would not be robbed on the journey, for deft pickpockets were known to be abroad. At last the train speeds across the bayou country of Louisiana, with the fighters, the seconds, the sponges, liniments and salves, and the purse for the fight; with the railway coaches filled to the top, and the overflow clinging to the roofs. Now comes the drinking, the shouting, and the laying of bets. Now the agreement that a good fighter must be fearless, agile, and game. Now the reminiscing about the good old days in New York when electoral campaigns were bare-knuckle affairs in the alleys; the stories retold of how a certain McCoy killed Chris Lilly in the ring, and how the bonfires burned along Park Row after Hyer defeated Sullivan "in a whirlwind fight," and how the huge sign hung for months on the famous old street where the post office now stands: "Tom Hyer, champion of America." Between swigs of burning liquor, some recall how Morrisey left Heenan for dead; others remember the blow to the forehead with which McCool felled Jones, that left him vomiting as if his brain had been shaken from its moorings; others remember Mace as a great slugger, who threw punches like a windmill and broke Allen's neck with one good blow. The morning sunlight streams through the coach windows!

At the scene of the fight, which was the city of Mississippi, the approaches to the ring site are already filled with people. Men are roosting in the trees, the curious peer from every balcony, and spectators stand embattled on the roof tops. The train unburdens itself of its human cargo. The ring is set up, with another larger surrounding ring, within which only the privileged may come. Singing happily, the newspapermen take their seats at ringside in a gleeful band, when suddenly hurrahs rend the air, and every hand is waving a hat, as the scowling Sullivan enters the ring in short pants and a green jersey, and the handsome Ryan, the Giant of Troy, takes his place in the opposite corner, attired in spotless white. There are ladies in the inner circle. The ruffians shake hands, and the blood that will soon stream from their wounds begins to boil. Squatted on the ground, their seconds count the money that has been bet on the two men. Why

look at them? In a moment one is down; he is dragged
to his corner and feverishly sponged. They rush at
each other again and deal each other mace-like blows;
their skulls resound like anvils beneath the hammer.
Ryan's jersey is crimson with gore, and he falls to his
knees. The Strong Boy skips back to his corner, laughing. The roar is deafening. Ryan rises shakily. Sullivan
moves in for the kill with his lips twisted in a smile.
They clinch and maul each other's faces; they stumble
back against the ropes. Nine times the assault; nine
times one goes reeling to the ground. Now the Giant
is staggered, now his cleated shoes no longer can help
him keep his footing, now he falls like a stone from a
blow to the neck, and on seeing him senseless, his
second throws the sponge in the air in token of defeat. Some $300,000 have been wagered across the
country on this fight; telegraph circuits have been set
up to every corner of the nation to speed a blow-by-
blow account to eager throngs that fill the streets of
the great cities and receive the news of the victory
with clamorous applause or angry mutterings. The
victorious Bostoner has been the toast of balls and
parties, and the Strong Boy and the Giant have toured
the country again to be feted and entertained in theatres and casinos. The sands by the sea are still red and
trampled in the city of Mississippi! This nation is
like a great tree: perhaps it is Nature's law that grubs
must nestle in the roots of great trees.

OKLAHOMA LAND RUSH

April 1889

New York has a short memory. Was the postmaster's death as much the result of sorrow as of sickness because his own Republican party stripped him of the job he had achieved rung by rung, from the mail route to the executive chair, to give it to a bearded ward heeler who spends his time in the saloons standing rounds of beer and toadying to the neighborhood leaders? Has City Hall refused to permit the extension of the elevated, which defaces the city and fills it with smoke and noise? Is the latest fad a stiff bow tie in the national colors? Are the streets almost impassable for the scaffoldings and half-finished stands, and is the air red, white, and blue calico and muslin because the flags and bunting for the centennial shut out the sky? Are seats for the parade going for $10 apiece, windows for $150, and boxes in the ballroom where the grand ball is to be held for $1,000? Was Good Friday a working day like any other, sanctified only by the beauty of the spring day which one drew in with every breath and which sparkled in women's eyes?

New York has a short memory. A fire worthy of the centennial consumes the grain elevators of the New York Central railroad. The river flows uselessly at their foundation. The fire engines huff and puff and spit out sparks, defeated. Six blocks are in flames. The black, scarlet, yellow, red flames snap at each other, embrace, and whirl up within the shell of the walls in tornadoes and fire spouts, like a solar disturbance. The glare extends for miles, silvering the steeples of churches, tracing the shadows on the pavement as sharply as inlay, and falling on the sign of a school front that says: "Girls." The hushed crowd of some 150,000 spectators watches the boiling sea of fire with the emotions of a Roman circus. Black smoke pours from a shortening refinery, with its thousand barrels in storage, and its tanks of crude cottonseed oil. Flames belch out of the main elevator. The roof, which touched the clouds, gives way with a roar, the asbestos falls in embers, and the steel girders twist and curl like wood shavings. A whole block of fire rages within the four walls. Burning oil spills from the piers and spreads over the river, surrounding a steamer that flees, pursued by the flames. The one who ventures to approach the inferno shielded by a fireman has no ears for the comments of the throng—the foolhardiness of permitting such a fire hazard to exist in the heart of the city; the loss, estimated at $3,000,000; the magnificence of the spectacle, more beautiful than the Chicago fire; the majesty of the human scene, the amphitheatre of marble faces transfixed by the conflagration. All he hears is the sobbing of the flames, like the sounds of a gale; and his heart is gripped by the sorrow a thoughtful person feels in the presence of destruction. One tower is already charred ruins, with glowing chinks from which smoke curls. Another tower is still ablaze, spreading a yellow pall over the city. The next morning, the motley crowd that always gathers to witness death, contemplated the burning shell in silence —pasty-faced youths with tobacco-stained lips, working girls in bedraggled silk and velvet, barefoot boys in hand-me-down coats, and dirty-faced hoboes, with brimless hats and shoes held together with string. A path opens before the director of an insurance company. His hands are burned.

The river was a riot of colors the next day, and Fifth Avenue a human sea for the Easter Parade. The millionaire patiently allows the Jewish shopkeeper to step on his feet. There are miles of people, each displaying a new outfit. The men wear lilac cravats and red carnations, light-colored coats and glistening top hats; the women, all finery and jewels, in the stylish jacket of the Directoire, with buttons the size of saucers and ornaments of braid, when not of gold and silver. Pearl and green are the colors in fashion; hussar caps, and hats that lack only cockleshells to match the pilgrim cape. The crowd along the curb is joined at one o'clock by those in silk and flowers who sang hymns in the Protestant churches, or heard Cherubini's mass in the Cathedral. The sidewalks are now choked, and carriages come to the rescue of swooning young ladies. The elaborate dresses sweep past, attracting eyes and envy, barely acknowledging the greetings of the plainer gowns, and making a display of their price. Bracelets are worn over gloves, and chains of silver, with endless links and adornments, jingle at the waist. Blue eyes are in a minority, and the Hebrew eye predominates. Stout women are the rule. There are few tall ones.

But over on Sixth Avenue there is a sight that warms the cockles of the heart. What if the young men dress with exaggerated elegance, in patent leather shoes with yellow spats, checked pants that suggest a chessboard, snug-waisted jackets with lapels like flower petals, and gloves that poke red fingers out from between lapel and vest! What if all the finery in the stores is not enough for their ladies, who wear purple frocks over red petticoats, or black and yellow shawls over a violet dress. The parents of these dandies and dudes, who greet each other with waist-deep bows, and these full-lipped beauties, with black faces and kinky hair, are those who twenty-five years ago, their cotton shirts stained with blood and their backs striped by the lash, sowed rice and tears in the same ground, and harvested the cotton with dragging steps. Thousands of well-to-do Negroes live in the vicinity of Sixth Avenue. They love without fear; they raise families and fortunes; they talk and make public their opinions; even their physical appearance has been altered by their spiritual change of state. It is a pleasure to see the respect with which they greet their bearded, frock-coated elders, and the courtesy with which the young men take leave of their sweethearts on the corner. They discuss the minister's sermon, the happenings at the lodge, the success of their lawyers, or the achievement of some Negro student who has just graduated from a medical school at the head of his class. All hats rise at once as one of their doctors rides past in a fine carriage.

And at that same hour homesteaders wait impatiently on the distant prairie for the stroke of noon on Monday when they will invade the new Promised Land and stake their claims in the ancestral hunting ground of the Seminole. They clean their rifles, pray, and carouse. All along that straining frontier, held in check only by the vigilance of the troops, one hears the shouted greetings of the penniless who are about to become landowners, of the speculators who see a froth of gold, of the adventurers who live by crime and death. Who will be the first to arrive? Who will drive the first stake on the plot that will front the main street? Who will lay claim with the heels of his boots to the fertile acres? Miles of wagons; a welter of horsemen; random shots fired in the air; songs and sermons; taverns and sporting houses; a coffin, followed by a woman and child; from the four corners of that land besieged by settlers one cry goes up: "Oklahoma! Oklahoma!"

The white invader is now rampant in the land of the Indian that was left as if without a soul when Osceola lay down and died in his war paint with his knife on his breast because he "did not have the heart to kill the white man like a bear or a wolf, although he comes upon us like a bear or a wolf, with friendship in one hand and a serpent in the other." So spoke Osceola, arrayed in his wampum belt and feathered head-dress in the hour of death, half his face painted red and his knife unsheathed. The Seminoles sold the land to the "Great White Father" in Washington with the understanding that other Indians or Negro freedmen might come and live there. Neither Indian nor Negro ever set foot on it, but cattlemen, who strung fences through it as if they owned it, and homesteaders who wanted it for fields to sow and a place to live, and not "so that these kings of the earth who have friends in Washington can fatten on pure gold." The blood of strife ran where only the blood of the hunt had flowed before. Federal troops forced out the trespassing cattlemen and settlers. The President finally proclaimed the area of the public domain, and set April 22 as the date for its occupation. Ready, on your mark! The first to drive the stake claims the land! A section by law to the first to arrive! After ten years of work, the railroads, the speculators, those who want to "grow with the country," those to whom the soil of Kentucky or Kansas has not been kind, those who want finally to settle down somewhere, who are tired of living on the move, hungry one day, begging the next, gather on the borders of the territory where many of them have already been squatters, raising children and grazing cattle on the very spot ambition has marked as the best site for the city, and where the only signs of man now are the ashes of the settlers' cabins, the tracks of the railroad and the red station.

The isolated towns along the frontier fill up with people; horses and wagons soar in price; bronzed faces, of dark and sinister eye, turn up where they were never seen before; there are hand-clasps in the shadows between those vowing aid to one another and death to their rivals. The settlers close in from every side until they are face to face with the cavalry guarding that million acres of free land. There they wait in silence, side by side, with their horses, their covered wagons, their rifles on their shoulders, and their wives beside them. Only the marshals named by the President are allowed within the territory, and persons authorized by the army, such as railroad workers laying track, a newspaperman setting up his press, a hotel man preparing his establishment, and the employes of the land office, where the eager throng must register its claims in orderly turn. But the word is going around that a suspicious number of marshals have entered the territory, that the railroads have hidden people in the underbrush, that the army has certified hotel men who have no hotel, and that the railroad owners have made a bargain with the government so that Guthrie, where the red station stands, will be completely staked out by the time the territory is legally opened.

But they continue to pour in from near and far. Whole towns have migrated. In clusters, in straggling lines, in cavalcades they come, amidst clouds of dust. The silent land stretches, virgin and green, with its grassland and bluffs, surrounded on all four sides by human masses, fenced off only by the flanks of the mounted troops. Burning eyes peer between the flanks. This is how the wilderness has been settled here, and how the wonder called the United States has come into being.

As the entry day approaches, the region is like an entire nation on the move, like a camp on the march, for miles around. There is no fear of the sun or the night, of death or rain. Railroads have extended their tracks into the famed territory; rival communities have sprung up to receive the caravans that come from afar, the horsemen carrying a deck of cards between their teeth, pistols at a hair-trigger, and their queans on the saddle behind them, pilgrim bands of army veterans, farmers, old men and widows.

Arkansas City has torn the awnings from its houses to make beds for the immigrants, and every saw in town is nicked and dulled from cutting up lumber for benches and tables. There is no milk left to sell a pioneer woman who steps down from the wagon where her husband watches over their only possessions—a tent, a stove, a plow, and the stakes with which to establish their claim to the land. There are seventy-five wagons in Arkansas City under lock and key ready to make the dash to Guthrie with the people that crowd its streets, beg, drink whiskey till it runs out of their ears, buy land now, sell it a moment later, and calculate their profit on the transaction. Land not yet owned is selling for two dollars an acre in Oklahoma City where speculators count on their agile rider, who will not hesitate to kill to arrive first and stake a claim. Night is converted into day in Purcell, where a thousand Texas cowboys are roaming the town, and there is not a man without a woman. Pistol shots and drunken guffaws are heard on every side: Heaven help the home-bodies in the wagons if they get in their way! The best land to the best rifle! "If they try to stop me with a child, Henrietta, I'll bring him back to you as beef-steak!" The carousing goes on until they fall asleep in their vomit.

The migrating towns, the towns on wheels, roll by toward the frontier. When the horses tire, the men put their shoulder to the wheel. If the men cannot do it alone, their wives get behind the other wheel. The beast's knees buckle, and the strapping son, his belt bristling with knives, kisses and caresses it. Day comes to a close, but not the journey. Now it is a thousand veterans, womanless and in good wagons, seeking land. Now it is a hundred men, with a Negro walking alone at their head. Now a group of cowboys on horseback in boots and blue shirts, four revolvers in their belt and a Winchester across the saddle, passing the bottle and mouthing oaths. Here come a hundred more, with a woman leading the way. There goes the Widow Dickinson, with three daughters and two rifles bouncing in the wagon. Many wagons carry a sign painted on the canvas: "Land or bust!" One wagon, from which boots stick out from under every flap as though it were filled with men stretched out, carries this sign: "There are plenty of damn fools like us!" Covered with dust, and with spades on their shoulders, a group of men plods forward under the command of a tall, spare man who is everywhere at once, with a spring in his step and a word of encouragement on his lips, hat pushed back, a few straggling hairs on his chin and two burning coals for eyes, in a faded shirt, and pants made out of an American flag tucked in his boots. Others come at a gallop with two bodies thrown across the saddle: two brothers who killed each other in a knife fight over which had the better "title" to a section that had already been picked out, "nobody knows where." Here comes the great caravan, that of the "old settlers" who had been living in the territory these ten years, headed by the man who pushed the land act through Congress. His voice is martial, his shoulders broad, and he stands six feet in his socks. The troop marches forward a thousand strong, determined to throttle anyone who stands in their way to the land they consider their own, to which they returned when they were ousted by the cavalry, and where they already have staked their claim. The clouds suddenly pile up and rain comes down in torrents. The wind tips over the wagons and rips off their canvas coverings, and frightened horses bolt from under their riders. The storm passes as quickly as it came, and the caravan proceeds. Here is an entire hotel of tents and folding chairs; here the newspaper press; here a wagon filled with coffins.

Only one day more, only one day to go! Reports of bad doings come in from Purcell and Arkansas City. They say a cowboy was found in the morning impaled with a knife to the saloon table; that fast ponies are being sold at fabulous prices for the hour of entry; that the speculators have joined up with the desperadoes, and the desperadoes with one another, to defend the land they take away from the first arrivals, who will have no defense but that which they carry in their cartridge belt; that some thirty trespassers forded the river and entered the territory through a wood, and surrendered, one with his arm shot away, another with his jawbone shattered, another dragging himself along with a bullet in his belly, to the troops that went to dislodge them from their parapet, from which a youth, whose face could not be seen for the blood, emerged carrying a white flag. But the horses graze peacefully on this side of the frontier, where the best of the settlers are gathered. The people come in their Sunday best from miles around to where an old man with a milk-white beard calls them to services with a cowbell, a soap box serving as his pulpit. The veterans tell how they broke down and cried and hugged each other when they saw the land, and sang and shot off their rifles. A group squats in a circle, chin in hand, listening to the old Negress, Aunty Chloe, who has already raised chickens and kept a dog in Oklahoma before the soldiers put her out, and is now going back to the "land of the Lord" to see if she can find her chickens. Another group is made up of women who have come alone, like the men, to stake a claim for themselves, or to speculate in land they buy from others, like Polly Young, the pretty widow, who has already speculated in Kansas. Some will pool the lands they get and hold with horse and rifle, like the nine girls from Kentucky, who are pledged to work together. Some are going back to their lands, like Nellie Bruce, who hid in the woods with the chickens, when the soldiers put her father off his place, and burned down the cabin he had built so she could teach school. Nanny Daisy is going back to see if anybody has taken down the sign she left on the homestead which said: "This belongs to Nanny Daisy, who knows her way around, and has two medals for sharpshooting. Beware!" Nanny takes out her medals, mounts bareback, without bit or bridle, slides off the neck or the croup, twirls her pearl-handled revolver, tells how she slapped the judge who tried to kiss her, and recalls her days as a schoolteacher, as a candidate for the post of librarian in Kansas, and as a newspaperwoman in Washington. From around the bend in the road comes the sound of the crack of the whip and a high-pitched, girlish voice: "Ehoe! Hooray! Here we come in calico dresses and shingle bonnets! Ehoe! Hooray! Tommy Barny ran off with Judas Silo's wife! Here is pretty Ella Blackburn, and her three sisters, with no men but these two Colts at my side."

By noon the next day everybody is ready, everybody is silent; 40,000 human beings and not a sound. Those on horseback are crouched forward on their horse's neck; those in wagons, standing with their foot on the footboard, the lines in their hands. Those with spavined beasts are to the rear, so they will not be trampled. The swish of the horses' tails driving away the troublesome flies is the only sound. A bugle note rends the silence, the cavalry turns aside, and from all sides at once that human torrent pours into the territory, spur to spur, wheel to wheel, without cursing, without talk, all eyes fixed on the dry horizon. From Texas, the horsemen at a dead gallop, firing their rifles, standing in their stirrups, yelling like mad, and slapping their horses with their hats. From the opposite direction, the ponies from Purcell, running flank to flank, without yielding their place, without surrendering their advantage. From Kansas, at full tilt, the heavy, bouncing, thundering covered wagons on the heels of the riders. Some stop, unhitch the horses, leave the women with the wagon, saddle a horse, and overtake the horsemen. They pour into the valley.

They are lost from sight behind the bluffs, they reappear and are lost again, they dismount, three at a time, on the same acre of land, and face each other, murder in their eyes. One suddenly reins his horse short, dismounts, and sinks his knife in the ground. The wagons gradually come to a halt, and their hidden occupants, the wives and children, spread out on the prairie, where the father drives his stakes. They do not climb down, they erupt. The children roll in the grass, the horses whinny and swish their tails, the mothers shout distractedly and wave their arms. One late arrival does not want to surrender his place, and the father fires his rifle point blank in his face, and returns to laying out his stakes, kicking the body aside with his foot to clear the line. The horsemen disappear from sight in the distance. The torrent continues to pour in.

The railroad station, the tents of the troops, and the registry office, flying the flag, are in Guthrie, which will be the principal city. All of Arkansas City and Purcell moves into Guthrie. The men throw themselves into the cars like madmen, fighting, punching and biting to keep their place, tossing out their knapsacks and suitcases to be among the first arrivals, riding on the roofs of the cars. The first train pulls out with shouts and hur-rahs; the first car is filled with newspapermen. Few talk; eyes are as big as saucers. A deer runs by, and is riddled with shots from the train. "Oklahoma now!" calls a voice and they go out on the back platform to fire off their guns; they shoot through the window and stand on the seats, shouting and shooting off pistols at each other's feet.

They arrive: they tumble through the windows, they scramble over each other, men and women go down to-gether in a heap: to the office, to get in line! to the office, to file the claim! But the first arrivals find to their amazement that the city is plotted, divided, occu-pied, with one hundred claims filed in the office, and men clearing brush from the land, with a rifle slung over their shoulder and a knife in their belt. Treachery! The troops have proved false! The troops have permitted their friends to hide in the underbrush! These names are those of the Federal marshals who are not allowed to take land, but have done so! "People began coming out of the ground at noon," they say in the office. Hurry for what is left! Some carry a sign that says "Bank of Guthrie" which they have to put up two miles from the station when they had planned to put it up right across the street. One gets down on all fours to have a better claim to a lot than one who simply stands on his two feet. One sells a corner lot at five dollars a foot. But how is it that in twenty-five minutes there are corners, avenues, streets, and squares? The truth comes out: there was trickery! The favorites, those hidden in the underbrush, the ones who "came out of the ground," the ones who entered in the guise of marshals and railroad workers, held their meeting at 10 a.m., when, legally, there was no land on which to hold a meeting, and divided up the city, marked out the streets and lots, assigned themselves the best plots, and at twelve noon were placing their privileged signatures in the registry book. The frock-coated lawyers with pistol at the hip go about drumming up suits. "What for, so the lawyers will wind up with the land?"

Bankers offer loans to the settlers in return for mortgages on their property. Those coming from the prairie ride in to register a claim on horses that drop to their knees. Two by two they stand in line, crowding through the door of the registry office where their claims and title to one of the free sections will be recorded. That is one way to obtain land; another, surer but more dangerous, is to occupy it, stake it out, clear it, fence it, take the wheels off the wagon and pitch the tent. "Bank of Oklahoma" it says on one big tent. "Guthrie's First Hotel!" "Rifles for sale!" "Water, a nickel a glass!" "Bread, a dollar a loaf!" Tents everywhere, with banners, signs, gambling tables, and banjos and violins at the door. *"The Oklahoma Herald,* with the announcement of elections for city officers!" The meeting is at four o'clock, and 10,000 men are present. At five o'clock *the Herald* gets out an extra with the list of elected officials.

Sandwichmen parade through the crowds advertising names of carpenters, hardware merchants, and surveyors. One cannot see the ground for the discarded handbills. At nightfall, the red railroad station is a living city. Forty thousand children sleep for the first time on the Oklahoma prairie. A muted sound, like the beating of the surf, is carried by the night wind from the prairie.

The black shadows of those still abroad are thrown against the tents by the light from the fires. All night a light burns in the registry office. All night the pounding of the hammer is heard.

II: OUR

AMERICA

OUR AMERICA

January 1891

The villager fondly believes that the world is contained in his village, and he thinks the universal order good if he can be mayor, humiliate the rival who stole his sweetheart, or add to the savings in his sock—unaware of the giants with seven-league boots who can crush him under foot, or the strife in the heavens between comets, which streak through space, devouring worlds. What remains of the parochial in America must awake. These are not times for sleeping in a nightcap, but rather with weapons for a pillow, like the warriors of Juan de Castellanos: weapons of the mind, which conquer all others. Barricades of ideas are worth more than barricades of stone.

There is no prow that can cleave a cloud-bank of ideas. An energetic idea, unfurled in good season before the world, turns back a squadron of ironsides with the power of the mystic banner of the judgement day. Nations that do not know one another should make haste to do so, as brothers-in-arms. Those who shake their fists at each other, like jealous brothers who covet the same land, or the cottager who envies the squire his manor, should clasp hands until they are one. Those who allege the sanction of a criminal tradition to lop off the lands of their brother, with a sword dipped in his own blood, had best return the lands to the brother punished far beyond his due, if they do not want to be called thieves. The honorable do not seek money in satisfaction of debts of honor, at so much a slap. We can no longer be a people like foliage, living in the air, heavy with blossoms, bursting and fluttering at the whim of light's caress, or buffeted and tossed by the tempest: the trees must form ranks so the giant with seven-league boots shall not pass! It is the hour of muster and the united march. We must advance shoulder-to-shoulder, one solid mass like the silver lodes in the depths of the Andes.

+

Only the seven-month birthling will lack the courage. Those who do not have faith in their country are seven-month men. They cannot reach the first limb with their puny arms, arms with painted nails and bracelets, arms of Madrid or Paris; and they say the lofty tree cannot be climbed. The ships must be loaded with these destructive insects, who gnaw the marrow of the country that nourishes them. If they are Parisians or Madrilenians, let them stroll along the Prado under the lamplights, or take sherbet at Tortoni's. These carpenter's sons who are ashamed of their father for his trade! These American sons who are ashamed of the mother that loves them because she wears an Indian apron, and disown their sick mother, the scoundrels, abandoning her

on her sick bed! Well, who is the man worthy of the
name? The one who stays with his mother to nurse
her in her sickness, or the one who puts her to work out
of the sight of the world and lives off her labors in the
decadent lands, affecting fancy cravats, cursing the
womb that carried him, displaying the sign of traitor
on the back of his paper cassock? These children of our
America, which will be saved by its Indians, and goes
from less to more, these deserters who take up arms in
the armies of North America, which drowns its Indians
in blood, and goes from more to less! These delicate
beings, who are men but do not want to do the work of
men! The Washington who forged this land, did he go
to live with the English, to live with them during the
years in which he saw them coming against his own
country? These *incroyables* of their honor, who trail it
through alien lands, like their counterparts in the
French Revolution, with their dancing, their affecta-
tions, their drawling speech!

For in what lands can a man take greater pride than
in our long-suffering republics of America, raised up
from among the mute Indian masses by the bleeding
arms of a hundred apostles to the sounds of battle between the book and the thurible. Never in history have
such advanced and unified nations been forged in less
time from such disordered elements. The fool in his
pride believes that the earth was created to serve him
as a pedestal because words flow easily from his pen,
or his speech is colorful, and he charges his native land
with being worthless and beyond salvation because its
virgin jungles do not provide him with means to travel
continually abroad, driving Persian ponies and lavish-

ing champagne, like a tycoon. The incapacity does not
lie with the nascent country, which seeks suitable forms
and greatness that will serve, but with those who attempt to rule nations of a unique character, and singular, violent composition, with laws that derive from
four centuries of operative liberty in the United States,
and nineteen centuries of French monarchy. A decree
by Hamilton does not halt the charge of the *llanero*'s
pony. A phrase of Sièyes does nothing to quicken the
stagnant blood of the Indian race. One must see things
as they are, to govern well; the good governor in America is not one who knows how government is conducted
in France or Germany, but who knows the elements of
which his country is composed and how they can be
marshaled so that by methods and institutions native
to the country the desirable state may be attained
wherein every man realizes himself, and all share in
the abundance that Nature bestowed for the common
benefit on the nation they enrich with their labor and
defend with their lives. The government must be the
child of the country. The spirit of the government must
be the same as that of the country. The form of government must conform to the natural constitution of the
country. Good government is nothing more than the
true balance between the natural elements of the nation.

For that reason, the foreign book has been conquered
in America by the natural man. The natural men have
vanquished the artificial, lettered men. The native-born
half-breed has vanquished the exotic Creole. The struggle is not between barbarity and civilization, but between false erudition and nature. The natural man is

good. He respects and rewards superior intelligence, as long as his submission is not turned against him, or he is not offended by being disregarded, a thing the natural man does not forgive, prepared as he is to regain by force the respect of whoever has wounded his pride or threatened his interests. Tyrants in America have risen to power serving these scorned natural elements, and have fallen the moment they betrayed them. Republics have paid in tyrannies for their inability to recognize the true elements of their countries, to derive from them the proper form of government, and govern accordingly. To be a governor of a new country means to be a creator.

In nations of cultured and uncultured elements, the uncultured will govern, because it is their habit to strike and resolve all doubts by force, whenever the cultured prove incapable in office. The uncultured mass is lazy, and timid in matters of the mind. It asks only to be well-governed. But if the government hurts it, it rebels and governs itself. How can the universities be expected to produce governors, if there is not one university in America that teaches the rudimentary in the art of government, which is the analysis of the elements peculiar to America? Young men go out into the world wearing Yankee or French spectacles, and hope to govern by guesswork a nation they do not know. In the political race, all entries should be scratched who do not demonstrate a knowledge of the political rudiments. The prize in literary contests should go not to the best ode, but to the best study of the political factors in one's country. Newspapers, universities, and schools should foment the study of their country's dynamic factors. They have only to be stated, straightforward and in plain language. For whoever disregards any portion of the truth, whether by ignorance or design, is doomed to fall; the truth he lacked grows in the negligence and brings down whatever was erected without it. It is easier to determine the elements and attack the problem, than to attack the problem without knowing the elements. The natural man arrives, indignant and strong, and topples the authority based on books because he was not governed according to the obvious realities of the country. Knowledge holds the key. To know one's country, and govern it with that knowledge, is the only alternative to tyranny. The European university must give way to the American university. The history of America, from the Incas to the present, must be taught until it is known by heart, even if the Archons of the Greeks go by the board. Our Greece must take priority over the Greece that is not ours: we need it more. Nationalist statesmen must replace cosmopolitan statesmen. Let the world be grafted on our republics; but the trunk must be our own. And let the vanquished pedant hold his tongue: for there are no lands in which a man can take greater pride than in our long-suffering American republics.

+

With the rosary as our guide, our head white and our body mottled, both Indian and Creole, we intrepidly entered the community of nations. We set out to conquer liberty under the standard of the Virgin. A priest, a handful of lieutenants, and a woman

raised the Mexican Republic on the shoulders of the
Indians. A few heroic students, instructed in French
liberty by a Spanish cleric, raised Central America
against Spain under a Spanish general. In the ori-
flammed habits of monarchy, Venezuelans and Argen-
tinians set out, from north and south, to deliver nations. When the two heroes collided, and the continent
almost rocked, one, and not the lesser, turned back.
But when the wars ended, heroism, by being less
glorious, became rarer; it is easier for men to die
with honor than to think with order. It was discovered that it is simpler to govern when sentiments are
exalted and united, than in the wake of battle when
divisive, arrogant, exotic, and ambitious ideas emerge.
The forces routed in the epic conflict sought, with the
feline cunning of their species, and utilizing the weight
of realities, to undermine the new structure, which em-
braced at once the rude and singular provinces of our
half-breed America, and the cities of silken hose and
Parisian frock coat, beneath the unfamiliar flag of
reason and liberty, borrowed from nations skilled in
the arts of government. The hierarchical constitution
of the colonies resisted the democratic organization
of the republics. The capitals of stock and collar kept
the countryside of horse-hide boots cooling its heels
in the vestibule. The cultured leaders did not realize
that the revolution had triumphed because their words
had unshackled the soul of the nation, and that they
had to govern with that soul, and not against it or
without it. America began to suffer, and still suffers,
from the effort of trying to find an adjustment between the discordant and hostile elements it inherited

from a despotic and perverse colonizer, and the imported ideas and forms which have retarded the logical government because of their lack of local reality. The continent, disjointed by three centuries of a rule that denied men the right to use their reason, embarked on a form of government based on reason, without thought or reflection on the unlettered hordes which had helped in its redemption; it was to be the reason of all in matters of general concern, not the reason of the university over the reason of the province. The problem of the Independence was not the change in forms, but the change in spirit.

It was necessary to make common cause with the downtrodden, to secure the new system against the interests and habits of rule of the oppressors. The tiger, frightened off by the powder flash, returns at night to the haunts of his prey. When he dies, it is with flames shooting from his eyes and claws unsheathed. But his step cannot be heard, for he comes on velvet paws. When the prey awakes, the tiger is upon him. The colony lives on in the republic; and our America is saving itself from its grave errors—the arrogance of the capital cities, the blind triumph of the scorned country people, the influx of foreign ideas and formulas, the wicked and unpolitic disdain in which the aboriginal race is held—through the superior virtue, backed by the necessary conviction, of the republic that struggles against the colony. The tiger lurks behind each tree, waiting at every turn. He will die with his claws unsheathed and flames shooting from his eyes.

But "these countries will be saved," as the Argentine Rivadavia announced, whose sin was to be gentlemanly in crude times; a silk scabbard does not become the *machete*, nor can the lance be discarded in a country won by the lance, for it becomes angry, and presents itself at the door of Iturbide's congress demanding that "the blond one be made emperor." These countries will be saved because a genius for moderation, found in Nature's imperturbable harmony, seems to prevail in the continent of light, where there emerges a new realistic man schooled for these realistic times in the critical philosophy, which in Europe has succeeded the literature of sect and opinion in which the previous generation was steeped.

We were a strange sight with the chest of an athlete, the hands of a coxcomb, and the brain of a child. We were a masquerade in English trousers, Parisian vest, North American jacket, and Spanish hat. The Indian circled about us in silent wonder, and went to the mountains to baptize his children. The runaway Negro poured out the music of his heart on the night air, alone and unknown among the rivers and wild beasts. The men of the land, the creators, rose up in blind indignation against the scornful city, against their own child. We were all epaulets and tunics in countries that came into the world with hemp sandals on their feet and headbands for hats. The stroke of genius would have been to couple the headband and tunic with the charity of heart and daring of the founding father; to rescue the Indian; to make a place for the able Negro; to fit liberty to the body of those who rose up and triumphed in its name. We were left

with the judge, the general, the scholar and the preb-
endary. As if caught in the tentacles of an octopus,
the angelic young men lunged toward Heaven, only
to fall back, crowned with clouds, in sterile glory.
The natural people, driven by instinct, swept away the
golden staffs of office in blind triumph. The European
or Yankee book could not provide the answer to the
Hispanic-American enigma. Hate was tried, and the
countries wasted away, year by year. Exhausted by
the senseless struggle between the book and the lance,
of reason against dogma, of the city against the country, of the impossible rule by rival city cliques over
the natural nation alternately tempestuous and inert,
we begin almost without realizing it to try love. The
nations stand up and salute each other. "What are we
like?" they ask; and they begin to tell one another
what they are like. When a problem arises in Cojimar,
they do not send to Danzig for the answer. The frock
coat is still French, but thought begins to be American.
The youth of America roll up their sleeves and plunge
their hands into the dough; it rises with the leavening
of their sweat. They understand that there is too much
imitation, and that creation holds the key to salvation.
"Create" is the password of this generation. The wine
is from plantain, and if it proves sour, it is our wine!
It is understood that the forms of government must
accommodate themselves to the natural elements of
the country, that absolute ideas must take relative
forms if they are to escape emasculation by the failure
of the form, that liberty, if it is to be viable, must be
sincere and complete, that the republic which does not
open its arms to all, and move ahead with all, must

die. The tiger within enters through the fissure, and
the tiger from without. The general restrains his cavalry to a pace that suits his infantry, for if the infantry be left behind, the cavalry is surrounded by the
enemy. Politics is strategy. Nations should live in continual self-criticism, because criticism is healthy; but
always with one heart and one mind. Go down to the
unfortunate and take them in your arms! Dissolve
what is clotted in America with the fire of the heart!
Make the natural blood of the nations course and
throb through their veins! Erect, with the happy,
sparkling eyes of workingmen, the new Americans
salute one another from country to country. The natural statesman appears, schooled in the direct study
of Nature. He reads to apply what he reads, not to
copy. Economists study the problems at their origin.
Orators begin to be lofty. Dramatists bring native
characters to the stage. Academies consider practical
subjects. Poetry shears off its romantic locks and hangs
its red vest on the glorious tree. Prose, lively and dis-
criminating, is charged with ideas. Governors study
Indian in republics of Indians.

+

America is escaping all its dangers. The octopus still
sleeps on some republics; but others, in contrast, drain
the ocean from their lands with a furious, sublime
haste, as if to make up for lost centuries. Some, forgetting that Juárez rode in a mule-drawn coach, hitch
their coach to the wind and entrust the reins to a soap-
bubble; poisonous luxury, the enemy of liberty, cor-
rupts the frivolous and opens the door to the outlander.

In others, where independence is threatened, an epic
spirit produces a heightened manliness. Still others
spawn a rabble-in-arms in rapacious wars against their
neighbors which may yet turn and devour them. But
there is yet another danger which does not come from
within, but from the difference in origins, methods
and interests between the two halves of the continent.
The hour is fast approaching when our America will
be confronted by an enterprising and energetic nation
seeking close relations, but with indifference and scorn
for us and our ways. And since strong countries, self-
made by the rifle and the law, love, and love only,
strong countries; since the hour of recklessness and
ambition, of which North America may be freed if
that which is purest in her blood predominates, or on
which she may be launched by her vengeful and sordid
masses, her tradition of expansion or the ambition of
some powerful leaders, is not so near at hand, even to
the most timorous eye, that there is not time to show
the self-possessed and unwavering pride that would
confront and dissuade her; since her good name as a
republic in the eyes of the world puts on the America
of the North a brake which cannot be removed even
by the puerile grievances, the pompous arrogance, or
parricidal discords of our American nations, the press-
ing need for our America, is to show herself as she is,
one in soul and purpose, swift conqueror of a suffocating tradition, stained only by the blood drawn from
hands that struggle to clear away ruins, and the scars
left us by our masters. The scorn of our formidable
neighbor, who does not know us, is the greatest danger
for our America; and it is imperative that our neighbor

know us, and know us soon, so she shall not scorn us, for the day of the visit is at hand. Through ignorance, she might go so far as to lay hands on us. From respect, once she came to know us, she would remove her hands. One must have faith in the best in men and distrust the worst. If not, the worst prevails. Nations should have a pillory for whoever fans useless hates; and another for whoever does not tell them the truth in time.

There can be no racial hate, because there are no races. The rachitic thinkers and theorists juggle and warm over the library-shelf races, which the open-minded traveler and well-disposed observer seek in vain in Nature's justice, where the universal identity of man leaps forth from triumphant love and the turbulent lust for life. The soul emanates, equal and eternal, from bodies distinct in shape and color. Whoever foments and propagates antagonism and hate between races, sins against Humanity. But as nations take shape among other different nations, they acquire distinctive and vital characteristics of thought and habit, of expansion and conquest, of vanity and greed, which from the latent state of national preoccupation could be converted in a period of internal unrest, or precipitation of the accumulated character of the nation, into a serious threat to the neighboring countries, isolated and weak, which the strong country declares perishable and inferior. The thought is father to the deed. But it must not be supposed, from a parochial animus, that there is a fatal and ingrained evil in the blond nation of the continent, because it does not speak our tongue, nor see the world as we do, nor resemble us in its political faults, which are of a different order, nor favorably regard the excitable, dark-skinned people, nor look charitably, from its still uncertain eminence, on those less favored by History, who climb the road of republicanism by heroic stages. The self-evident facts of the problem should not be obscured for it can be resolved, to the benefit of peaceful centuries yet to come, by timely study and the tacit, immediate union of the continental soul. The hymn of oneness sounds already; the actual generation carries a purposeful America along the road enriched by their sublime fathers; from the Rio Grande to the straits of Magellan, the Great Semi, seated on the flank of the condor, sows the seed of the new America through the romantic nations of the continent and the sorrowful islands of the sea!

SIMÓN BOLÍVAR

Address before the

Hispanic American Literary Society

October 1893

With the contrite brow of the American who has yet to enter America, serene in the knowledge of the true place and worth of the great son of Caracas in the spontaneous, manifold achievement of the Independence, with the awe and reverence of one who still sees before him, demanding his due, that man whose majesty and amplitude were like the *samán* of the savannahs, the mountain river plunging through the gorge, and the red thunder of the crater, I bring the meager homage of my words, less profound and eloquent than my silence, to him who tore Pizarro's ensign from the skies of Cuzco. Above the carping and criticism, above the passions of praise and abuse, above even the shortcomings of that prince of liberty —black flecks on the condor's breast—the real man emerges radiant. He sears and enthralls. Reflect on him, scan his life, read one of his speeches, surprise him, ardent and breathless, in a love letter, and thought soars on golden wings. He burned with our own ardor for liberty; he spoke with the voice of our nature; his zenith was our continent's finest hour; his fall stills the heart. Speak Bolívar's name, and visions swim in the mind of the mountain crowned less by snow than by the caped horseman, or of steaming jungles through which the liberators swirl forward, three republics in their knapsacks, to strike the last chains from a continent. Oh, no! That life that never knew repose cannot be discussed with calm; one must speak of Bolívar from the tribune of a mountain, or amidst thunder and lightning, or with a fistful of free nations in one's grasp and tyranny beheaded at one's feet! No one need shrink from just admiration because it is perennially fashionable among a certain human type to belittle the extraordinary; at the same time, a low desire for applause should never allow the swollen phrase to silence the voice of sober judgement. Words can never express the mystery and sublimity of that mind at the disaster of Casacoima, when fever-ridden and deserted by his scattered army, he saw, as in a vision, the roads across the Andes over which he would carry liberty into the valleys of Bolivia and Peru. But whatever we said tonight, even were it exaggerated, would befit the occasion, for all of us gathered here are children of his sword.

Nor need the fear of offending our ladies stifle the tribute on our lips, for among American women one may speak of liberty without qualms. It is their glory to be descended of women like the daughter of Juan de Mena, the indomitable Paraguayan, who laid aside her widow's weeds and put on her finery when she learned that her countryman, Antequera, was to be hung as a patriot because "the day a just man dies gloriously for his country is a day of celebration"; and the Colombian girl, in homespun and calico, who anticipated the patriots, tore down the insolent edict on taxation in El Socorro, and set 20,000 men fighting; or the wife of Arismendi, pure as the finest pearl of Margarita, who told her captors when led out on the battlements in clear view of her husband shelling the fort: "You will never force a word past my lips to sway him in the performance of his duties"; and the noble Pola, who sent her sweetheart into battle, and shared death beside him on the gallows; or Mercedes Abrego, of the flowing tresses, who was beheaded because she embroidered the Liberator's uniform with her finest gold thread; and the loyal companions of Bolívar's soldiers, who rode with their men when they breasted the furious streams that plummet in foaming torrents from the Andean peaks, the milestones of Nature, on Liberty's march to Boyacá.

Of no man can it be said with more truth that he was in all ways extraordinary. He lived as if among flames, and he was flame. He loved, and spoke flowers of fire. He revered friendship, and the death of a loyal companion silenced all activity about him. He was weakly, yet with the speed of the fastest post his untried army swept all before it from Tenerife to Cúcuta. He led in battle, and in the darkest moment, with all eyes pleadingly upon him, he ordered his horse unsaddled. He wrote, and it was the gathering of a mountain storm that bursts suddenly over the gloomy valley; and then the sunlight slants through blue rifts in the black overcast, the clouds drift around the peaks, and the valley below sparkles with fresh colors. He was anchored like a mountain at his base, with roots deep in the ground, and rose to a lofty peak, as if to pierce the sky. One can see him knocking at the gates of glory with the golden hilt of his sabre. He believed in Heaven, in gods, in immortals, in the god of Colombia, in the genius of America, in his destiny. He laid siege to glory and took it by storm. Is it not a mark of divinity to have conquered? He conquered men, swollen rivers, volcanoes, centuries, Nature! Could he have undone the work of centuries if it were not that he would set new ones in motion? He unfettered races, disenthralled a continent, summoned up nations, and covered more peoples with the flag of liberty than ever a *conquistador* covered with that of tyranny! Did he not address eternity from Mt. Chimborazo with Potosí, one of history's most audacious and enduring creations at his feet, beneath the condor-studded flag of Colombia? Did not cities open their gates to him, and the powers of this earth? Did not all rivals submit to him in fear or adoration, and all the gifted sons and beauties of the New World? He came to think of himself as the sun in his power to thaw and give life, to illuminate and sear. If there is a Senate in Heaven, he is there. He now sees that world, golden with sunlight, and the seat of the rock of creation, the floor of clouds and the roof of stars, reminding him with their glinting light of his lances at Apure when they threw back the noon-day sun; from those heights, happiness and order descend on men as if from a paternal hand. But that is not so in this world, where the sum of divinity rises from the bloody and painful sacrifice and ordeal of all

men! He died in Santa Marta from the shock and hor-
ror of seeing the design he had thought immortal
broken in pieces. He confused his truly divine glory
of having served, which grows and is a crown no hands
can take from his brow, with the mere accident that
human power was his to wield. For power, which is
nearly always the corrupt employment and pursuit of
those who seek it for themselves with neither merit
nor courage, the barren triumph of one faction over
another, or the pawn of interests and passions, only
falls to virtue or genius in moments of crisis or reform, when nations, moved by danger, acclaim the idea
or unselfish motive in which they see their salvation.
But Bolívar is there in the American heaven, seated
on the rock of creation, vigilant and stern, with the
Inca at his side and flags clustered at his feet; he is
there, still wearing his campaign boots, because what
he did not complete has yet to be accomplished; because Bolívar still has work to do in America!

America seethed at the turn of the century and he
was like its crucible. That America still stirs and rears
its head, a huge creature, as yet undefined, like the
larvae one discovers beneath the bark of old roots.
The revolutionary message came from France and
North America under the priest's cassock and in the
minds of the cosmopolitan statesmen to sharpen the
discontent of the educated and well-bred Creoles, governed from across the seas by the law of tribute and
the gallows; in the measure that the rebellion grew
in high places, leavened by the rebellious and in a sense
democratic unrest of the second-born, disinherited
Spaniards, the Argentine *gaucho,* the Chilean *roto,*

the Peruvian *cholo*, and the Venezuelan *llanero*, chafed in their manhood, swallowed their sullen anger with new displeasure each day; abandoned in the cruel upheaval, the Indians, their defenseless faces furrowed with tears, wandered in bands through the forests, taking the small comfort of pillage, like tongues of fire licking at some huge pyre. The Independence of America had been shedding its blood for a century: our America springs neither from Rousseau, nor Washington, but from itself! In the scented evenings in his garden at San Jacinto, or along the banks of the mirrored waters of Anauco, where he may have guided the tiny feet of the bride plucked in first bloom, Bolívar, with clenched fist against his bosom, saw the terrifying procession of the forerunners of the Independence: the spectres come and go through the air, and there can be no rest until his task is finished! In the sunset against Mt. Avila he surely saw the bloody events to come . . .

The Paraguayan Antequera appears, first before any, raising his severed head; the whole family of the poor Inca, dismembered in the presence of their fettered father, advances, gathering up their quartered limbs; Tupac Amaru passes; then the king of the Venezuelan half-breeds, adrift in the air, like a phantom; then Salinas, asleep in his gore, Quiroga, pitched forward over his plate, and Morales, a living slaughter, because in Quito's prison their love of country never flagged; and León, dead in the cave, without a home to call his own, for they sowed his lands with salt; there on hooks come the limbs of Juan España, who died smiling on the gallows, and there the smoking torso of Galán, burned on the gibbet; Berbeo passes, most cruelly dead of all, though the executioner spared his life from fear of the patriots, because for one who has known the joy of fighting for the honor of his country, there can be no greater death than to live while the national shame continues. The hero wrapped himself in this soul, Indian, half-breed, and white merged into one flame, and found it constant and in-extinguishable. He fused disparate components in the brotherhood of the common cause by the flame of glory; he curbed or removed rivals; he crossed the timberline and humbled mountains; he sowed republics through the watershed of the Andes; and when he drew rein on his march, because the Argentine revolution opposed its collective and democratic endeavor to the Bolivarian drive, fourteen Spanish generals, huddled on the slopes of Ayacucho, had laid down their swords!

From the palms along the coasts, placed there as if to intone an endless paean to the hero, the land rises in terraces of silver and gold to the broad plateaus, slashed with blood by the American Revolution. The sky has rarely witnessed more beautiful scenes, for the determination to be free never stirred so many hearts, heroism never knew a setting of such natural grandeur, and the soul of a continent never entered so fully into that of one man. Heaven itself seems to have played a role, for those were battles worthy of Heaven; it was as if all the heroes of liberty and all the martyrs of the earth gathered in that beautiful firmament and hovered like a protective shield over the straits in which our souls struggled, or fled aghast through the unjust Heaven when the battle went

against us! Heaven must have paused, in fact, to
see such beauty: breath-taking waterfalls plunge like
runaway horses from the eternal snows; hoary trees
cling to the dark ravines like down or curled fleece;
the ruins of Indian temples keep a silent vigil over
the desert of lakes; the spires of Spanish cathedrals
pierce the fog in the valleys; the craters smoke and
erupting volcanoes reveal the bowels of the earth. All
the while, in every corner of the land, Americans are
fighting for liberty! Some gallop over the savannahs
and are snuffed out in the shock of combat like candles
in a wind; others, the reins gripped in their teeth,
swim swollen rivers with their cartridge belts held
over their heads; others scale a volcano and plant the
flag of liberty atop the flaming crater. But none so
beautiful as that man of high forehead above a face
devoured by eyes indifferent to steel or tempest, whose
cape billows behind him on his flying horse, and whose
sword sheds the light of freedom on five nations! He
draws rein on his black stallion, his hair wind-blown
by the tempest of victory, and reviews the ranks of
those who helped him crush tyranny: Ribas' republican cap, Sucre's gentle horse, Piar's curly head, Páez's
red cloak, Córdoba's slashing quirt, and the flag-
shrouded corpse of the colonel carried by his troops.
He stands breathless in the stirrups as Nature pauses
to see Páez and his wraith-like lancers charge at Las
Queseras and scatter the enemy ant hill in the dust
and shadows beneath the flying hooves of their mounts.
He looks on with moist eyes as his army makes merry
on the eve of Carabobo, pennants and ensigns flying,
masses of men rallying around the tattered battle flags,

music from every quarter, the play of the sun on steel, and through the whole encampment runs the mysterious joy that fills a household where a child is about to be born! But he was most beautiful at Junín, wrapped in the shadows of night, where the last Spanish lances splintered in the pale silence against the triumphant arm of America . . .

. . . And then, a little later, the shadow of death on his face, his hair clinging to his sunken temples, his feverish hand in a gesture of rejection of the world, the hero said on his death bed: "José! José! Let us go, for we are not wanted here; where can we go?" His government had fallen, but he may have thought the Republic was collapsing; local jealousies and rivalries had been largely submerged in the enthusiasm that surrounded the Independence, and he may have lost sight of, or discounted, these realistic forces which reappeared after the triumph; he may have been fearful that rival ambitions would wreck the new nations, and by hateful subjection he sought that political equilibrium which is constant only when based on freedom, and inevitable in a regime of justice, with the fewer restraints the better. Perhaps in his dream of glory for America and himself he did not see that the unity of spirit indispensable to the survival and happiness of our American states suffered more than it benefited from his union based on theoretical and artificial forms without roots in reality; perhaps the foresighted genius who proclaimed that the salvation of our America lies in the joint, unified action of our republics with respect to the rest of the world and the course of our future, was unaware, because it was foreign to his temperament, class, and education, of the moderating force of the popular will, the open struggle between sectors of opinion, which requires only the law of true liberty to be the safeguard of republics. The anxious father erred perhaps at the critical moment for all political creators when the voice of prudence counsels him to yield the helm to new leaders, that the title of usurper shall not sully his creation, while another voice, perhaps welling up from the mystery of the master creative idea, bids him suffer even the dishonor of being held a usurper for its sake.

For they were the daughters of his heart, which bled themselves white without him in a prolonged, accursed conflict; which took their life from his magnanimity and perseverance, and wrested from him, because theirs was the strife and the future, the power to rule themselves according to the needs and aspirations of their peoples! The relationship as basic as the attraction between stars that joined Bolívar and America for the work of the Independence disappeared, and the disaccord between Bolívar, determined to unite far-flung countries under a remote, central government, and the many-headed American Revolution, born of the desire for local self-government, became manifest. "José! José! Let us go, for we are not wanted here; where can we go?" . . .

Where will Bolívar go? To the respect of the world and the affection of all Americans! To this loving home, where every man is indebted to him for that ardent satisfaction of feeling himself in the arms of his own people whenever he is among Americans, and every woman adoringly remembers that man who al-

ways dismounted from his horse of glory to give
thanks for a wreath or flower received from beauty's
hands! To the justice of nations, which can see beyond
the possible error of hasty and personal measures,
and recognize the impetus Bolívar gave to the basic
ideas of America through these very measures, like a
powerful hand shaping molten lava! Where will Bolívar
go? Arm and arm with men of good will to defend
from new greed and old prejudices that land where
human life will be happier and more beautiful! To
peaceful nations like a father's kiss! To men without
horizon and triflers, to paunchy burghers and crop-full
Harpagons, that by the light of the blaze that was his
existence, they may see the brotherhood indispensable
to the continent, and the dangers and greatness the
future holds for America! Where will Bolívar go?
The life-blood of the last Spanish viceroy spilled from
his five wounds, three centuries were dragging from
the tail of the hero's horse, and wearing the cassock
of victory and small clothes of luxury, the Liberator
rode at the head of his army, as if bound for a ball.
Crowds gazed down from the overhanging ledges
amidst clusters of flags like flowerpots in a balcony.
Postosí appears at last, bloody and scarred. The five
flags of the new nations blaze with real fire atop a
resurrected America. The cannon boom the hero's approach, and over the mass of heads bared with respect
and fear, the thunder echoes and re-echoes from hillside to hillside as each mountain takes up the salute.
So, while America lives, shall the echo of his name
pass from father to son in what is best and manliest
in us!

JOSÉ ANTONIO PÁEZ

An American Hero

March 1888

Why this laughing sun, these thronged streets, this thunder of artillery and blare of bugles, this coming and going of aides on horseback? Carriages surround the armory of the Twelfth Infantry Regiment. It is a cold morning, but the turnout is large. Who is arriving now that everybody makes way and friendly greetings rise on every side? He carries a black-plumed tricorne in his hand; how can such spindly legs bear the weight of that massive torso? He is burdened by a huge chest and broad back; the epaulets square on his shoulders like the silver corner guards of an old-fashioned prayer book; whoever has faced a bull about to charge has seen his eyes. But as he has rubbed elbows with death and seen his cheering squadrons fall smiling at his feet; as he has gained his greatness in the clutch of danger, the audacity of his gaze is tempered by a magnificent benignity: his inscrutable eyes are deep, and flecked with gold. A pair of drooping black moustaches fall on either side of his beard. Who is this then who commands everyone's attention? It is Sheridan, and now Sherman, who helped Grant corner the exhausted Confederate forces near Richmond! And here is his brother, John Sherman, the able presidential candidate; and Sickles, who led the charge that wrested victory from the Confederates at Gettysburg, where he lost a leg, but gained glory; and Flower, who rose from the streets to become a powerful impresario; and Hewitt, who challenges Depew for the right to represent the Yankee spirit against the rising tide of Europe; and so a hundred more, the toast of Congress, the Church, Finance, the Army and the Republic, who have gathered, braving the biting cold, to accompany to the pier where the launch of a warship bound for Venezuela awaits them, the remains, forgotten long enough, of José Antonio Páez, who with no school but his savannahs, no discipline but his will, no strategy but his genius, and no army but his hordes, freed Venezuela from Spanish rule in a horse race that lasted sixteen years.

The procession moves down Fifth Avenue. Yesterday the corpse lay in state with a guard of honor at City Hall where for some years a picture has hung of the *llanero* as he appeared in later years: a well-set head with short, gray hair; a kindly, sensual mouth; marvelous, radiant eyes; a gold chain across his white vest. On the casket there were only five wreaths! There goes the procession, starting from the barracks at ten o'clock and reaching the pier at four.

The mounted police come first, led by Sickles in an open carriage with a blue cape over his shoulders and his crutch by his side; then the batteries, with their gleaming pieces; the infantry battalions; the regiments of the city's militia; Sheridan at the head of the cavalry; the Seventh Regiment, the pride of New York, guarding the black funeral coach; and finally Sherman and the Venezuelan officials, the generals, the magistrates, the Congressmen, the ministers, the consuls, prominent New Yorkers and loyal Spanish Americans in a double line of carriages. The bands strike up. Some Venezuelan women in a balcony flutter a salute with their handkerchiefs.

The sidewalks are crowded with the curious. This heroic music, this clank of gun-carriages, this clatter of cavalry, these gallooned uniforms, these public figures in carriages, are a fitting tribute to one who with the water to his chest and the lance between his teeth came out of the wilderness to gain the ranks and riches in the defense of liberty that others gain oppressing it, and died recommending to his countrymen that "unless it be to defend yourselves from foreign attack, never take up your arms!" Later, he erred, to be sure, in thinking that mind and muscle are the same thing, that to conquer is the same as to legislate, that to fight is the same as to govern, and that to be a *caudillo* of plainsmen is the same as being president of the republic: but who will look at the sun and see its blemishes before its light? When his extraordinary accomplishments are praised here in a foreign tongue, will we not praise them in that same language in which he commanded: *Strip!* at Cople . . . *About lances!* at Queseras. May heroes long be remembered!

He is remembered well by his old friends here, who are now bankers, pillars of the church, commanders

of militia, and presidential candidates, and who as
youths first heard with amazement of the deeds of the
epic *llanero*, who, later, by the manliness of his con-
duct, knew how to maintain during twenty years of
exile in New York, the admiration for the private citizen the warrior had commanded. "We still seem to
see him," they will tell you, "courteous and affable, better versed in battles than in the law, punctual in his
appointments, neat of dress, warmhearted and enter-
taining, a man of favor with the ladies and in the ballroom, with only an occasional imperious gesture or
flash of his eyes to remind one of the president and
general in him." They still remember the old hero
spinning tales on snowy nights of those incredible
battles with men like Sánchez who would charge uphill
into a cannon's mouth, and those women, like Alme-
dilla's wife, who would tell their husbands: "I would
rather see you agonizing in your own blood than defeated and a prisoner"; and those horsemen who broke
the broncos at daybreak with which in the afternoon,
lance in hand, they gave chase to the enemy.

So it was that his old friends wanted to bid a majestic farewell to one whom they had seen so often in
that light. Thus they honored that tireless old lance in
this nation which for the sake of expediency opposed
the liberation of the Antilles with which he had hoped
to crown his labors.

+

Nobody ever began life in more humble circumstances,
nor so distinguished it with those qualities that seem
to appear, through life's mysterious process, in those

men privileged to embody the very spirit of the land
which gave them birth. He saw the light by the edge
of the water in which he would fight a cavalry engagement as readily as on dry land. His parents had
enough to eat, and little more. He was taught the
Catechism and his first letters by dint of the rod in
Dame Gregoria's school; paper sacks and brown sugar
cakes were his first arms when he worked as a boy
in his uncle's general store, and in the afternoon he
helped plant the fields of cacao; he worked as a ranch
hand in his youth, fetching and carrying buckets of
hot water for the nappy-haired foreman, who looked
resentfully on the lad's blond hair, to wash his feet;
bareback, with only the mane for reins, he began breaking the wild, bucking, snorting ponies, jumping ditches,
touching the sky, flying. During the few moments of
pleasure Manuelote allowed him, he braided horsehair
into halters and mended saddles, seated on the skull of a
horse or crocodile which were the only chairs they knew
there: "I'm not asking you if you know how to swim,"
Manuelote would tell him, "I'm telling you to jump in the
river and guide the herd." His food was a chunk of freshly killed steer roasted on the open fire, with neither bread
nor salt, his drink was water from the gourd passed
from hand to hand, and his bed a hide. The soles of
his feet were his shoes, the rooster his timepiece, and
the lance his law. On Sundays and holidays he sang at
his sweetheart's door those rustic and poetic songs
the jealous rival interrupts with another song, and
sometimes with death. And suddenly, like the scorched
and parched plains harboring only the sluggish crocodile and coiled snake, which burst into beauty, fra-

grance and color after the first rain, and the colt whin-
nies, and the bull feels the old desire again, and the
birds, winged emeralds, sing, and the grand concert of
life emerges sparkling and thundering, so Dame Gregoria's pupil, the choreboy of the country store, the
youth who fetched and carried water, laid his ear to
the ground, and off in the distance, summoning to
triumph, heard the hoofbeats of Bolívar's horse. Leaping to saddle, he rallied, recruited, assailed, dazzled,
rode a white horse and wore a red cloak, and emerged
in his full stature at Queseras del Medio, leading his
150 heroes, slashing the enemy, rounding them up as
in a rodeo, goading the malevolent forces of Morales
with the lance, like lagging cattle. He fords the river
and attacks them, taunts them, and tickles the lips of
their horses with his lances: he feigns flight and lures
all their cavalry into the draws. "About lances," he
commands, and by the light of the sun that halted in
its course to see the wonder, his hundred odd impaled
six thousand mercenaries against the jungle, leaving
them sprawled in the dust, dragged by their own
mounts, crushed by their cannon, tangled in their
weapons, more the victims of fear than of the havoc
worked by the lances! That is how he won the day
in the Mata de la Miel, his first formal battle, and so
his last, thirteen years later, when he assured the independence of the continent at Carabobo. "To avenge my
horse," he said at Mata and he brought back all the
riderless horses of López! "To avenge my black Camejo," he said at Carabobo: he charges with his six hundred, wins the day, scatters the enemy, returns with
every lance red, and America is free!

He served as a soldier for three years in the first war, and when he was only a sergeant in his own ranks, the enemy, victorious in 1813, wanted him as a captain of cavalry. Was it not he who unseated thirty riders in one encounter? Was he not the "pal," the "old man," the "boss" of the plainsmen whom he dazzled with his bravery, strength and shrewdness? Was it not he who could see a league's distance, kill the wild boar with a single arrow, master the wild pony with a fixed look, and send the bull sprawling with a twist of the tail? But he slipped away through the mountains to become a captain of the patriots. Their interest soon flagged, however, and soon they were twenty, and then two, and then he was alone. He was disarmed by trickery, because face to face not even the whole town of Canagua could have taken his sword from him! In Barinas they shackled him with irons: "The heaviest for me," he said. They would have killed him, lancing him with the rest of the prisoners that night, if his pleas, and those of a companion, had not softened the jailer who removed their irons. Where would Páez go now? To find his horse and arms and return alone to rescue his companions! "Who goes there?" the guards challenge him. "The devil, who will soon be back to make off with some of you," he replies. "This way; forward!" he shouts at an invisible battalion. The guards scatter. A blow from the flat of his sword reconciles the hesitant jailer. He frees 115 prisoners. He opens another jail full of women.

Accompanied only by a gallant Spaniard who did not know him, and to whom he later gave his purse as though to punish himself for having considered venting on him all his pent-up indignation, he sets out again, refusing the certain sacrifice of the people of Barinas who hail him as their chief, to raise an army out where freedom is surer than in the cities, in the plains: the plains loyal to the crown, but he will raise an army! His first soldiers were five Royalists who had first demanded his surrender. When pressed by his five recruits about a company he says he has in the offing, but which never arrives, he takes to the road again: he comes upon a band of Indians; he terrifies them; makes them drop their arrows: tying arrows and bows into a bundle, he packs it on his back, and rides into town. With the captive Indians, and the plainsmen Garcia de Sena holds in contempt, he organizes his first company in Mérida.

With the prisoners taken by his lieutenant in Banco Largo, he organizes "Páez's Bravos"; with rum and words he so inflames the Indians of Canabiche, that the Indians, usually afraid of gunfire, are transformed, prick their tongues with arrowheads, daub their faces with the blood from their wounds, and die embracing the cannon.

If no others will join him, he goes on campaign with three lancers and a rifleman; but if he needs horses for the people that come to him, do not the Royalists go mounted? If he needs boats to defend the river, have not the Spaniards gunboats that outdistance cannon fire waiting upstream? For that reason Páez chose gray horses for his thousand plainsmen, because the gray is the swimming horse. He was above betrayal by man, beast, or elements, because he, who sometimes in battle was so eager to meet the first blows that he fell in a swoon from his saddle; he, who finding himself alone, attacked, and in attacking, triumphed; he, who, blinded by the combat, gave chase to the enemy with only a boy at his side, while his troops hung back dividing the spoils; he, who at Mata de la Miel warned his troops: "Whoever returns without a victim goes before the firing squad!": this same man never humiliated a brave man or wreaked vengeance on the defeated! He did unseat the proud Sánchez with his lance and finished him off with another thrust because, as he lay at his feet, he "broke into a babble of words inappropriate to the condition in which he found himself." But, when a blood-thirsty patriot dishonored his arms by beheading defenseless prisoners, as the fifth head rolled, he could contain his indignation no longer, stopped the brute, applied to his superior officer, and defended the prisoners before the troops. "No: not even the strictest military obedience," he wrote later, "can make an executioner's knife of the soldier's sword."

+

Then he became an independent commander, somewhat freer than at the beginning of treacherous friends and jealous superiors, and rode at the head of the lancers who loved him, who stopped his horse to ask him what he wanted, who took from his hands the slice of meat they carried to their lips. They traveled by night down the rivers, shouting to scare off the crocodiles; through the swampy estuaries, dragging their half-drowned horses out of the mire by the strength of the muscle in their arms; across the scorched plains, through fire, smoke, and choking dust. There was no food but the steer they killed; and the hatless soldiers would dismount, lance in hand, to argue over the fresh hide. The troop kept a steady pace, singing, sharpening or securing their lance heads. Páez rode in front, "barefoot and ill-clothed," with his coarse trousers hanging in tatters halfway down his leg.

They crossed rivers with their weapons and saddles on their heads; they made coracles of hide for those who did not know how to swim; if there was too much to carry, they would tie up the edges of a hide with rawhide thongs, throw the heavy stuff inside, and jump into the river with the reins in one hand and the thongs between their teeth. Entering a settlement they found a man squatting with his hands buried in his tangled hair staring at the ground: at his feet, stripped clean of flesh, were the bones of his own son. Time and again they came upon the head of a patriot fried in oil and left hanging in a cage or impaled on a pike; one day, after a victory, they took down the head of Aldao, and out of the skull flew a bird, yellow like his flag, which had nested there.

What were Monteverde, or Calzada, or Correa, or Latorre, or Boves, or Morillo, against Páez? While plans were still taking shape in their heads, Páez was already at their heels undoing them. He divined all the tricks and stratagems of the Spaniards and calculated their every move with exactitude from a knowledge of their weaknesses and strength. He followed his intuition and he won.

He left nothing to chance and provided for everything before entering into an engagement; but once in the fray he took advantage of every new turn. He improvised with striking resourcefulness in the moment of greatest danger. He outwitted his most astute opponents. He always hit on what the enemy could not foresee. He carried meat for three days so that the buzzards, who circle a fresh kill, would not give him away. Each encounter schooled him further in the ways of victory.

His strategy was original, striking, and simple. No one surpassed him in the feint followed by the crushing attack; in pretending to flee with his cavalry, dividing his pursuers, and then turning with all his forces first on one group and then on the other; in drawing the enemy into terrain where the infantry became immobilized; in tipping the scales in his favor with an unexpected charge. What hand-to-hand battles, those of La Miel, Los Cocos, Macuritas, Queseras, Carabobo!

His thousand men seemed one man: they hurtled across the plains, their hoofbeats one, they undulated like a ribbon, converged into a single column, raced away flank-to-flank and split into four groups, only to come together again and fall on the divided enemy; they dashed away after the victory, flourishing their lances.

As late as 1814 they were still only a hundred, and Páez went out boastfully to challenge the Royalist chief. Defeated, the chief plunged into the river, and Páez, plunging in after him, crossed it first and awaited him on the other side to accept his surrender. But his exhausted horses collapsed and the fight continued on foot. The Spaniard was threatening one flank and they lay hour after hour on the necks of their horses await-

ing him. The number of their adversaries endangered
them and they spent the night in the swamp.

The Spaniards came after them in boats: Páez's men
took to the water, approached the gunwales, dove under
water when they saw the flare of the gunner's match
touching the fuse, ran the gunners through with their
lances, and naked, lance in hand, boarded the deserted
gunboats. Morillo prepared under the cover of night
to throw his main force against them. Páez, who had
never heard of Hannibal and his 2,000 oxen, tied dried
skins to the tails of four horses, and loosing a volley
of gunfire, he sent the frenzied horses charging into
the Spanish camp, which withdrew in confusion. With
the enemy downwind he fired the savannah, and
through the blistering fire and between the columns
of smoke and licking flames made fourteen cavalry
charges. He took Puerto Cabello by way of the ocean
on horseback one night after a series of false maneuvers. And in 1818, a few hours after embracing Bolívar
for the first time, Páez learned that the impatient hero
wanted to ford the Apure River under the shadow of
the Spanish cannon at Cople. "I will take the cannon,"
said Páez; he ordered his *bravos* to strip, and they
jumped into the river with their barebacked horses,
their lances in their teeth; they swam with one hand
and guided their horses with the other; they reached
the breastworks, leapt from the water to their horses'
backs, from the backs to the emplacements, from the
emplacements to victory! The batteries are theirs!
Bolívar crosses the Apure in triumph.

Páez was great by the light of the flames consuming
San Fernando, put to the torch by its inhabitants so

Morillo would be unable to make it a fortress against
the patriots; he was great at Queseras raining blows on
the forces of Morales with the shafts of lances blunted
while his horsemen wounded 6,000 of the enemy; he
was great at Carabobo, when, pointing to the red-
crested enemy rallying his demoralized cavalry, he
saw the bravest of his men coming, the black Camejo,
whose horse, dead like his rider, fell at his feet; summoning his remaining riders with a whirl of his arm
he charged, and when a compassive Royalist lifted him
from the earth where he had fallen in a swoon, all that
was left of Spain's power in America were the hooves,
red from the blood that soaked the plain, of the horses
of Valencey de Barbastro! But the *llanero* formed in
the command of his overpowering horde was never
greater than the day when he ordered a priest brought
from a distant town to witness his oath of allegiance
to Bolívar in the presence of his troops; or on that
other day, after being greeted for sixteen years by the
heads of his lieutenants impaled on pikes or hung in
baskets, when he saw the last Spanish sword broken
with honor at Puerto Cabello, and neither humiliated,
nor took vengeance, nor hung heads in baskets, nor
impaled them on pikes, but to the roll of drums and
with flags unfurled he gave the garrison free passage
from the fortifications.

+

Now the procession has reached the pier, through
streets where curtains were drawn aside to see the
passing stranger. In the poorer sections, the Poles, the
Italians, and the Negroes crowded to the curb to hear

the music, to see what was happening, to cheer their tired eyes with the colors of the uniforms, the crests, and the cavalry. The children in the windows applauded the one-armed veterans. A Colombian Negro, who made his way through the crowd, stood on the sidewalk with tears streaming down his face. The infantry, the batteries and the cavalry troop come to attention. Is it the soul's fond desire, or is it that when the coffin is removed from the hearse the air seems somehow more luminous, and the horses cease to paw the ground, and all is silence? Eight sailors lift the coffin to their shoulders. The band plays "Nearer My God to Thee." Sherman lowers his eyes. Sheridan raises his head. Hats off, gentlemen!

SAN MARTÍN

1891

One day, while stones in Spain started to the tramp of French boots, Napoleon fixed his eye on a lean, sunburned officer wearing a blue and white uniform; he approached him and read on a button of his coat the name of his corps: "Murcia!" It was the boy of the frontier village of Yapeyu, grown up in the open among Indians and half-breeds, who, after twenty-two years of peninsular wars, laid hold of the crumbling insurrection in Buenos Aires; bound the rebellious creoles to a solemn oath; scattered the royal flotilla at San Lorenzo; built the army of liberation in Cuyo; crossed the Andes to appear with the dawn at Chacabuco; from Chile, freed by his sword, proceeded by Maipú to the liberation of Peru; decreed himself Protector in Lima and wore a uniform with gold palms; yielded, self-defeated, before the ascending might of Bolívar; abdicated; withdrew; passed alone through Buenos Aires; and died, his daughter's hand in his, in a little French cottage filled with light and flowers. He dangled kings before America, and artfully sought

to use the resources of his country for his own glory.
He clung to his dictatorship, in visible or dissembled
form, until his own blunders forced him to give it up;
unquestionably, he never attained the sublime merit
of voluntarily surrendering his natural dominion in
the sight of all men. But it was his creole head that
nurtured the epic idea that gave urgency and balance
to the independence of America.

The blood of a soldier of León and a granddaughter
of *conquistadores* mingled in his veins; he was born
while his father was military governor of Yapeyu,
on the banks of one of America's mighty rivers; he
learned to read in the lap of the mountains and was
brought up in town as a gentleman's son in the shade
of the palms and the *urundayes*. He was taken to Spain
and taught dancing and Latin at the academy for the
sons of noblemen, and at the age of twelve the boy
"who laughed little" became a cadet. When he returned,
a thirty-four-year-old Spanish lieutenant colonel, to
fight against the crown, he was not a man formed by
the wind and rain of his native American backlands,
but a soldier, warmed by boyhood memories, who
worked in the shadows of secret Masonic lodges, among
noblemen of Madrid and young gentry, to forge the
will to work with a plan and system for the independence of America. Under the command of Daoiz and
in the war with Napoleon he had learned from Spain
how to defeat Spain. He fought against the resourceful
Moors, the showy Portuguese, and the brilliant French.
He fought beside the Spanish, when Spaniards fought
with their teeth, if necessary, and with the British,
who die at attention, with tunics buttoned, so as not to

break the battle line. When he stepped off the boat in Buenos Aires he brought with him nothing but his Moorish sabre that had flashed at Arjonilla, Bailén, and Albuera, and a reputation for fearlessness; he asked for nothing but "unity and direction," a "system that will save us from anarchy," and "a man capable of placing himself at the head of an army." The war was going the way of wars when they are not founded on a firm political plan, more a skirmish than a war, and a breeding-ground for tyrants. "There can be no army without officers." "A soldier must be a soldier from head to toe." San Martín arrived from Spain with Alvear, the ambitious son of an influential family and a patriot. Eight days later he was given the task of organizing the corps of mounted grenadiers, with Alvear as his sergeant major. The skill of the military man dazzles the wavering heroes of a revolution, the incomplete heroes who do not know how to put an idea on horseback. Professional skills are taken for genius, and the well-intentioned, but ignorant, person mistakes procedure for greatness. Among recruits, a captain is a general. San Martín was in the saddle and he was not to dismount until he reached the palace of the vice-roys of Peru; he selected his officers from among his friends, and these only from people of quality; the regulars remained lieutenants; the cadets came from the first families; the soldiers, of a good stature and strong; and all of them, at all hours, "Head up!" "The soldier must keep his head up!" He did not address them by their right names, but by a *nom de guerre* he gave each one. With Alvear and the Peruvian Monteagudo he founded the secret lodge of Lautaro, "to

work with a plan and system for the independence of
America, and her happiness, acting with honor and
proceeding with justice"; so that "when one of the
brothers assumes the supreme authority he will not be
able to name for himself diplomats and generals, governors, judges, or high ecclesiastical and military officials"; "to work toward winning over public opinion";
"to mutually assist each other and honor our vows,
under pain of death." He built his squadrons man by
man. He himself instructed them in the use of the sabre:
"The first *godo* you come upon, split his head open like
a watermelon." He organized the officers in a secret
body; he accustomed them to accuse one another and
bow to the will of the majority; he laid out the penta-
gon and the defenses with them on the drill field; he
dismissed whoever showed fear under fire, or laid
hands on a woman; he developed the salient quality in
each man; he cloaked the military life in religious
ritual and mystery; he turned out each of his men with
precision instruments, and each was placed like a jewel
in a setting. He appeared with them in the square when
the lodge of Lautaro rebelled against the government
of the triumvirate. He rode at their head on a magnificent bay when they attacked the Spaniards dis-
embarking at San Lorenzo; he closed his right and left
flanks upon them; with "spear and sabre" he sent
them tumbling from their mounts; pinned beneath his
horse he still gave orders, sword in hand; one grenadier
fell clutching the Spanish colors; the grenadier who
raised the horse and freed him dropped at his feet;
Spain fled, leaving behind her artillery and her dead.

But Alvear was jealous, and his faction in the lodge

of Lautaro, "which governed the government," proved
stronger than San Martín's. San Martín corresponded
voluminously with the political figures: "the first thing
is to exist, afterwards we will see how we are to exist";
"an army is needed, an army with officers who are
mathematicians"; "we must rid ourselves of the last
Royalist"; "I will resign my military commission when
America no longer has any enemies"; "let us make a
united effort, and we will be free"; "this does not
seem a revolution of men, but of sheep"; "I am a republican by conviction, as well as by principle, but I will
sacrifice even this if it is for the good of my land."
Alvear was sent as general against the enemy in Monte-
video, and San Martín was sent as general to Upper
Peru, where not even the patriotism of Salta could
keep spirits at a fighting pitch; he was transferred to
Cuyo as administrator of the province. And that was
the place for him! Those were his people; that exile
would become his fortress; from those heights he would
pour himself out over all the Americans. There, in
that corner, with the Andes for his staff and council,
alone, he created the army with which he would tra-
verse them; alone, he conceived a family of nations
covered by his sword; and he alone saw the danger
liberty ran in every American country while all were
not free: while there is one enslaved country in America, the liberty of all the rest is in jeopardy! He made
the devoted region the hard core of power upon which
anyone must depend who hopes to make his influence
felt in public affairs. He thought of himself, and of
America: because his enduring glory, the unalloyed
gold of his character, is that in the affairs of America

he never thought of one nation or another as separate entities, but by the light of his vision saw only one American nation stretching across the continent. He was aware of the local political realities and the hidden purpose of actions, as is the case with all men of instinct; but, like all of them, he failed by allowing his native sagacity to be clouded by success and flattery, and in confusing his faith in himself with that knowledge and art of manipulating the intangible and determining factors in a nation, which are attained, through a combination of innate qualities and cultivation, only by the highest genius. That same redeeming concept of America, which would lead to the effective unity in spirit of the sister nations, hid from him the differences, necessary for liberty, between the American states, which make a formal unity impossible. He did not see, as would the profound statesman, the nations already formed, each with its past; he saw only the nations of the future struggling to emerge in his mind; and he dealt with them in his mind as a patriarch deals with his sons. There is something truly formidable in the collision of men of will with the accumulated work of centuries!

The administrator of Cuyo saw only that he had to forge the independence of America. He had faith and he commanded. Assigned, through the design of destiny, to a province as spare as himself, he quickly won over a people who happily recognized in him their own qualities. He became a natural king without a crown. Perfect government stems from the identity of a people with a man who rules with sympathy and a noble purpose; for the identity is insufficient if the

noble purpose is lacking, since nobility is innate in
every people. Dizzied by the heights, the day came
when San Martín sought to rule in Peru with a vision
muddied by the fear of losing his personal glory; for
the sake of his waning authority, he exaggerated an
honest belief in the need for kings to rule in America;
he fatuously put his own interests ahead of America's,
when the first thing a public figure must do in times
of creation or reform is renounce the personal, without
thought of himself except in relation to the good of the
nation; he sought, without means, to entertain a highly
cultivated nation, albeit lacking the strength of its
native originality, with a government of phrase-makers. But in Cuyo, still touched by the justice and
freshness of Nature, there were no obstacles to the
triumph of this man who ruled realistically, prepared
his own breakfast, sat down with the workingmen,
saw that the mule was painlessly shod, received official
visitors in the kitchen over a bowl of stew and a black
cigar, and slept in the open on a cowhide. The well-
tended earth was like a garden there; the clean houses
stood white among the olive groves and vineyards; the
men tanned the hides which the women stitched; even
the mountain peaks seemed scoured by hand. He stood
out among those industrious people, a harder worker
than they; among those marksmen, a better shot than
any of them; among those early risers, knocking at
their doors in the morning, dispensing justice on the
basis of common sense, deriding and punishing only
the lazy and hypocritical. Silence came over him like a
black cloud and he spoke like the lightning. To the
priest: "There is no bishop here but me; preach that

the independence of America is holy." To the Spaniard: "Do you want me to have a good opinion of you? Then get six creoles to vouch for you." To the gossipy mistress of the market stall: "Ten pairs of shoes for the army for having spoken badly of the patriots." To the sentinel he pushed out of the powder mill for entering with spurs on: "One gold doubloon." To the soldier who said his hands were tied by an oath taken before the Spaniards: "The firing squad will untie them for you!" He leaves a group of ransomed prisoners penniless "in order to ransom other prisoners!" He ordered an heiress to pay a tribute: "The deceased would have given more to the revolution!" All around him the American revolution was crumbling in the face of the Spanish campaign of reconquest. Morillo came; Cuzco fell; Chile fled; from Mexico to Santiago the cathedral bells tolled the Te Deum of victory; the broken rebel regiments took to the mountains in tattered bands. At that moment of continental catastrophe, San Martín decided to build his army around the handful of Cuyanos, and inviting his officers to a banquet he gave the toast in a voice as vibrant as a bugle: "To the first shot fired against the oppressors of Chile across the Andes!"

Cuyo was his, and he rose up against the dictator Alvear, the rival who blundered when he rashly accepted the resignation San Martín sent him with his plan already in full swing. Cuyo kept its governor, who pretended to cede his office to the replacement, who kept offering his verbal resignation to the provincial council, who allowed the militia to go into the square, out of uniform, demanding the fall of Alvear.

Cuyo angrily expelled the emissary who came with a paper appointment to succeed Nature's appointee and Cuyo's choice; for him there could be no withdrawal, for he carried within him the salvation of the continent: the friend of the harness makers, to whom he returned the saddles borrowed for the cause in good condition; of the mule drivers, whose mules he returned after army service; of the small farmers, who proudly brought him their seed corn for the soldiers to plant; of the men of substance, who trusted the honest administrator and placed in him their hopes of freeing their heads and ranches from Spain. San Martín levied taxes virtually on the air the people of Cuyo breathed; every root that sprouted was subject to a duty. But first he had fired their souls with such a passion for the liberty of their country and pride in Cuyo, that whatever tax he imposed seemed tolerable, particularly since San Martín, who understood men, did not offend their local customs, but raised new revenues by the old methods: by decision of the members of the Council. Cuyo was to save America. "Give me Cuyo and I will ride into Lima!" Cuyo returned the faith placed in it, and raised to the heavens the man whose opinion of it was so high. In Cuyo, the gateway to Chile, he built an army complete from shoes to boats, with which to liberate her. Soldiers, the defeated; money, from the Cuyanos; meat, ground charqui, which lasts eight days; shoes, sheepskin boots, stitched over the instep; clothing, tanned hides; canteens, cow-horns; sabres, razor-sharp; music, bugles; cannons cast from bells. Daybreak found him in the arsenal counting pistols; in the ammunition depot where he knew each shell, weighing them, inspecting the powder, carefully returning each to its pile. He placed a friar who was an inventor in charge of the arsenal, which outfitted the army with gun carriages and horseshoes, canisters and cartridges, bayonets and machinery; and the friar, a lieutenant at twenty-five pesos a month, shouted himself hoarse for the remainder of his life. San Martín erected a saltpeter plant and a powder mill. He drew up the military code, and organized the medical corps and the commissary. He established an officers' academy because "without officers instructed in mathematics, there can be no army." In the mornings, with the sun touching the peaks of the Andes, they held field maneuvers, with San Martín's flashing sabre everywhere, among the raw platoons, the grenadiers, and his beloved Negroes. He would take a drink from his canteen and say: "Here now, let me fix your rifle!" or, "Let me shake your hand, soldier, that was a fine shot," or, "Come on, *gaucho*, cross sabres with the governor!" At the sound of the bugle he was off, galloping like the wind from group to group, hatless and radiant with satisfaction: "Faster, faster, while there is still daylight: battles are won on the drill field!" He set his officers bullfighting: "These are the madmen I need to defeat the Spaniards!" He fused and transformed the stragglers from Chile, the freed slaves, the conscripts, and the vagrants into an army of 6,000 soldiers. He marched them into Mendoza one sunny day when the city was filled with flowers; he placed his general's baton in the hand of Our Lady of Carmen; in the silence that followed the drum-roll, he dipped the blue colors three times: "This, my soldiers, is the first flag of independence to be blessed in America; swear, as I swear, to die defending it!"

They set out over the Andes in four columns: 400 battle cavalry, with one groom for every twenty horses; 1,200 militia men; 250 gunners, with 2,000 rounds of artillery, and 900,000 of ammunition. Two columns went in the middle with two guarding the flanks. Friar Beltran was at the head, shouldering his crowbar, with his 120 pioneers, his drays and beams to safely transport the twenty-one cannon, rope bridges for the river crossings, and grapples and cables to recover those that fell. At times they skirted the precipice; at times they climbed with their chests touching the mountain. They lived among the lightning and struck as one man in the valley of Chacabuco like a bolt from above. Aconcagua rose shimmering from the snowy expanse. Below them the condors circled among the clouds. Beyond them waited the rattled Spaniards, not knowing from which side the blow would fall, their forces divided and scattered by San Martín's clever espionage and divisive politics, so that he might avoid a battle with their concentrated forces. San Martín dismounted from his mule, wrapped himself in his cape, and slept, with a stone for a headrest, surrounded by the Andes.

It was on the morning of the twenty-fourth day that O'Higgins, his column in friendly rivalry with Soler's, gained the heights commanding the road by which the Spaniards might escape the trap. Back in Cuyo, San Martín had already hemmed them in mentally, ridge by ridge. Battles are won in the mind. To wage a campaign one must know the terrain by heart. At noon, the worried Spaniards began to retreat before the skirmishers in the valley, only to find the cavalry at their rear on the ridge. The liberating cavalry whirled through the enemy infantry like a windmill, and left the gunners draped across their pieces. San Martín threw his full force against the ineffectual ranch walls that were the enemy's fortifications. The last of the Royalists took to their heels through the potato fields and marshes. San Martín sat down after the battle that freed Chile and assured America's liberty, wrote a letter carrying the news to "admirable Cuyo," and ordered the cloth of his cape turned.

Chile wanted to make him governor with absolute powers, but he declined; he returned his commission as brigadier general to Buenos Aires "because I have given my word not to accept any military ranks or political offices"; the city fathers enshrined his portrait in Santiago with trophies of the battle, and his countryman, Belgrano, ordered a pyramid erected in his honor. But what he wanted from Buenos Aires was troops, armament, money, and ships with which to cut off Lima by sea as he planned to by land. He revisited the battlefield of Chacabuco with his Irish lieutenant, and wept over his "poor blacks" who fell there in defense of the liberty of America. He set in motion the secret power of the lodge of Lautaro in Buenos Aires; he backed his friend O'Higgins, whom he installed as Director in Chile, against the rival ambitions of his enemy, Carerra; from his house in Santiago where he tolerated no "silver service" or salaried retainers, he set about undermining the influence of the viceroy of Peru; he sighed, from the depths of the "disappointments that gnaw at my existence" for "two months of peace in the good city of Mendoza"; from the arch-bishop's doorway, astride his charger, he rallied the Chileans routed at Cancharrayada, and surged trium-phant, with Lima before him, from the bloody field of Maipú.

He leaped from his battle steed to an Andean mule; with the threat of his resignation, he forced Buenos Aires, prodded by the lodge, to send him funds for the Peruvian expedition; he corresponded with his loyal friend Pueyrredón, the Argentine Director, con-cerning the plan which finally sent a member of the lodge to the courts of Europe in search of a king; at the same time, the Chilean fleet controlling the Pacific came under the command of the Englishman Cochrane, who had left his country rather than "see it oppressed without mercy" by a monarchy, and Bolívar swept for-ward planting the republican colors in country after country. And when Chile and Buenos Aires, faced with San Martín's threat of withdrawing his army across the Andes, leaving O'Higgins without support and the road to Chile and Argentina open to the Spaniards, were forced to submit to his demands for further help; when Cochrane had opened the sea route to Peru with his daring raids; when he was finally on the point of falling on the palaces of Lima with his reinforced army, assuring America of independence and himself of glory, Buenos Aires recalled him to throw back an expedition from Spain that was thought to be on the high seas, to protect the government against the rebellious federalists, and to support the monarchy which San Martín himself had recommended. He refused. He rose up with the army he could never have assembled without the help

of his country, was acclaimed the supreme commander
by his troops at Rancagua, and as an independent
captain, carrying the Chilean colors, he turned toward
Peru to rout the Spaniards, leaving his strife-torn
country at his back: "The war will not end until Lima
is in our hands!" On this campaign "hang the hopes of
this continent." "I must follow the call of destiny . . ."

+

Who is that in the golden uniform riding through
effeminate Lima in a carriage with six horses? It is
the Protector of Peru, the self-proclaimed absolute
governor, who wrote a constitution fixing all power in
his hands and establishing the political system, who
freed the unborn children of slaves, did away with the
lash, abolished all tortures, and accomplished both
good and evil through his fiery minister, Monteagudo;
who on the very day the constitution was put in effect,
created the ranks of nobility, the Order of the Sun;
who ordered inscribed on the ribands worn by the
ladies of Lima, "to the patriotism of the gentler sex";
the "emperor," who was mocked in the songs of
the people; "King Joseph," laughed at behind his back
by his brothers in the lodge of Lautaro. It is San Martín, abandoned by Cochrane, denied by his own troops,
hated in Buenos Aires and Chile, thrown into confusion
at a meeting of the "Patriotic Society" where he alone
applauded a speech in favor of monarchy by a priest;
whose dream of a king for Peru went begging at
the courts of Austria, Italy and Portugal. Who is that
emerging solitary and sombre, after the titanic meeting at Guayaquil, from the dance where Bolívar, the

unchallenged leader of the armies descending from
Boyacá, sweeping the Spaniards before them, waltzes
aglow with success among ladies vying for his favor
and gay soldiers? It is San Martín, who summoned
delegates to Peru's first constitutional convention and
stripped himself before them of his red and white
sash; who stepped down from his coach, with Peru
in an uproar against the Protector, because "the presence of a successful soldier is frightening to infant
countries, and I am tired of hearing it said that I want
to make myself a king"; who left Peru to Bolívar,
"who beat me with the first gambit," because "there
is not room enough in Peru for Bolívar and me, without a conflict ensuing that would be the scandal of the
world, and San Martín will not be the one to give the
Royalists a Roman holiday." He quietly took his leave
of a faithful officer in the shadows of the night; he
arrived in Chile with 120 gold doubloons in his purse
to find himself hated; he appeared on the streets of
Buenos Aires and was met with derisive whistling,
without his countrymen recognizing that by his calm
acceptance of defeat he had gained a greatness to which
his ambition had pretended in vain.

Cured of the temptation and madness of power, his
character emerged in all its beauty. This instrument
of Nature's design had secured the triumph of the continent so well that even his own defection could not
imperil the American achievement. He, who by his
vision brought three free nations into being, lived in
dedicated exile, studiously removed from the affairs
of men. He learned from his own experience that a
caudillo's strength is not in his own person, although

it may seem that way, but in the degree to which he serves his people: he rises when he is in step with them, and he falls when he tries to take them in tow. Tears would spring to his eyes when he met an old friend; he died facing the sea with his heart in Buenos Aires, seated erect in an armchair, white-haired and serene, with that majesty of the snow on Aconcagua in the silence of the Andes.

ABORIGINAL AMERICAN AUTHORS

April 1884

Such Indian writings as we know, the fragments that escaped the episcopal hands of the Landas and Zumarragas, are informed with the splendor of the *samán,* the elegance of the palm, and the brilliance and variety of the flora of the American uplands. The rays of the Persian sun do not shatter in richer hues against the silver saddles and precious gems of the paladins of tempered sabre and silk tunic than those abundant and vivid colors rendered by the Indian phrase, ample and pliant as a robe. Who that has read an account of battle or title of property of the Guatemalan Indians will deny it? The *Mahabharata* is more sententious; the *Schahnameh,* more grave; the prophesies of Chilam Balam of Yucatan are more serene and profound; the odes of the Mexican Netzahualcoyotl, more sublime; the dramas of Peru have more passion, the *Apu Ollantay,* perhaps the *Uska Pankar;* the traditions of Tingal shimmer like a tunic spangled with diamonds. But the legends of the Quiche and Zutugil are like a brook, like a young stallion of winged gait and flaming mane, like a magician's rope that grows upon itself in endless coils, like an ocean newly formed that sparkles in pure, virgin light, like a chattering troop of Indian girls tinkling with little blue bells, and warriors in plumed headdresses cavorting under the blazing sun of a summer morning, or a river of jewels, as if a maiden had set her thoughts adrift on the limpid waters of a forest stream. The tremendous "Jonatin," the handsome Alvarado, surprised them while they quarreled among themselves and conquered them. The despot laughs in the shadows when a people become disunited.

Literature is simply the expression, form and reflection of the vital spirit and natural setting of the people who create it. How, then, could our indigenous literature run counter to this universal law, and lack the beauty, harmony and color of the American scene? We who love the Indians as one loves a broken lily are not the only ones who see this. The purpose of these lines is to report the publication of an interesting book in which a North American author discovers these qualities in the fragments of pre-Colombian literature that we know, and in all the literature after the conquest in which the native genius demonstrates its richness and character, both in the native languages, and the language of the *conquistadores*. What institutions were Tlaxcala's! What warriors, Mayapan's! Teotitlan, what schools! What a circus in Copan! Mexico, what workshops, plazas, and aqueducts! What temples in Zempoalo! The Andes, what highways! What does it matter that we come of fathers of Moorish blood and fair skin? The spirit of a people resides in the land in which they live and is drawn in with the air one breathes. One may descend from fathers of Valencia and mothers of the Canary Islands, yet one feels the blood of Tamanaco and Paracamoni run hot through one's veins and regards as one's own the blood of the heroic, naked Caracas warriors which stained the craggy ground of Mount Calvary where they met the armored Spanish soldiers hand to hand! It is good that canals be dug, schools built, steamship lines organized, good that we keep abreast of the times and in the vanguard of the beautiful human march; but if we are not to fail from the lack of a living spirit, or the pursuit of false values, we must drink deeply at the springs of the Nature into which we were born, which is strengthened and animated by the spirit of men of all races who spring from its soil and return to it. Politics and literature prosper only when they are a direct expression of their people. The American intelligence is an Indian headdress. Is it not yet apparent that the blow that paralyzed the Indian, paralyzed America? Until the Indian marches again, America will limp.

There are excellent Americanists in the United States, and Daniel G. Brinton is among the best. He has just published a study he read before the Congress of Americanists in Copenhagen last year containing all that is known of indigenous works. He demonstrates how broad, adaptable, and flexible was the vocabulary of the aborigines. He discovers a powerful literary capacity in them, and vigorously points it out. Since they dealt in living impressions, their need for expression was immediate. They liked to narrate, and they did it with both abundance and grace. Color was always essential to them, and an indispensable part of their stories. An ingenuous soul and vivid imagination are the hallmark of what we know of the Indians. Their relish for symmetry and ornament is apparent in their manuscripts, as in their ruins. The Greeks had their Atriums and Niestes, and easily swayed Europa; the Indians also had theirs, and their feuds between rival houses and families, which, to judge by the scant pages translated from their letters and symbols, are told with greater flourish and passion in their parchments and tablets than the rivalry of Atrides and Pelopides in the glorious Greek romance. How august, the Iliad of Greece! How brilliant, the Indian Iliad! Homer shed golden tears; the Indian verses are palm fronds, alive with hummingbirds.

Brinton's book contains not only facts and deductions, but a list of documents: he has included an appendix cataloging all the works that are known and considered of authentic indigenous authorship. The Indian in the North, subjected to a struggle for survival against wild beasts and the cold, had little time to leave a painted or written record of his life; a poor people, constantly at war, and on the march toward the warm lands, they wrote more with the arrow than with the quill. But in the tropic lands, where all men will eventually seek a haven, the poetry that springs from repose and imagination, which is sumptuous in lands of natural richness, flowered in all its magnificent colors. Nature placed a wondrous mantle on America's shoulders! The world will witness an imposing spectacle the day it discovers its strength and awakes. What silver fringes, our rivers! Our mountains, what roses! What embroidery, our thoughts! Our souls, what eagles! Nature placed a wondrous mantle on America's shoulders!

THE PAMPA

May 1890

The gaucho crosses the plain at full gallop with a wary backward glance over his shoulder. His warrior horse, ears pricked and sharp-eyed, springs forward on slender forelegs that stem from its powerful chest like pointed lances. The poncho, caught about the saddle stock, flaps blue and gold in the breeze. The gaucho is of those born to the saddle; he guides his companion with his knee more than with the reins. He wears blue pants and a white shirt, a red kerchief at his neck, and a soft, narrow-brimmed hat held snug to his head by a strap under his beardless chin. This is the frontispiece of *The Pampa,* a book on the Argentine published in Paris by the Frenchman Alfred Abelot.

It is not a shameful book on coarse paper with pre-Raphaelite prints, but as handsome a book as comes from the press, with pages that invite the reader, and delicate sketches that present in all its tenderness and ferocity the life of the pampa, that awesome and melancholy plain crowned to the north by the tropical palm and luxuriant carob of Brazil, and bounded to the south by the sullen hills of Patagonia. There, the hard life under the open sky, with saddle and sheepskin for gear and gable, and everywhere the horizon broken only here and there by an ostrich's silhouette. There the *pulperia,* the club of the desert, with its gin and conversation, teamsters and song, hub-bub and trade, wakes and verse. There, in the sea of grass, the chase with the balled lariat, the *boleada;* the *baqueo,* tracking the deadly Indian by his trail through stone and water; the fight between the soldier posse and the gaucho outlaw, who gives them the slip, parrying their bullets with the point of his knife. There the Indian on horseback, who raises his sons to exterminate the white invader and the horses that are his livelihood and fortune—or die under hoof as the riders, guns blazing, raze the Indian wigwams. There, the primitive life, and a whole epoch dying now under the wheels of the locomotive.

In those 700 leagues of solitude, which reach to the gates of the university cities, there still exists an untamed, natural caste of a motley Spanish and Indian tradition, children of the castle and the wigwam, reared on horseback and schooled in bloodshed, who descended on the city, lance in hand, to unseat their despoilers from authority—the frock-coated bureaucrats, the land surveyors, the *botavacas. La Cautiva* of Esteban Echevarria and *Celiar* of Magarinos Cervantes relate in verse the life of those centaurs; their courtships in the saddle with their *"china,"* and the duels to the death between those knights of the knife, of leonine soul and regal presence. Rafael Obli-

gado describes that life in his colorful verse. The great
Sarmiento, in the work of a founder of nations, *Civilization and Barbarity*, paints the bloodthirsty monk,
Aldao, and the "tiger," Facundo Quiroga. Now Abelot
presents the pampa that is disappearing: the last wake,
the last *pulpería*, the last gaucho outlaw, his poncho
wrapped around one hand, his flashing blade in the
other; the last *mate* sipped at daybreak while squatted
in a circle around the fire before the horse race, the
roundup, or the chase with the *bolas*. "Pampa" is the
horse that does not shy from a tiger; "pampa," the dog
that breaks the leg of the running ostrich with one
snap; the Indian girl, whose head is turned after a
month in town by the beaded necklaces and red shawls,
no longer wants to be called "pampa"; "luluhuu!"
cries the naked Pampa Indian riding after the lank-
haired *guanacos* with the balled lariat whirling over
his head. The pampa is the poem of the man who rises
at daybreak as in the Golden Age; who wrests the
hunting ground from the puma he kills with his bare
hands; who copies trees, battles, or clouds on hide with
the point of his knife; who sings his songs, the *triste*
and *cielito*, under the stars; who slashes the face of
whomever offends him or challenges his place, and
sinks at the feet of civilization, hamstrung by the plow-
share. Why read Homer in Greek when he still lives,
roaming the American wilderness with the guitar over
his shoulder?

The Pampa is not a thick book, which it could have
been if the author had simply set down the salient and
characteristic aspects of that natural existence with
art, but without comment, so that it revealed itself,

and the character of its inhabitants become manifest
from the environment that surrounded and educated
them. The prompter is as annoying in books as in the
theatre. The important thing is what is seen, not who
sees it. Art demands objectivity of an author. It is like
the appearance in the Chinese theatre of the stage
manager in clogs and shirtsleeves, shifting the proper-
ties among the gossamer princes and winged generals
while the dance of fury or the swordplay are in progress. The shortcoming of this well-intentioned book is
that the author introduces his second-hand, precon-
ceived opinions into the testimony of the facts, which
is what the reader looks for in a book. These are times
for men to think for themselves, needing and demanding facts on which to base their judgements, without
literary frills and useless digressions; there is justified
impatience at the complacent, gratuitous intrusion of
the judgements of others. There are books of a dis-
cursive and personal character that collapse when the
opinions of the author are not well premised, and
whose charm resides in the art with which his reason-
ing is employed as argument, and the subtlety with
which he sways and persuades the reader toward the
desired view, never offending his sight with clumsy
pomposity or his reason with dogmatism. What men
want to know is what life teaches, and it is infuriating
not to be permitted to see life as it is, but through
spectacles of this or that hue. Despite all that is being
written today, the literature that is useful and strong
is still in swaddling clothes.

It is true that the author of *The Pampa* relates what
he saw in the manner of a witness, and expresses him-

self with ease, honesty, and that spirit of nature that makes us all one, in the words of the English poet. But his subject matter is so interesting and lively—the stagecoach carrying gentlemen, country girls, and criminals all together is so noisy; the race between the high-strung horses is so hotly contested; the sixth sense of the *rastreador* on the trail of the "Black Wildcat" is so uncanny; so dazzling, with the sun setting in the distance and the blood quickened by the *mate,* is the return of the hunters from the *boleada* with the ostrich hanging from the saddle stock, or the pelt dripping blood down the horse's flank; so picturesque and novel the battle in which whoever wants a lance to fight takes it from his enemy with the *bolas,* that it is jarring when the French gentleman appears in his smoking jacket, seizes the bridle of the lathered horse with its rider in a white shirt and red headband like a Greek runner, and turns loose on the open plain the latest metaphysical concept, or removes from his lips the silver *bombilla* with which he sips the strong, bitter *mate* to utter the unpardonable artistic and philosophical anomaly of yoking Darwin and Haeckel with that free life, which must be approached with a mind as untrammeled as itself. One does not renounce one papacy to embrace another!

Where he could, and should have seen the heroic aspects of primeval society—the primary combat between man and beast, the pervading sadness and violent pleasures of the nomad life, the submission of the rootless lancers to the cunning and Herculean captain, the conflict between the raw, yet powerful gaucho hordes and the cultured, legalistic cities, and the final triumph of a beautiful, useful civilization over a dazed barbarity—he sees heredity, variations, selections, and reversions. He follows a theory, which is like walking blindfolded. He sees only primitive barbarity and a ferocious instinct in the Indian, descended of generations cowed and butchered by the white man, who gathers his children around the bound white captive that they may mete out the Indian justice the earth of their fathers—stained with blood by the invader—cries for. He attributes the gaucho's traffic in blood, which he considers a relish for gore, to an animal crudity and an outcropping of the bestial in human nature, without recognizing this as a consequence of the gaucho's life as a slaughterer, for, in civilized communities, he is always to be found in the stockyard, wedded to his knife; he forgets that bravery is a quality which all men like to display, anxious as they are to demonstrate prowess and manliness; human blood is red, no different from the bull's; if the bull falls under the knife through no offense of his own, what then of him who offends the punctilio and vanity of the savage? His theories lead him into pitfalls of his own making, such as declaring that the closer man is to the primitive state "the greater his passion for gambling and drinking"; he thinks, in keeping with his naturalist theories, that gambling, which is simply the violent, uncultured form of hope abounding in societies of cravat and casino, is a throwback and a periodic reappearance of the barbarian.

The attraction of the bottomless pit, the vertigo caused by the sea and heights, man's constant endeavor to fathom the absolute, to transcend and diffuse himself, he regards, with scholastic blinders, as a return to the chaotic thinking of the primitives. One has only to see the world in graduated social stages identical to one another at the same level of evolution, modified only by place and environment, to have at one's command a great and ample philosophy which comprehends every social development and permits one to enjoy them all, never being saddened, like our Frenchman, because the carnivals of the Buenos Aires of yesteryear, when ladies and gentlemen engaged in ferocious water fights, are become a thing of the past. Changes are a matter for concern only when they are produced by factors not native to the country, and run counter to the enduring and nourishing characteristics that are the salt and leavening of a country, and without which its personality is soon sapped. Why seek to convert into local peculiarities things that are common to all societies in their early stages? The Argentine gaucho has wakes; so does the Canary Islander and the Irish peasant. On the pampa, a dead infant is dressed in holiday clothes, and in Colombia, in golden slippers, for the road to Heaven has sharp stones and the mother pleads that her child not bruise its feet. The hunters of the pampa make their meat into charqui; so do the North American Indians. The gaucho of Choel-Choel knows no law; the Yankee cowboy knows no law. Fired with gin at the *pulpería,* the gaucho fills the air with shots and is ready to take on the house to see who is the best man, and the Colorado miner, when the whiskey goes to his head, makes the tenderfoot dance to the tune of his revolver. The gaucho outlaw counts his dead as an honor, and the *llanero* of Uputa in Venezuela told the teacher: "Mister teacher, what I like is to hear the crunch when I bury my knife in a man's back."

Whoever knows the unsubdued, wandering Arabs, knows gauchos. Are not the towers of the pampa forts the same as those of North Africa? Man is one, and order and unity are the changeless, irrefutable laws of Nature.

+

These limitations of prejudice, as harmful when they stem from the passion for science as from ignorance of it, are mitigated in the author of *The Pampa* by the fact that he is clearly a good man, which is the first condition of true intelligence. It is apparent that his sincere heart compels him to love those things which he condemns in theory as bestial. He says he likes the *pulperia.* The gauchos, in all fairness, "are good people if one knows how to treat them." The "Black Wildcat" swore death to the justices of the peace, and he killed five in one knife fight. But the justices stole his beloved horse, which was his "credit," his silver-trimmed saddle and bridle, and his girl. The author is "sorry" to see the gaucho disappearing. Who will ride out with him now for the pure love of the fight against the cunning Indian, and who will secretly leave the kerchief with the last *mate* leaves hanging from his saddle stock? Who will make him a present of the still warm pelt of the tiger—"because he would have liked it for himself"—killed and skinned with the same knife that disposed of a "weak-sister" in an argument? These gauchos are good people. A *china* catches their fancy, and they swing her up behind them, galloping

off to live where the sky is a jewel-box, with a single
diamond by day and a thousand gems at night. They
have the habit of the knife and hate the dandy from
the city. But when the poet Echeverria, pale and sickly,
traveled among the gauchos, they would doff their hats
and rise when he spoke to them, whispering to each
other: "This is no dandy! This is a poet." Good people, those gauchos!

We first see them in the book at a wake. The horsemen arrive at the *estancia* of a wealthy landowner of
the region, and tie their horses to the hitching rail, for
to pass beyond the rail on horseback would be a dis-
courtesy dearly paid. The little angel has died in his
fourth year and the neighbors are holding a wake to
celebrate his journey to Heaven. The rain is pelting
the roof outside; there are flashes of lightning and
claps of thunder. Inside, clasped together in an *haba-
nera* or face-to-face in the dextrous steps of the *zama-
cueca,* sweethearts dance in couples and cross themselves each time they pass in front of the chair atop
a pedestal of boxes where the infant is seated, surrounded by thirty-six wax candles, with the old, gray-
haired gaucho on one side, strumming the guitar, and
on the other the dry-eyed mother, her hands folded
in her lap. Celebrations are few and far between on
the pampa, and the keeper of the *pulperia* hires the
dead child from the penniless gaucho, who gratefully
rents it out to him so the little angel may have candles,
and go to Heaven in proper fashion, with song and a
wake.

Morning comes. Squatted in a circle around the dung
fire, the gauchos sip the steaming *mate.* The saddle

and sheepskins spread on the ground have served as a bed for a short sleep. Now the saddle gear, with its folded blanket, its leather pad to keep out the dampness, wooden saddle, bound stock and frame in leather, silver stirrups, and sheepskins, ceases to be a bed and becomes a saddle again. The girth is of leather and the overgirth of wool; the bit and bridle are in the Moorish style, of silver and tooled leather; wherever he can insert the point of his knife, the gaucho carves flowers, leaves, heads, and whimsies. He tucks his baggy pants into his horsehide boots and pulls on the *chiripá*, tied at his waist in the manner of short, outer loincloth; he slips the poncho over his head and pulls his hat down over his eyes. The party of gauchos is setting out as a posse on the trail of an assassin who killed the "Old Cowpuncher," a venerable gaucho who was the pride and glory of the region, for he could tell you in a wink where any *estancia* lay, how far it was to the next one, or how many days off the Indians were. The *rastreador*, who has studied the welter of hoofprints at the door of the old gaucho's ranch, sets out at the head of the group in search of the assassin who fled eight days before, riding through the high grass, doubling back on his tracks, taking to the river, and returning to dry ground in a stony place to give no clue of where he left the water. The posse arrives at a town where a fair is underway, with wagons, tents, knots of traders and strings of horses. The *rastreador* approaches a teamster showing a horse to a circle of traders. "This is the horse," says the *rastreador*, looking at the hoofprints in the mud. And it was. The assassin had traded with the teamster. They return to the point of the trade; the horse, left to its instinct, picks up the trail of its master and presently the *rastreador* drops his hand on the assassin's shoulder. He confesses. Who can withstand the *rastreador*? Even on cobblestone streets the sons of the gauchos can tell if the priest rode past on his mule, or if the horse of the tax collector has passed through, or if the teacher went out wearing rope-soled shoes or boots; they can read in the trampled grass the number of horses in a herd, which are mares and which are colts; it is useless for the fugitive to go on tiptoe, or gallop away to a far off place and continue on foot, for before the year is out the impassive *rastreador* will have picked up the trail.

If a hunt with the *bolas* is organized, who will not stay to see it? It is supposed to be for ostrich and antelope, but the wealthy gauchos are trembling because the hunters are just as likely to send their *bolas* whirling after a horse that catches their eye, or a brindle steer, "for love of the hide." The *boleadores* ride to the gathering place on their horses, in holiday trappings. The morning sun begins to streak the sky. The water for the *mate* bubbles in the kettle. The lean dogs lick their chops. The hunters mount. Off they go to the four winds in search of game! They return with the evening shadows from the four winds, their horses loaded with bloody pelts and dead ostriches in bunches; the muzzles of the dogs are red. Stretched out on their saddle gear, squatted around the fire, seated on the skulls of steers, they pass the long night as if in conversation with the stars. The *payador*, his fingers playing lightly across the guitar, sings of his misfortunes, of the sad death of the gaucho Santos Vega, of the *china* he loved but who was stolen from him, of the sadness that filled him when a rival *payador* sang better than he, of the battle between the gauchos and the Indians, of the tenderness a man feels within when he sees the starlit heavens at night.

When they reach the *pulpería*, they boast of their exploits in song, sit in the shadows on the benches that run the length of the wall carving the brands of the region in the wall with their knives or stand elbow-to-elbow at the bar, chatting with the keeper who serves them from behind the sturdy counter. And then, their pockets filled with the money the *pulpero* gave them for the pelts and ostrich feathers, they all go outside as the racers begin to gather from near and far, on their silver-studded saddles. The clearing has been carefully prepared as if for a big race. The horses that are going to race are led past the public by their leather halters. Some observe them closely, comment and bet; others are more interested in the *chinas* who have come in their Sunday dresses and yellow or violet shawls. They wear gold and glass earrings, and their hair is carefully combed, drawn back, and caught in a ribbon. Look, there are the riders in white shirts, and brightly colored headbands! Everybody stands back now, for the race is about to begin. From the waist down, there are no holds barred. A rider can catch his opponent's horse at the withers with his knee to break his stride, or hook his rival's leg with his own and suddenly unseat him, or lead him toward a hidden gopher hole. They are off in a tangled, straining pack! Now they return and thunder back at a breakneck speed, a mêlée, horse against horse!

The *chinas* gossip about the expedition that passed through the week before on the road to Juárez. They drove an impressive herd of reserve horses and there were more women than ever, for the expedition is not to return until the last Indian has been cleared from the frontier. Many old women went with the troop, those who make the tarts the soldier likes, and many a new born babe, too. All the women rode good horses, loaded with stoves, pots, baskets, bundles and irons, with which to earn pin money doing the officer's wash, so their man "will see that he is loved for his courage and merits, and not for what he can give on pay-day, because if he has nothing to give, the industrious woman finds a way to buy her handkerchiefs, pins, and perfumes." That is the way of the women who follow the troop in the field, of whom there are not so many now with the railroad and organized troops. The soldier does not fare well in the lonely desert without his woman. He leaves her behind, and then he must send for her. The dog is loyal to the battalion; but the woman is more so. If tempers are quick after the rum has flowed too freely and there are blows, a tasty tart comes on the heels of the whipping as the bread of peace. If there is fighting, she puts on a spare uniform and guards the horses, driving off the Indians.

The betting, the conversation, the cock fights are suddenly cut short. With a swing of the axe, the losing gaucho lops off the head of the bastard cock that crowed. The riders rein their horses off to one side. The stagecoach thunders in. The postilions, one for each pair of horses, spring from their exhausted beasts. Down from his seat atop the coach clambers the stage driver who is the hero there and who has left his mark on many an insolent face. His beard is black and his shoulders broad above a flat, tapering waist. His legs are thin and long-striding. He is curt of speech and a stranger to laughter. While the horses are changed in the bustling corral filled with dust and shouting, chairs and *mate* are brought out for the ladies traveling on the stage; the ladies are fashionably dressed, but they talk easily with the common folk. The keeper of the *pulpería* outdoes himself in his attentions toward the owner of the *estancia,* who wears patent leather boots and a fine-spun poncho. Among the passengers there is a gaucho wearing a fancy *chiripá* and a curly-haired Italian with a valise filled with the jewelry and trinkets that are the delight of the *chinas.* There is also a gaucho in irons guarded by two policemen, an "unfortunate" who killed his friend "because he ran too hard against his knife and the wound festered." For him there is a double portion of *mate* and the good rum; he is given a silk handkerchief so that he will remember in his sorrow that there is a compassive *china* somewhere. There is singing and dancing, and the *payador* sings of the sufferings of men of honor pursued by the law, and of the caution the stagecoach should take on the road to Juárez because the frontier is aflame and there is a scalped white man's skull bleaching out there for every steer's skull; the women listen and sip their *mate.* The stage driver and the *pulpero* throw a box of rifles into the back of the stagecoach that is about to proceed on its journey.

The stagecoach is taking a road of no return! The Indians, the last savages, will attack, leaping on the galloping stage horses; the driver will tumble from his seat, killed by the first shot; the Indians will carry off the women on their horses, leaving the naked corpses scattered around the stagecoach. But out there on the frontier there is now an Indian chief who is the son of a Frenchman and lives among the huts of his Indians in a brick house with his Spanish wife; he sports a pair of trousers like those the Argentine top sergeants wear, with gold braid down the side. Beyond, in the sandy hills of Patagonia covered with wind-tortured shrubs, the remotest city in the world, Our Lady of Carmen, there are now bankers, farmers and loving husbands and fathers where only short years ago there were highwaymen, forgers and murderers, sent there by the government to start life anew with women whose sin was to have loved without measure.

III: LITERARY

PORTRAITS

EMERSON

May 1882

There are times when the pen trembles, like a priest who feels himself capable of sin and unworthy to perform his ministry. Agitated, the soul flies upward. It wants wings to soar, not a quill to trim and taper into a graver. It is painful to write, and in a sense, humiliating, like yoking a condor to a wagon. For when a great man disappears from the earth he leaves behind pure splendor, a desire for peace, and a hatred of noise. The universe is like a temple where the commerce of the cities, the tumult of life and the uproar of mankind are a profanation. One feels the desire to shed one's feet and grow wings. It is as if one were seated by starlight in a meadow of white flowers. Pale, pure fire fills the immense silence of the atmosphere. Everything converges toward a summit, and we are astride it. The earth is at our feet wrapped in shadows like some land of long ago and far away. And the rumble of the wagons, the shouting of the shopkeepers, those tall chimneys that puff out great blasts on the air, and that coming together, strutting, arguing and living of men, seems to us in our still, pleasant retreat, like the sounds of a barbaric army that invades our heights, camps on our foothills, and angrily scouts the great shadow, behind which rises, like a colossal battle-ground, the grand, tumultuous, magnificent city where warriors of stone carry red lances and wear helmets and breastplates of gold. Emerson is dead, and sweet tears fill the eyes. His death causes envy rather than pain, and tenderness, not anguish, fills the breast. Death is a victory, and when one has lived well, the hearse is a triumphal chariot. The tears are of pleasure, not of mourning, because the wounds life inflicted on the hands and feet of the deceased already are covered with rose petals. The death of a just man is a day for celebration on which the whole world watches to see how the heavens open. And the faces of men are radi-ant with hope, and in their arms they carry sheaves of palm, with which they carpet the earth, and with battle swords raised on high, they make an archway beneath which passes the body of the victorious warrior, cov-ered with boughs of oak and golden straw. He who gave everything of himself, and did good to others, goes to his rest. He who labored badly in this life, goes to labor anew. And the young warriors, having feasted with envious eyes on the passing of the peerless victor, whose still warm corpse radiates the greatness of peace, turn again to the tasks of the living, to earn their right some day to strewn palms and arches on high.

Who is he that died? Well, the whole world knows that. He was a man who found himself alive, who shed from his shoulders all the mantles and from his eyes all the bandages that the past lays upon men, and lived face to face with Nature, as if all the world were his homestead, the sun his sun, and he a patriarch. He was one of those to whom Nature opens and reveals herself, extending her multiple arms as if to enfold within them the whole body of her son. He was of those to whom is given supreme knowledge, supreme calm, and supreme joy. All Nature trembled before him like a new bride. He lived happily because he put his love outside the world. His whole life was the dawn of a wedding night. What raptures filled his soul! What visions swam before his eyes! His verses, what flights of angels! He was a timid and slender child, and to those who looked on him he seemed a young eagle, a young pine. Later he became serene, kindly and radiant, and children and men alike stopped to see him pass. His step was firm, as of one who knows where he is going; his person was tall and slight, like those trees whose tops are rocked by pure zephyrs. He had the lean face of a man made to withdraw within himself in order to transcend himself. His forehead was like a cliff. His nose was like the beak of birds who dwell on the mountain-tops. And his eyes were captivating, like those of one who is filled with love, and tranquil, like those of one who has seen the unseen. It was impossible to see him without wanting to kiss his brow. Carlyle, the great English philosopher who turned against the earth with Satanic brilliance and strength, called Emerson "a beautiful transparent soul." Whitman, who has discovered a new poetry in Nature, thought time spent with him "a long and blessed evening." Stedman, a good critic, saw "an elemental light" burning in the town of the Concord seer.

Alcott, the sage of youthful spirit who thinks and sings, considered it "misfortune to have lived not knowing thee!" One came away from him with the feeling of having seen a living monument, or a supreme being. There are men like mountains who level the land before and after them. He was not familiar, but he was kind, for his was the imperial family where all men were to be emperors. He loved his friends like sweethearts; friendship for him had something of the solemnity of twilight in the forest. Love is superior to friendship in that it produces children. Friendship is superior to love in that it creates no desires, nor the fatigue of having satisfied them, nor new desires. Wherever he was, charm was there. His voice was like that of a messenger of the future speaking from out of luminous clouds. It seemed that an impalpable strand of moonlight bound the people who assembled to hear him. Wise men would go to see him and come away from him as if both chastened and delighted. Young men would walk long miles to see him, and he received the trembling pilgrims with a smile, made them sit down at his sturdy mahogany table covered with great books, and served them himself, standing like a servant, of his generous, aged sherry. And he is accused of being aloof, by some who read him and fail to understand him, because, made for permanent communion with the great, he considered his personal matters of little consequence, things of chance and unessentials that did not bear repetition. These tearful little poets of woe! Men should be told of manly matters, capable of uplifting them! It is work for ants to relate one's petty cares in swooning rhymes! Grief must be dignified.

His mind was priestly, his gentleness, angelic, and his anger, Mosaic. When he saw men enslaved, and reflected on them, his utterance made it seem that the tablets of the Law were again being shattered on the slope of some new biblical mountain. As a lion scatters flies with a toss of his mane, so Emerson rid himself of the trivialities of vulgar minds. Argument for him was time stolen from the discovery of the truth. Since he said what he saw, he was impatient with those who questioned what he said. His was not the choler of vanity, but of sincerity. Was he to blame that others did not possess the radiant light of his eyes? Will the caterpillar not deny that the eagle flies? He disdained sophistry, and since the commonplace was the extraordinary for him, the necessity of having to demonstrate the extraordinary amazed him. If men failed to understand him, he shrugged his shoulders: Nature had spoken to him and he was a priest of Nature. He did not trump up revelations; he did not construct worlds of the mind; he did not inject the effort or conflict of his mind into the prose and poetry he wrote. All his prose is verse and his verse and prose seem to echo each other. He saw behind him the creative Spirit that spoke to Nature through him. He considered himself a transparent pupil that saw everything, reflected everything, and was nothing but pupil. What he writes seems like fragments of shattered light that fell upon him, bathed his soul, intoxicated him with the intoxication light induces, and emanated from him again. What was he to think of those vain little minds that walk about on the stilts of convention? Or those unworthy men who have eyes and will not see? Or those idlers and conformists who, instead of using their own eyes, see through the eyes of others? Or those figures of clay who stride about the earth molded by tailors, shoemakers, and hatters, adorned by jewelers, endowed with senses and speech, and nothing else? Or those pompous phrase-makers who do not know that every real thought is a travail of the mind, a flame kindled with oil extracted from one's own life, and a mountain peak?

No man ever lived freer of the pressures of men or of his moment. He did not tremble before the future, nor did he pass through it blindly. The light he carried within brought him safe through that journey among the ruins we call life. He knew nothing of bounds and fetters, not even those of country, because he belonged to the community of mankind. He saw the earth, found it out of tune with himself, felt the sorrow of answering the questions that men do not ask, and turned in toward himself. He was educated to teach a creed, and he turned over his vestments to the subscribers to the creed because he felt that upon his shoulders had fallen the august mantle of Nature. He neither obeyed nor created systems, for the one seemed to him an act of servility and blindness, and the other the work of a shallow, base and invidious mind. He submerged himself in Nature and emerged resplendent. He felt himself to be a man, and therefore, a God. What he saw, he related, and where he could not see, he was silent. He revealed what he saw, and he venerated what he could not see. He looked on the universe with his own eyes, and spoke his own language. By not wishing to be a creator, he became one. His were the joys divine, and his commerce was with the delightful and heavenly. He knew the ineffable sweetness of ecstasy. His mind, his tongue, and his conscience were never for hire. Light emanated from him as from a star. Human kind reached its fullest dignity in him.

He spent his life beholding the invisible and revealing it. He lived in a sacred city, because it was there that men, tired of being slaves, decided to be free, and with one knee on Concord ground, they fired the first shot, from which iron this country has been forged, on the English redcoats. He lived in Concord, which is like Tusculum, where thinkers, hermits, and poets live. His home was roomy and solemn, like himself, surrounded by tall pines, like a symbol of the owner, and shady chestnut trees. In his room, the books had more the look of guests than of books: all wore an every-day appearance with discolored pages and worn bindings. He read everything, like a preying eagle. The roof of his house was peaked like the dwelling place of one who lives in continual upward flight, and plumes of smoke emerged from the high roof like the vapor of ideas one sometimes sees emerge from a great pensive forehead. There he read Montaigne, who saw things for himself and spoke true words; Swedenborg, the mystic with the oceanic mind; Plotinus, who searched for God and came close to finding him; the Hindus, who humbly and a-tremble attend the evanescence of their own souls, and Plato, who looked without fear, and with unequaled harvest, on the divine mind. Or he would close his books, and the eyes of the body, and give himself the supreme pleasure of seeing with his soul. Or when an idea, seeking its exact expression, struggled on his lips like an animal caught in brambles trying to fight its way clear to the open air, then, all ablaze, he would pace agitated and uneasy, like someone who is moved by a will not his own. Or he would sit down exhausted and smile sweetly, like one who sees something solemn, and gratefully strokes his spirit, which has found it. Oh, what fruition to think clearly! And what joy—the joy of a monarch—to understand the purposes of life! One smiles at the appearance of a truth as on a beautiful maiden. One trembles as if exchanging some mysterious vows. Life, which is usually awesome, becomes ineffable. The ordinary pleasures are the birthright of knaves. Life contains more delicate pleasures, which come from loving and thinking. For what clouds in the sky are more beautiful than those which form, float and ascend in the soul of a father when he looks at his child? And why should man envy woman because she suffers and gives birth, if a thought, in its torments before birth and the satisfaction it brings afterward, is a son? The moment of knowing the truth is intoxicating and august. It gives a sensation, not of rising, but of being at rest. One feels a filial tenderness and a father's confusion. The joy brings to the eyes a heightened brilliance, peace to the soul, and a caress of soft wings to the mind. It is as though the brain were populated with stars: an inner firmament, silent and vast, that illuminates the tranquil mind in a solemn night! Magnificent world, from which one turns and gently leads away by the hand all that has been man's handiwork, as if with pity for the small and a plea that it not disturb the sacred bliss. The books that seemed moun-

tains now seem withered grapes; men seem invalids
to whom one brings a cure. And the trees, the mountains, the immense sky, and the surging ocean seem
like our brothers and friends. And man feels himself
somewhat the creator of Nature. Reading stimulates,
fires, quickens, and is like a gust of fresh air that scatters the ashes from banked embers and bares the fire
to the air. One reads the great, and if one is capable
of greatness, one is better fitted to be great. The noble
lion awakes and from his mane, vigorously shaken, fall
thoughts like flakes of gold.

He was a subtle observer, who saw how the delicate
air became melodious and wise words in the throats of
men, and he wrote as an observer, not as a meditator.
Everything he writes is a maxim. His quill is not a
brush that dilutes, but a chisel that sculpts and trims.
He renders the pure phrase as the good sculptor renders the pure line. An unnecessary word seems to him
a wrinkle in the contour. And with one blow of his
chisel, the wrinkle flies into pieces and the pure phrase
stands clear and limpid. He abhors the superfluous,
and when he speaks, he gives the full measure of what
he means to say. Sometimes, he seems to jump from
one thing to another, and at first one does not see the
relationship between two consecutive ideas. But what
is a leap for others, is his natural gait. He moves from
peak to peak, like a giant, and scorns the roads and
footpaths where the pack-burdened pedestrians plod,
to whose remote eyes the towering giant looks small.
He does not write in rounded periods, but rather in
terse keystones of thoughts. His works are summaries,
not demonstrations. His thoughts seem isolated, for he

sees much at one time, and wants to say it all at once, and say it as he sees it, like a page read by lightning, or something seen in a light so beautiful that one knows it must disappear. He leaves analysis to the rest; he cannot take the time; he announces. His style is not rich, but crystal clear. He purifies, refines, tests, distills, and takes only the essence. His style is not a green hillock covered with fragrant, flowery plants; it is a cliff of dark marble. He made his tongue his servant, not he the servant of his tongue. Language is the creation of man, and man should not be a slave to language. Some fail to understand him well; that is because you do not measure a mountain in inches. And they say he is obscure; but when have great minds not been accused of this? It is less mortifying to say that what we read is incomprehensible, than to confess our own inability to understand. Emerson does not argue; he sets forth. He prizes Nature's teachings above man's. He thinks that a tree knows more than a book, that a star teaches more than a university, that a farm is a gospel, and a farmboy is closer to the universal truth than an antiquarian. For him there are no candles like the stars, no altars like the mountains, no preachers like the profound and tremulous nights. He is filled with angelic emotions if he is present when morning steps naked, rosy and happy from among her veils. He feels more powerful than an Assyrian monarch or a king of Persia when he witnesses a sunset or a laughing dawn. He needs only to see the beautiful to be good. These are the flames by which he writes. His ideas fall into the mind like white pebbles into a green sea: what sparks! what lightning!

what veins of fire! One feels dizzy as though one were astride the haunches of a flying lion. He felt that himself and emerged strong. And one presses the book to one's breast like a good and kind friend: or one caresses it tenderly like the spotless forehead of a faithful woman.

His mind touched on everything profound. He wanted to penetrate the mystery of life: to discover the laws of the existence of the universe. As a child, he felt strong and went out in search of the Creator. And he returned happy from his journey, declaring that he had found Him. He spent the rest of his days in the state of blessedness that follows such a colloquy. He trembled like the leaf of a tree in those expansions of his spirit and those mergings into the universal spirit; and he would return to himself, fresh and fragrant as the leaf of a tree. When he was born he was confronted with all those obstacles that centuries filled with presumptuous men have accumulated before the cradle of the newborn. The books are full of subtle poisons that inflame the imagination and sicken the judgement. He drained all these cups and walked by himself, scarcely touched by the poison. It is a torment of man that to see well he must be wise, and then forget that he is wise. The possession of truth is nothing more than a struggle between the revelations imposed on men. Some succumb, and become mere voices of another spirit. Others triumph, and add a new voice to that of Nature. Emerson triumphed: there is his philosophy. *Nature* is the title of his best work; in it, he gives himself up to those exquisite delights, he relates those marvelous walks, he turns with magnificent energy on those who ask for eyes to see, forgetting that they have eyes; he sees man the master, the universe meek and mild, and everything alive surging from the breast and returning to the breast, and above everything else he sees the Soul that will live, and in its arms, man. He gives account of himself and what he has seen. Of what he has not felt, he gives no account. He prefers to be thought inconsistent rather than fanciful. Beyond his range of vision, he says he cannot see. He does not deny that others may see; he only defends what he has seen. If in what he saw there are contradictions, let another comment and draw the distinctions: he simply narrates. He sees only analogies; he finds no contradictions in Nature, considers everything in it a symbol of man, and sees that everything in man is in Nature. He sees that Nature influences man, and also that man makes Nature happy or sad, eloquent or mute, remote or present, according to his mood. He considers the human idea master of the material universe. He sees that physical beauty strengthens and prepares men's souls for moral beauty. He sees that a barren soul conceives a barren universe. He feels that the universe that refuses to answer man in formulas, answers him by inspiring in him sentiments that soothe his fears and allow him to live strong, proud and happy. And he maintains that there is a similarity between everything, that everything has the same objective, that everything affects man, who beautifies everything with his mind, that all the currents of Nature pass through every child; that every man has within him the Creator, and everything will eventually come to rest in the bosom of the creative

Spirit; that there is a central unity in events—in thoughts and in actions; that the human soul, in traversing Nature, discovers itself in every part; that the beauty of Nature was created to arouse desire, to soften the trials of virtue, and to spur man to seek himself and know himself; that "Everything in Nature contains all the powers of Nature. Everything is made of one hidden stuff." Life does not dismay him; he is happy in the certainty that he acts rightly; the important thing is to be virtuous: virtue is "that Golden Key That opes the Palace of Eternity": life is more than the buying and the selling and the danger; it is commerce with the forces of Nature and government of oneself, of which the last follows from the first: the universal order inspires personal order: happiness is real, and the highest affection; therefore, whatever the truth about all the mysterious things, it is rational that one must do that which will produce the state of true happiness, above all other forms of happiness, which is virtue: life is nothing more than a way-place in Nature. The eyes of the reader fly over these radiant and serene pages, which seem to have been written, by some divine favor, atop mountain peaks and by a light not of men's eyes. Ablaze with the desire to see those bewitching marvels and walk through the palace of all these truths, one's eyes fix on those pages that entrance and sparkle like mirrors of steel reflecting glorious images to eyes already smarting from so much light. Oh, to read when one feels the flame hammering in the brain—it is like impaling a live eagle! If the hand were only lightning and could annihilate the skull without committing crime!

And what of death? Does not death afflict Emerson? Death afflicts or frightens only those who have reason to fear death, never those who have lived nobly; immortality will be attained by those who deserve it; death is a return of the finite to the infinite. Emerson does not consider it good to rebel: life is a fact, and is its own reason for being; it is a toy only for imbeciles and for real men it is a temple: it is better to live improving oneself through honest exercise of the thinking, feeling spirit than to rebel.

And science? Science confirms what the spirit possesses: the analogy between all the forces of Nature; the similarity between all living beings; the identity of composition of all the elements of the universe; the superiority of man, whose inferiors are known, but no superiors. Theories only ratify what the soul foreknows. Submerged in the abstract, the soul sees the whole; science, measuring the material like an inchworm, sees nothing but the detail. The fact that the universe has been formed by gradual, methodical and analogous steps neither reveals the finality of Nature nor refutes the existence of spiritual facts. When science runs its cycle and has recorded as much as there is to know, it will not know more than the soul knows now, and it will know what the soul knows. It is true that the foot of the saurian resembles the human hand, but it is also true that the soul of man reaches the grave with its youth while the body is wasted. The soul, in its immersion in the universal soul, feels such pervading and compelling pleasures, and energy so fresh and powerful, a serenity so majestic, and such a vital desire to love and forgive, that this is as truly the law of life for those who see it, as the resemblance between the foot of the saurian and the human hand, although this truth may elude those who do not see.

And the object of life? The object of life is to achieve the dream of perfect beauty because virtue makes beautiful the places where it works, and places of beauty influence virtue. All the elements of Nature have a moral character, for since all heighten this character in man, since all produce it, all elements must have it. Therefore, there is a oneness in truth, which is beauty in judgement; goodness, which is beauty in the affections; and pure beauty, which is beauty in art. Art is nothing more than Nature created by man, and this relationship is inescapable. Nature opens itself to man and shows him its variety so that he can perfect his judgement; its marvels, to stimulate his desire to imitate them; its difficulties, to educate his spirit for work, for disappointments, and in the strength to overcome them. Nature gives men its objects, and these are reflected by the mind which governs his speech in sounds that convey each object. The stars are messengers of beauty, and the eternal sublime. The forest is eternal youth and returns man to reason and faith. The forest lifts the spirits like a good deed. Nature inspires, heals, consoles, fortifies and prepares man for virtue. And man does not feel complete or revealed to himself, nor does he see the invisible, except through his intimate relation with Nature. The universe reaches man in multiple forms, as the radii meet in the center of a circle, and man, in the endless action of his will, exerts an influence to the circumference of the universe like radii from the cen-

ter. The universe is multiple, yet one: music can imitate
the movement and color of the snake. The locomotive
is the elephant of man's creation, potent and colossal
like the elephants. Only a degree of heat makes the
water that runs through the river bed different from
the stones it bathes. And in all this endless universe, as
though symbolic of the human being, everything takes
place as it takes place in man. Smoke rises on the air
like thoughts into infinity. The waters swing and seethe
in the deep like the affections of the soul. The mimosa
is frail, like a sensitive woman. Every quality of man
is represented in some animal of Nature. The trees
talk to us in a language we understand. The night
whispers something in our ear, for the heart that entered it heavy with doubt, awakes filled with peace.
Truth's appearance suddenly illuminates the soul, as
the sun illuminates Nature. Morning makes the birds
chirp and men talk. Evening stills the wings of birds
and the words of men. Virtue, toward which all Nature
conspires, leaves man at peace, as if he had finished
his work, like a curve that finds itself; and the circle
closed, need travel no further. The universe is a servant
and man is the king. The universe has been created to
instruct, nourish, delight and educate man. In the presence of variable and decaying Nature, man feels a certain stability. He feels eternally young and immemori-
ally old at the same time. He learns that what he
knows he did not learn here: this reveals to him a
prior life in which he acquired that knowledge he
brings to this life. He turns his eyes toward a Father
he cannot see, but of whose presence he is certain, and
whose kiss, which fills space and comes to him on the

night air charged with scent, imprints on his forehead
a flame by whose pale light he sees confusedly revealed
the interior universe—which is a reflection in miniature of the external universe—and the external, which
is a magnification of the internal, and the dreaded and
beautiful universe of death. But is God outside the
earth? Is God the earth itself? Is he above Nature?
Is Nature creative, and is the immense spiritual being,
whose bosom the human soul seeks, without existence?
Did the world in which we live spring into being of its
own accord? And will it move forever as it moves now,
or will it evaporate and will we in its vapors be lost
in an august and delightful union with a being of
whom Nature is a mere apparition?

With such thoughts this giant of a man bestirs his
powerful mind and seeks with open eyes the divine
mind, and he finds it complete, invisible, uniform and
alive in the light, the earth, the waters, and in himself,
and he feels that he knows what he cannot say, and that
man will eternally touch, but never feel, the pinions of
the golden eagle on which he will finally be borne. This
man has stood before the universe and has not swooned.
He has dared to analyze the synthesis and he has not
gone astray.

He has stretched out his arms and held the secret
of life within them. From his body, the frail basket
of his winged soul, he has ascended through painful
labors and mortal fears to those pure heights from
which the devotion of the traveler is rewarded by a
view of the outline of the tunics bordered in starlight
of the infinite beings. He has felt that mysterious overflowing of the spirit in his body, that solemn experi-

ence that fills the lips with kisses, the hands with caresses, and the eyes with tears, and seems like the sudden swelling and overflow of Nature in the spring-time. And then he felt that calm that comes after conversation with the divine, and that magnificent arrogance of a monarch which the consciousness of his own power gives man. For what man who is master of himself does not laugh at a king?

Dazzled at times by those shining books of the Hindus who believe that the human creature, purified by virtue, flies like a radiant butterfly from its earthly dross to the bosom of Brahma, he sometimes allowed himself to do that which he criticized, and looked on Nature through the eyes of others because he felt those eyes to be in keeping with his own, and then he saw darkly and made out his own visions. For that philosophy of India intoxicates, like a forest of orange blossoms, and it fires one with the desire to fly, as when one sees birds take wing. The man who enters into it feels gently annihilated and consumed by blue flames in his journey to the heights. Then he asks himself if Nature is not some fantasy, and man the fancier, and the whole universe an idea, and God the pure idea, and man the aspiring idea which will ultimately end in the bosom of God like a pearl in the shell or the arrow-head in the tree trunk. And he begins to erect a scaffolding and sets about constructing the universe. But he tears down his scaffolding at once and is embarrassed by the meanness of his edifice and the poverty of the mind which, when it turns to building worlds, seems like an ant trying to drag a mountain range on its back.

And once more he feels the mystic and vague currents course through his veins; and he sees again how the storms of the soul die away in the friendly silence, charged with promise, of the forest; and he sees that when the mind goes aground like a ship on a reef, the intuition springs up, like a caged bird seeking the sky, and escapes from the sprung mind; and in a language uncompromising, brutal, and refractory as stone, he translates the lucid transports, the chaste ecstasies, the soothing delights, and rapturous joys of the tremulous spirit which captive Nature, surprised by the daring lover, admits to her affections. And he announces to every man that the universe has revealed itself to him fully and directly, and that with him is revealed the right of each to see it for himself, and slake with his own lips the burning thirst it inspires. And having learned in those colloquies that pure thought and pure feeling produce such vital joys that the soul feels a sweet death in them and then a radiant resurrection, he proclaims to men that they can only be happy by being pure.

And when he had discovered this, and was sure that the stars are man's crown and that when his brain had turned to clay his serene spirit would cleave the air wrapped in light, he laid his hand affectionately on his tormented fellow men and turned his sparkling and penetrating eyes on the rude combats of the earth. His looks swept rubbish aside. He sat at ease at the table of heroes. He narrated with Homeric tongue the episodes of nations. He showed the ingenuousness of a giant. He allowed himself to be guided by his intuition which opened for him the bosom of graves and of

clouds. Having sat in the parliament of stars and returned strong, he sat in the parliaments of men as
though he were in his brother's house. He recounts the
history of the ancient and of the modern. He analyzes
nations as a geologist might analyze fossils. And his
phrases are like the vertebrae of mastodons, gilded
statues and Greek porticos. Of other men one can say:
"This is a brother"; of Emerson one must say: "This
is a father." He wrote a wonderful book, a sum of human experience, in which he studied and enshrined,
each in his type, the great men. He saw the native England of his Puritan fathers and drew on his visit to
write another powerful book which he called *English
Traits*. He grouped the vital facts of existence, studied
them in magical "Essays," and gave them laws. All his
laws of life turn about the axis of this one truth: "all
of Nature trembles before the conscience of a child."
Religion, destiny, power, wealth, illusion, greatness—
he analyzed them all and broke them down with a
chemist's hand. He leaves the beautiful intact, but the
false he razes. He does not bow to usage. What is base
remains base for him no matter how wide its acceptance. Man should range himself with the angels. Tenderness, resignation and prudence are the new law.
These essays are codes. They are overwhelming in the
abundance of their wisdom. They have the grandiose
monotony of a mountain range. There is no contradiction for him between the great and the small, between
the ideal and the practical, and he says that the laws
which will give the final victory, which give man the
right to crown himself with stars, are the laws which
give happiness on earth. There are no contradictions in

Nature, but only in man's inability to find her analogies. He does not depreciate science for being false, but for being slow. His books abound in scientific truths. Tyndall says he owes his science to him. The whole doctrine of evolution is contained in a handful of Emerson's phrases. But he does not think the understanding alone is enough to penetrate the mystery of life, bring peace to man, and place him in possession of all his faculties of growth. He believes that intuition finishes what the understanding began. He believes that the eternal soul divines what science can only suspect. The latter trails like a hound; the former crosses the gorge in which the naturalist stands bemused, like a powerful condor. Emerson constantly observed, jotted down everything he saw, grouped together in his notebooks all analogous facts, and when it came time to reveal, he raised his voice. There was in him something of Calderón, of Plato and of Pindar. He has something of Franklin. He was not a leafy bamboo that comes to earth beneath its heavy foliage, ill-supported on a hollow trunk; he was like a baobab, or juniper, or great *samán* whose abundant crown spreads from a strong trunk. Little loved by the guardians of respectability, he seemed to disdain the earth, and walked in the land of idealism. Emerson has made idealism human: he did not wait for science, because the bird has no need of stilts to reach the heights nor the eagle of rails. He leaves science behind like an impatient *caudillo* who mounts a flying horse and leaves behind the plodding soldier loaded down with weighty armament. Idealism is not in him a vague desire for death, but a conviction in the after-life which is to be gained by the serene practice of virtue in this life. And life is as beautiful and ideal as death. Do you want to see how he conceives things? Like this: he holds that man does not dedicate all his powers to the study of Nature, but only that of understanding, which is not his strongest, and as a result he does not penetrate very far into it, and he says: "The axis of vision is not coincident with the axis of things." And he wants to explain that all the moral and physical truths are contained in one another, and each contains all the others, and he says: "It is like a great circle on a sphere, comprising all possible circles; which, however, may be drawn and comprise it in like manner. Every such truth is the absolute Ens seen from one side. But it has innumerable sides." Do you want to hear how he talks? He talks like this: "To a man laboring under a calamity, the hearth of his own fire hath sadness in it." "We are not built like a ship to be tossed, but like a house to stand." "Cut these words and they will bleed." "To be great is to be misunderstood." "Leonidas . . . consumed one day in dying." "All facts in natural history taken by themselves, have no value, but are barren like a single sex."

And his poetry is constructed like those palaces of Florence, with massive, irregular stones. He pounds and surges like ocean waters. At other times he seems a naked boy holding a little basket of flowers in his hands. His is a poetry of patriarchs, primitive men, cyclops. Some of his poems are like an oak grove in bloom. His poetry is the only one that consecrates the greatest struggle on earth. And other poems of his are like brooks of precious stones, or patches of clouds, or a bolt of lightning. Is it not clear yet what his verses are? Sometimes they are like an old man with a curly beard, matted hair, and a piercing look, who leans on a live oak staff and sings in front of a cave of white stone, and at other times he is like a gigantic angel with golden wings who plunges from the tall green mountain into the abyss. Marvelous old man, at your feet I lay my sheaf of green palms, and my silver sword!

THE POET, WALT WHITMAN

April 1887

He seemed a god last night, seated in a red velvet armchair, with his shock of white hair, his beard spread on his chest, his eyebrows as thick as forests, his hand resting on his cane." That is what to-day's newspaper said about Walt Whitman, the patriarch of seventy whom the discerning critics—always the fewer—assign an extraordinary place in the literature of his country and his time. Not since the sacred books of antiquity has there been a doctrine comparable in its apocalyptic language and sinewed poetry to that of this old poet whose grandiose and priestly utterances erupt like sun-bursts through the pages of *Leaves of Grass*, his astonishing book whose sale is prohibited.

And why not, since it is a natural work? The universities and schoolmen have brought men to the pass where they no longer know each other; instead of embracing, attracted by the essential and eternal in them, they draw apart, insulting one another like fishwives over purely circumstantial differences. As a pudding conforms to its mold, so men take their shape from

the book or the enthusiastic teacher who first introduced them to the fad or fashion of the moment. The
philosophical, religious, and literary schools straiten
men with the liveried confinement of the lackey; men
allow themselves to be put to the iron like horses or
bulls and then they parade about the world displaying
their brand; so that in the presence of the naked, original, loving, sincere, potent man—who travels, loves,
fights, rows—the man who accepts sorrow and reads
the promise of final triumph in the balance and fullness
of the world—face to face with the vigorous and angelic he-man of a Walt Whitman, they flee as from
their own conscience and refuse to recognize in that
vital and superior manhood the true type of their faded,
domesticated and dwarfed species.

The newspaper said that yesterday, when that other
venerable elder, Gladstone, had finished lecturing his
parliamentary opponents on the justice of conceding
self-government to Ireland, he seemed a bristling mas-
tiff, rampant without rival above the crowd cringing
like curs at his feet. Thus Whitman appears with his
"natural person," his "nature without check with original energy," his "myriad youths, beautiful, gigantic";
with his belief that "the smallest sprout shows there is
really no death," his formidable review of peoples and
races in "Salut au Monde," his assurance that "knowing the perfect fitness and equanimity of things, while
they discuss I am silent, and go and bathe and admire
myself"; that is the Whitman who "does not say these
things for a dollar," who says "I am satisfied—I see,
dance, laugh, sing," who has "no chair, no church, no
philosophy"; so stands Whitman compared with those

rachitic poets, one volume reputations, hirelings, and philosophers of one convention—the literary and philosophical mannequins.

Whitman must be studied because if he is not the most tasteful poet, he is the most fearless, comprehensive, and spontaneous poet of his age. In his little frame house, where poverty seems no stranger, Victor Hugo's picture is enshrined in a border of black mourning; Emerson, whose writings purify and exalt, threw an arm about his shoulder and called him his friend; Tennyson, who is of the company of those who see to the core of things, sends tender greetings to the "grand old man" from his oaken chair in England; Robert Buchanan, the outspoken Englishman, takes the North Americans to task: What can you know of letters—he exclaims—when you are letting the old age of your colossal Walt Whitman slip by without paying him the eminent honors he deserves? The truth is that to read him, although it may be astonishing at first, leaves a delightful sensation of new strength in the soul tormented by the general pettiness. He creates his own grammar and logic. He reads in the ox's eye and the sap of the leaf. "That one who cleans the filth from your house, he is my brother." Whitman's apparent irregularity, which is disconcerting on first impression, is later seen, except for brief instants of monstrous exaggeration, to possess that sublime order and composition with which the mountains range themselves against the horizon.

Whitman does not live in New York, his "beloved Manahatta," his "superb-faced," "million-footed Manhattan," where he comes when he wants to intone "the

song of what I behold, Libertad." Since his books and
lectures earn him barely enough to buy bread, "loving
friends" care for him in a little house nestled away in
a pleasant country corner from which he rides out in
an old-fashioned carriage drawn by the horses he loves,
to see the "athletic young men" at their virile pastimes,
to the *camerados* who are not afraid to rub elbows
with this iconoclast who wants to establish "the in-
stitution of the dear love of comrades," to see the
bountiful fields, the friends who pass by singing arm
in arm, the lovers gay and animated as quail. He tells
of it in his "Calamus," that enormously strange book in
which he sings the love between friends: "City of
orgies . . . Not the pageants of you, not your shifting
tableaux, your spectacles, repay me . . . Nor the pro-
cessions in the streets, nor the bright windows with
goods in them, Nor to converse with learned persons
. . . Not those, but as I pass O Manhattan, your fre-
quent and swift flash of eyes offering me love . . .
Lovers, continual lovers, only repay me." He is like the
old men he announces at the end of his *Leaves of Grass;*
"I announce myriads of youths, beautiful, gigantic,
sweet-blooded, I announce a race of splendid and savage old men."

Whitman lives in the country, where the natural man,
his peaceful horses nearby, tills the generous earth
beneath the burnishing sun; but yet, not far from the
inviting, ardent city, with its noises of life, its varied
occupations, its Protean epic, the dust of the wagon
wheels, the smoke from the gasping factories, the sun
that sees it all; "the loud laugh of work people at their
meals"; "exclamations of women taken suddenly who

hurry home and give birth to babes"; "the flap of the
curtained litter, a sick man borne inside to the hos-
pital." But yesterday Whitman came from the country
to recite before a gathering of loyal friends his oration
on that other natural man, that great and gentle soul,
"that great star early droop'd in the western sky,"
Abraham Lincoln. Rapt, in religious silence, the audience followed the brilliant discourse, which seemed at
times like the whispering of the spheres with its sudden changes, vibrant tones, hymn-like sweep, and
Olympic familiarity. Perhaps those who have drunk
only at the Classic or Gallic springs cannot understand
that heroic manner, but the free and fitting life of men
in a new continent has produced a fresh and robust
philosophy which is going abroad in athletic lyrics.
The largest body of freemen and workers the world
has ever seen require a befitting poetry of faith and
of the whole, tranquil and grave, a sun that rises from
the ocean kindling the clouds, touching the crests of
the waves with fire; bringing to life the sleeping flowers and nests in the rank jungles along the shore. The
pollen scatters; the cooing and billing are hidden among
the pleached branches; the leaves seek the sun; all ex-
udes music; in this language of raw light Whitman
spoke of Lincoln.

Whitman's dirge on the death of Lincoln is one of
the most beautiful creations of contemporary poetry.
All of nature accompanies the lamented bier on its
journey to the grave. The stars portended the event and
the clouds rolled darkly a month before. The poet
wanders down the shadowed fields, close-flanked by
the thought and knowledge of death. With musical art

he brings together, fuses, and reproduces these sad elements in a perfect harmony of twilight. The poem ends and the whole earth seems dressed in mourning, covered from ocean to ocean by the corpse. One sees the clouds, the heavy moon announcing the catastrophe, the long wings of the gray bird. It is much more beautiful, strange and profound than Poe's "The Raven." The poet brings a branch of lilac to the coffin.

That is his poem.

The willows no longer sigh over the graves; death is "the harvest," "the opener and usher to the heavenly mansion," "the great revealer"; apparent contradictions and sorrows are resolved in the fullness of the heavenly spring; a bone is a flower. Close at hand comes the thunder of suns moving with majestic purpose toward their final station; life is a hymn and death is a hidden form of life; blessed is sweat and blessed is the one-celled creature; men should kiss each other on the cheek when they meet and the living should embrace with ineffable love; they should love the grass, the beasts, the air, the ocean, sorrow, death; souls that possess love suffer less; life holds no sorrow for those who solve its meaning betimes; honey, light, a kiss have a common origin; in the shadowed vault of the night a-glitter with clustered stars, a peaceful and gigantic lilac tree lifts itself with the most gentle music over sleeping worlds stretched like hounds at its feet.

Every form of society brings its own expression to literature in such a way that a truer account of the history of nations can be drawn from the stages of literature than from the parchments and chronicles of history. There can be no contradictions in Nature; the human aspiration to find an ideal type of grace and beauty in love during life and in the unknown in the after-life demonstrates that in the totality of life there is a pleasing union of those elements that in our earthly span seem disunited and hostile. The literature that announces and prepares for the final happy concert of the apparent contradictions; the literature that emerges like Nature's spontaneous counsel and instruction proclaiming the oneness in a higher peace of the dogmas and rival passions that divide and bloody nations in their primitive states; the literature that fixes in the timid souls of men a conviction in the ultimate justice and beauty so deeply rooted that it cannot be galled or disheartened by the miseries and deformities of life will not only reveal a social state closer to perfection than any we have known, but happily uniting grace and reason that literature will provide mankind, thirsting for poetry and wonders, with a religion which it has gropingly awaited since it discovered the hollowness and insufficiency of its ancient creeds.

Who is the fool who maintains that poetry is not indispensable to a people? There are those so short-sighted that they mistake the rind for the fruit. Poetry, whether it unite or divide the soul, comfort or afflict it, uplift or cast it down, whether it give men faith and hope or take them away, is more necessary to a people than industry itself, for while this gives men the means of subsistence, poetry gives men the desire and strength to live. What is to become of a nation whose people have lost the habit of thinking with faith in the significance and latitude of their actions? The better part, those whom Nature endows with a sacred hope for the future, will lose, through a blind and painful annihilation, the incentive to deal with the ugly aspects of life; and the mass, the vulgar, the people of appetites, the average, will breed without sanctity a race of empty children, they will raise to the level of essentials faculties that should serve only as instruments, and they will bemuse the incurable torment of the soul, which is satisfied only by the beautiful and the grand, with the bustle of an ever incomplete prosperity.

Liberty should be blessed, apart from other reasons, because its enjoyment brings to modern man—deprived from birth of the tranquility, the stimulus and poetry of existence—that supreme peace and religious well-being that those who live with assurance and serenity of will find in the order of the world. Look beyond the hills, you poets who water the deserted altars with vain tears.

You thought religion lost because it was changing form above your understanding? Arise, for you are the priests. Liberty is the definitive religion and the poetry of liberty is the new cult. It calms and beautifies the present, it foreshadows and illuminates the future, and it explains the ineffable purpose and the seductive goodness of the universe.

Hear this hard-working and satisfied people singing; hear Walt Whitman. He elevates the exercise of self to majesty, tolerance to justice, and order to happiness. He who follows an autocratic belief lives like an oyster in its shell seeing only the prison that encloses him and in his darkness believing it to be the world: liberty gives wings to oysters. That which seemed an ominous conflict within the oyster shell turns out in the light of day to be the natural flow of the sap in the vibrant pulse of the world.

For Walt Whitman the world has ever been as it is today. It is enough that a thing is, that it should have been, and when it no longer should be, it will cease. Whatever no longer exists, the unseen, is proved by what is, and is seen; because everything is in everything, and the one explains the other; and when what is now is no longer, it will receive proof in turn from what is then. The infinitesimal collaborates with the infinite, and everything has its place, the tortoise, the ox, the birds, "wing'd purposes." It is as lucky to die as to have been born, because the dead are alive: "(No array of terms can say how much I am at peace about God and about death)." He laughs at what they call dissolution and he knows the span of time. He contains everything in his person; all of him is in everything; whoever degrades another degrades him; he is the tide, the ebb and the flow; how can he not have pride in himself, feeling himself to be a living and intelligent part of Nature? What does he care if he returns to the womb from which he was born and at the kiss of the moist earth is converted into a useful vegetable or beautiful flower? Having loved men, he will now

nourish them. His duty is to create; the atom that
creates is essentially divine; the act of creation is exquisite and sacred. Convinced of the identity of the
universe, he sings the "Song of Myself," weaving his
song out of everything—the beliefs that rise, struggle
and pass, the man who breeds and works, and the animals that help him. Ah! those animals of which "not
one kneels to another . . . not one is respectable or
unhappy . . . they do not sweat or whine about their
condition." He considers himself the heir of the world.

Nothing is alien to him, and he reckons everything
—the snail dragging itself along, the ox who gazes on
him with his mysterious eyes, the priest who asserts
part of the truth as though it were the whole truth.
Man should open his arms and clasp everything to his
breast, the wicked as well as the righteous, the filthy
as well as the clean, ignorance as well as wisdom; he
should fuse everything in his heart, as in a crucible;
but above all, he should let his white beard grow. And,
he adds: "We have had ducking and deprecating about
enough"; he scolds the skeptics, the sophists and the
talkers; procreate instead of complaining and add to
the world! Believe with the devotion of the devout
kissing the altar steps!

He belongs to all castes, creeds and professions and
he finds justice and poetry in all of them. He judges
religions without anger, but believes the perfect religion to be in Nature. Religion and life join in Nature.
Where there is one sick he tells the physician and the
priest to "go home": "I seize the descending man and
raise him with resistless will . . . I dilate you with
tremendous breath, I buoy you up, every room in the

house do I fill with an armed force, Lovers of me, baf-
flers of graves." The Creator is the "Lover divine and
the perfect Comrade"; men are *camerados,* and the
more they believe and love the greater their worth,
although everything that occupies time and space is
worth as much as everything else; but each must see
the world for himself because Walt Whitman, who feels
in himself the world since its creation, knows from
what the sun and the open air have taught him, that
a dawn is more revealing than the best book. He considers the orbs, he desires women, he feels himself
possessed by a frantic and universal love; he hears a
concert rising from the scenes of the creation and the
employments of man that overwhelms him with happiness, and when he goes to the river at that hour
when the shops and offices close and the setting sun
fires the water, he feels that he has an appointment
with the Lord, he acknowledges that man is definitely
good, and he sees spokes of light diverging from round
the shape of his head in the sunlit water.

+

But what can give the measure of his vast and burning
love? This man loves the world with the fire of Sappho.
He sees the world as a gigantic bed and for him the bed
is an altar. He says he will make illustrious the words
and ideas that men have prostituted with secrecy and
false modesty: he will chant and consecrate what Egypt
consecrated. One of the sources of his originality is the
herculean strength with which he wrestles with ideas
as though to violate them, when actually all he desires
is to give them a kiss with saintly passion. Another

source is the earthy, brutal and corporeal form in
which he expresses his most delicate ideals. That language has seemed lewd to those who are incapable of
comprehending its greatness; fools, with the affected
modesty of prurient schoolboys, have thought to see a
return to those low desires of Virgil for Cebetes and of
Horace for Gyges and Lyciscus in those most ardent
images of the human language with which Whitman
celebrates the love between friends in "Calamus." And
when he sings the divine sin in "Children of Adam" in
pictures before which the most vivid evocations of The
Song of Songs seem pale, he trembles, he gathers, he
overflows and swells, he is mad with pride and satisfied
virility, he recalls the god of the Amazon who passed
over the forests and rivers sowing the seeds of life
through the land; "singing the song of procreation."
"I sing the body electric," he says in "Children of
Adam"; and to find a counterpart to the satanic force
with which he reviews the parts of the feminine body,
one must have read the patriarchal genealogies of
Genesis in Hebrew and have followed the naked and
cannibal bands of primitive men through the virgin
jungle. But do you say this man is brutal? Listen to
this composition, "Beautiful Women," which like many
of his poems is only two lines: "Women sit or move to
and fro, some old, some young, The young are beautiful
—but the old are more beautiful than the young." And
this other one, "Mother and Babe": "I see the sleeping
babe nestling the breast of his mother, The sleeping
mother and babe—hush'd, I study them long and long."
He foresees that just as virility and tenderness are
combined to a high degree in men of superior mind,

so the two energies which have had to be divided in order to carry on the work of creation will be joined in that delightful peace where life finds its final rest with all the solemnity and rejoicing of the universe.

When he goes into the grass, he says the grass caresses him, that he feels the moving of its joints; and the most restless novice could not find such burning words to describe the happiness of his body, which he considers part of the soul, at feeling the ocean's embrace. Everything in existence loves him; he is loved by the land, the night, the ocean; "You sea . . . Dash me with amorous wet." He savors the air. He offers himself to the atmosphere like a trembling lover. He wants doors without locks and bodies in their natural beauty; he is "Walt Whitman, a kosmos, of Manhattan the son, Turbulent, fleshy, sensual, eating, drinking and breeding, . . . no stander above men and women or apart from them." He describes truth as a passionate lover who invades his body and unbuttons his clothing in the anxiety to possess him. But on the clear midnight, his soul, free of books and occupations, emerges whole, silently and in contemplation from the day well spent and meditates on the subjects that please her: on night, dreams, and death; on the song of the universal for the benefit of the common man; on the sweetness "to die advancing on," falling at the foot of the primeval tree with ax in hand, bitten by the last serpent in the forest.

Imagine what a new and strange effect is produced when that language dilated with proud animality celebrates the love that will bring men together. In one of the compositions of "Calamus" he names the deepest joys he owes to Nature and homeland; but he finds only the waves of the ocean by moonlight worthy of chorusing his joy at seeing the friend he loves asleep at his side. He loves the humble, the defeated, the wounded, even the wicked. He does not despise the great, because for him only the useful are great. He throws an arm about the shoulder of teamsters, sailors, and workers. He hunts and fishes with them, and in haying time he climbs to the top of the wagon and rides there with them. The powerful Negro poised behind the team of percherons guiding his dray calmly through the maelstrom of Broadway seems more beautiful to him than an emperor coming in triumph. He understands all virtues, receives all rewards, works at all employments, suffers all pains, and he feels a heroic pleasure when he stops at the threshold of the smithy and sees the young men bare to the waist swinging the sledges over their heads and each striking in his turn. He is the slave, the prisoner, the fighter, the fallen, and the beggar. When the slave comes to his door, pursued and sweaty, he fills the bath tub and sets a place for him at the table; he has his loaded gun in the corner ready to defend him; if they come to attack him, he will kill his pursuer and return to the table, as if he had just killed a serpent.

Walt Whitman is satisfied. What vanity can torment him, knowing that the end is grass or a flower? Where is the vanity of a carnation, a sprig of sage, or

the honeysuckle? How can he look on human sorrows
except with calm, knowing that after them there is an
existence without end for him who awaits a happy
fusion with Nature? What can hurry him, with his
belief that everything is where it should be and that
the will of one man cannot change the course of the
world? He suffers, yes; but he considers that self within
him that suffers, secondary and temporal, and he feels
that he contains another self that is above fatigues and
miseries and free of suffering because it sees the universal greatness. It is enough for him to be as he is,
and he looks with serenity and contentment on the
course of his life, whether it be silent or acclaimed.
He casts aside at one stroke the romantic lament as a
useless excrescence stating that he is "Not asking the
sky to come down to my good will." And what majesty
there is in that phrase in which he says he loves animals because "they do not whine about their condition."
The truth is that there are already too many prophets
of doom; one must see the world as it is, to avoid
making mountains out of molehills; give men strength,
rather than take away with laments what little sorrow
leaves them; do the maimed go about the streets displaying their scars? Not even the doubts raised by
science disturb him. To the scientists he says: "Gentlemen, to you the first honors always! Your facts are
useful, and yet they are not my dwelling, I but enter
by them to an area of my dwelling," "How beggarly
appear arguments before a defiant deed!" "Lo! keen-
eyed towering science . . . Yet again, lo! the soul,
above all science." But it is in that phrase, touched
with the melancholy of the defeated, with which he

uproots the cause of envy that his philosophy shows
that complete mastery of hate that the wise men order:
why should I be jealous, he asks, of my brother who
does what I cannot? "He that by me spreads a wider
breast than my own, proves the width of my own."
"Let the Sun interpenetrate the Earth until it all be
sweet and pure light, like my blood! Let the rejoicing
be universal. I sing the eternity of existence, the happiness of our life and the beauty beyond change of the
Universe. My signs are the calfskin shoe, the open
collar and a staff cut from the woods."

+

He expresses all this in apocalyptic phrase. Rhymes or
accents? Oh, no! his rhythm, amidst that apparent
chaos of superimposed and violent phrases, lies in the
arrangement of his stanzas in a profound pattern of
composition that distributes his ideas in great musical
groups. This is the natural poetic form for a nation
that builds not stone by stone but in enormous blocks.
Walt Whitman's language differs entirely from any
used by poets until the present and its wildness and
potency accords with his cyclical poetry and is well-
suited to this new humanity congregated on a fertile
continent whose vistas, actually, are such that they
cannot be accommodated in genteel or rhyming lyrics.
It is no longer a question of unspoken loves, inconstant
ladies, the sterile complaints of those who lack the
energy to tame life, or the circumspection that becomes
cowards. It is not jingling rhymes, or sighs in the al-
cove, but the birth of an era, the dawn of the definitive
religion, and the renovation of man that are involved;

it is a question of writing the sacred books of a people who, in falling away from Europe, bring to the flowing breasts and embrace of wild Nature all the virgin energies of liberty; it is a question of finding words to match the noise of masses taking root, cities at work, oceans enthralled and rivers harnessed. Will Walt Whitman pair consonants and confine in tame couplets these mountains of goods, forests of masts, communities of ships, battles in which millions fall that right may prevail, and the all-imperious sun that streams limpid fire across the horizon of the vast scene?

Oh, no! Walt Whitman speaks in verses that seem bereft of music until one has listened to them a little and then one perceives in them that sound of the vibration of the earth when it is being crossed by the glorious and unshod triumphal hordes. Whitman's language seems sometimes like a meat-market window hung with carcasses; sometimes it seems like the song rising from the elders seated in a circle, with that gentle sadness of the world, at the hour when the smoke loses itself in the clouds; sometimes it sounds like a rough kiss, a ravishment, or the crack of the desiccated hide that bursts beneath the sun; but his phrases never lose their rhythmic swing of the waves. He himself tells how he talks: in "prophetic screams," expressing "one or two indicative words for the future." That is his poetry, an indication; a sense of the universal pervades his book which gives it a grandiose regularity underlying the superficial confusion; but his disjointed phrases—sharp-sided, incomplete, adrift—effuse rather than express: he sends his musings over the hoary mountains; "Earth! . . . Say, old top-knot, what do

you want?"; "I sound my barbaric yawp over the roofs
of the world."

He is not one to turn out a beggarly idea in regal
trappings and send it stumbling and weighed down
beneath its outward opulence. He does not inflate sparrows so they will look like eagles; every time he opens
his hand he casts forth eagles like the sower scatters
his seed. One verse has five syllables, the next forty,
and the next ten. He does not force comparisons and, in
fact, he does not compare. He tells what he sees or remembers with a graphic and incisive touch, always
the sure master of the impression of unity he sets out
to create. He employs his art, which is completely submerged, to reproduce the elements of his picture with
the same disorder in which he observed them in Nature. If he raves, it is without dissonance, because that
is the way the mind wanders through analogies from
subject to subject without order or constraint. Moreover,
when suddenly, as if he had simply loosed the reins without laying them aside, he gathers them in and close-reins
his rearing four-in-hand with a driver's grip, his verses
go galloping in earth-devouring strides. Sometimes they
neigh eagerly, like the lordly stallion; sometimes, lathered and white, they put their hoofs over the clouds;
sometimes, bold and black, they plunge into the bowels
of the earth, and the rumble is heard for a long time.
He sketches, but always one would say with fire. He
gathers all the horrors of war into five lines like a
bundle of rawly gnawed bones. He needs only an ad-
verb to dilate or clinch a phrase, and an adjective to
transfigure it. He needs a method that is large because
that is his effect; but it might be thought that he

proceeds without any method whatsoever, above all in the unprecedented daring with which he uses words, placing the august and nearly divine ones beside those which are considered least appropriate or proper. At times, he paints pictures without his ever lively and incisive epithets, employing only sounds which he introduces and removes with perfect skill, and with this variety of techniques he maintains an interest which would be imperiled by the monotony of a single style. He evokes melancholy by the use of repetition, like the savages. His unexpected and compelling caesura changes constantly and without any formal pattern, although a conscious order can be found in its evolutions, pauses and breaks. He considers accumulation the best method of description, and his reasonings are never reduced to the ordinary form of argument or the pompous form of oratory, but instead find expression in the mystery of insinuation, the fervor of conviction, and the fiery turn of prophecy. At every step, one finds these words of ours in his book: *viva, camarada, libertad, americanos*. But what shows his character better than the French words he embeds in his verse with evident rapture, as if to exaggerate their meaning: *ami, exalté, accoucheur, nonchalant, ensemble; ensemble* particularly entrances him because he sees the heaven of the life of nations and of worlds. He has taken one word from the Italian: *bravura*.

So, celebrating muscle and boldness; inviting passersby to put their hand in his without fear; listening to the song of things, with palms turned out to the open air; discovering and proclaiming with delight gigantic fecundities; gathering in epic verses the seeds, the bat-

tles, and the orbs; he points out to amazed ages the
teeming hives of men extending across the valleys and
mountains of America where their bee's-wings touch
the skirt hem of ever-vigilant liberty. Shepherding
the friendly ages toward the eternal calm of the final
fold, Walt Whitman stops with his friends while they
serve him wine and the first catch of the spring at
rustic boards. Having revealed to the world a complete, loving, and truthful man, he awaits the happy
hour in which the material will depart from him, and
given up to the purifying airs, he will become germ
and fragrance in its swells, "disembodied, triumphant,
dead."

OSCAR WILDE

January 1882

We who speak the Spanish tongue live steeped in Horace and Virgil and the frontiers of our spirit would seem to be those of our language. Why must foreign literatures be virtually forbidden fruit for us, rich as they are today in the natural setting, honest strength, and contemporary spirit so lacking in modern Spanish literature? Byron's reflection in Núñez de Arce, the influence of the German poets on Campoamor and Bécquer, and the smattering of pallid translations from the German or English hardly convey an idea of the literature of the Slavs, the Germans or English whose poems contain at once the snowy swan, castle ruins, rosy-cheeked maidens in flower-filled balconies, and the serene and mystic light of the aurora borealis. The knowledge of different literatures frees one from the tyranny of a few, just as the danger of blind subjection to one philosophical system is best escaped by feeding on all. It is then one realizes that in all systems one spirit prevails, confronted by the same problems, whatever the form the human imagination, soaring or restrained, according to climate, takes to express its faith in the infinite, the desire to transcend itself and that noble non-conformity with one's own existence which is engendered by all philosophical schools.

Consider Oscar Wilde: he is a young Englishman who writes excellent verse. He is a dissenter who accuses English art of having broken with the church of beautiful universal art. An elegant apostle, brimming with faith in his message and scornful of those who criticize it, he is traveling about the United States at this moment, telling, in his suave and discreet manner, why he abominates societies that make a cult of material well-being to the neglect of the well-being of the soul, which so lightens human shoulders of the burden of living, and lends charm to all tasks and endeavors. Beautify life and you give it meaning. The desire to rise above oneself is an unrelenting human longing, and he who beautifies man's existence serves him well, for he reconciles man to live within himself. It is a way of blunting the beak of the Promethean vulture. This is the sort of thing Wilde says, although he may fall short of that precision and scope. He is a rebel who would shake from his cultivated attire the oily smoke and soot that grime the sky of the English cities where the sun is an opaque red disk struggling against dense fog to send its life-giving rays to the harsh, rude-limbed, dulled northerners. So the poet born in those lands intensifies his precious faith in the neglected, unloved things of the spirit. One must live under tyranny to learn to really hate it, and nothing so quickens the poetic fire as to dwell among those who lack it. But the poet suffocates who lacks the vessels of companionable souls in which to pour his overflowing spirit.

Now see Oscar Wilde! He is in Chickering Hall, with its spacious rooms where New Yorkers gather to hear lectures. It is the tribune for the fashionable lecturers of established fame and fortune. There, Christian dogma is attacked and defended, the traditional is affirmed and the new proclaimed. Travelers describe their journeys with lantern slides and drawings on a great blackboard. A critic analyses a poet. A lady discusses the merits or defects of this or that dress. A philosopher expounds the laws of philosophy. In one of these rooms, Wilde is about to read his lecture on the great rebirth of art in England, of which he is the so-called guide and master, although actually he is no more than a spirited adept and an active and fervent disciple. He is a fighter for his faith. There were others who died for it—but we will come to that later. The hall is crowded with elegant ladies and distinguished gentlemen. The major poets are absent, perhaps from fear of being taken for accomplices of the innovator. Men love the dangerous truths in secret, and their fear of defending them before they become accepted is matched only by the tenacity and enthusiasm they display in supporting them once the danger of controversy has passed. Oscar Wilde comes from an excellent Irish family and he has purchased intellectual independence with his personal wealth. For here is one of the evils that beset men of genius: it often happens that the consuming and illuminating truth they bear is too new and revolutionary for the public, and their poverty does not permit them to be its champion. So they must bury within themselves the revelation of which they are the messengers in order to survive, and from the pain caused by this, they die. The carriages jounce and jostle before the wide doors of the stately lecture hall. A lady enters carrying a lily, which is the emblem of the new doctrine. The women have spared no effort to bring elegance and ornateness to their dress. Like the esthetes who are renovating art in England, they aim at a perfect harmony of color in the arrangement of their adornments and clothes. The stage is simple and neat.

A high-backed chair with thick arms, like our choir stalls, awaits the poet. The chair is of dark wood, with back and seat of dark morocco. As a backdrop there is a curtain of lighter chestnut. On an elegant table next to the chair sits an artistic pitcher in which the pure water sparkles like trapped light. Here comes Oscar Wilde! He is dressed in singular fashion, not at all like the rest of us. His dress immediately betrays the flaw in his persuasion, which is not so much to create the new, of which he feels himself incapable, as to recreate the old. His abundant hair, parted in the middle, falls to his shoulders in the manner of Elizabethan courtiers. He wears a dress coat; a white silk vest; knee breeches; black silk stockings and buckled shoes. His shirt collar is open, like Byron's, and held together by a carelessly knotted white silk tie. A diamond stud adorns his gleaming shirt front and an artistic watch-chain hangs from his vest. For it is necessary to dress beautifully and he sets the example. However, art demands a unity of time in all its works, and it is distressing to see this young man dressed up in the latest waistcoat, outmoded breeches, an antiquated hairdress, and a foppish watch-chain of the turn of the century. The young poet's face radiates noble sincerity. He is dignified in the display of his eccentricity. He respects the sublimity of his aspirations and they in turn command respect for him. He smiles confidently. The select audience is a-whisper. What does the poet say?

He says that Goethe has defined beauty beyond need of further definition; that the great English renaissance of this century unites a love of Grecian beauty, a passion for the Italian Renaissance, and a desire to avail itself of all the beauty brought to its works by the modern spirit. He says that the new school has come into being, like the euphony of Faust and Helen of Troy, through a union of the spirit of Greece, where everything was beautiful, and the individualism of the modern romantics, burning, searching, and rebellious. Homer preceded Phidias; Dante anticipated the wonderful renovation of the plastic arts in Italy; the poets always form the vanguard. The Pre-Raphaelites, painters who loved the real, natural, naked beauty, preceded the esthetes, who love beauty in the art and culture of all times. But Keats, the exuberant and plastic poet, came before the Pre-Raphaelites. These advocates of the techniques used by the forerunners of melodious Raphael wanted those painters to step aside who slavishly taught the ways of the old masters, and with palettes full of color they insisted on copying objects directly from nature. They were sincere to the point of brutality. From hatred of convention in others, they fell into a convention of their own. In their impatience with excessive rules, they came to disregard all rules. Improvement cannot be a turning back; nevertheless, if the Pre-Raphaelites were incapable of constructing, at least they tore down some dusty idols. After them, and largely as the result of their efforts, liberty and truth in art came to be esteemed in England. But, said Oscar Wilde: "Don't ask the English who those worthy Pre-Raphaelites were: knowing nothing about its great men is one of the fundamentals of English education. Back in 1847, the admirers of Keats gathered and were witness to his awakening of English poetry and art from its stony slumber. But one does this in England at the expense of one's rights as a citizen. They had what an Englishman never can forgive: youth, strength, and enthusiasm. They were satirized, because satire is the tribute envious mediocrity always pays genius. The reformers should have been very pleased with themselves at this, for there is no more legitimate cause for self-satisfaction than to be in disagreement on all points with three-quarters of the English people, and in times of spiritual depression this must be a great source of comfort."

Now hear Oscar Wilde talk of that other most harmonious poet, William Morris, author of *The Earthly Paradise,* who prided himself on the great beauty of his person, and the majesty of his verse, vibrant and limpid as Japanese porcelain. Hear Wilde say that Morris believed that the detailed copy of Nature stripped her of the most beautiful of her attributes which is that exhalation which surrounds her objects

like a luminous halo. Hear him say that English literature owes to Morris that precise method of rendering
the images of fantasy into poetry, for he knows of no
English poet who surpasses Morris in the polished
phrase and the pure image. Hear him recommend that
maxim of Gautier, who held that there was no book
more worthy of the poet's attention than the dictionary. "Those reformers," Wilde said, "hailed the beautiful wherever they found it, whether of their own time,
or of any of the ages of the earth." They wanted to
say everything, but say it beautifully. Beauty was their
only check on freedom. They were guided by a profound love of perfection.

They did not stifle inspiration, but clothed it in
beautiful raiment. They did not want it to go slovenly
through the streets, or dressed in bad taste, but well
turned out. And Wilde said: "We do not want to clip
the poet's wings, but we have learned to count their
innumerable pulsations, to calculate their unlimited
strength, to govern their ungovernable liberty. Let the
poet sing everything, if what he sings is worthy of his
verse. Everything enters within the poet's province.
He lives by the Spirit, which is eternal. For him no
forms are worthless or subjects barren. But with the
calm of one who feels himself in possession of the
secret beauty, the poet should accept whatever he finds
unquestionably beautiful in every age, and reject whatever falls short of his highest standard of beauty. Another great English poet, Swinburne, whose imagination sowed countless riches through his musical stanzas,
says that art is life itself, and that art knows nothing
of death. Let us not reject the ancient, for in the an-

cient is the perfect reflection of the present. Life is various in its forms, but perpetual in essence, and seen in the past it is free of that blur of familiarity and personal concern that beclouds life for the living. But the selection of a proper subject is not sufficient to move men's souls; it is not the subject on the canvass that commands and holds the eye, but the exhalation of the soul which emerges from the skillful use of colors. Therefore, the poet who would create a noble and lasting work must acquire that craftsmanship, purely technical, that gives to his songs the spiritual fragrance which enraptures. Let the critics frown! Whoever is capable of being an artist does not limit himself to being a critic, and artists who stand the test of time are comprehended in their full worth only by other artists. Our Keats used to say that he venerated only God, the memory of great men, and beauty. That is what we esthetes came for: to demonstrate to men the utility of loving beauty, to stimulate the study of those who have cultivated beauty, to revive a taste for perfection and the abhorrence of all ugliness; to return to fashion the admiration, knowledge and practice of everything mankind has admired as beautiful. But how shall we restore the dramatic form to its proper eminence, as was attempted by our poet Shelley, sick with love for the sky in a land where it is not loved? What does it avail us that we eagerly pursue the improvement of our conventional poetry and pale arts, seek to beautify our homes, and bring charm and quality to our dress? There can be no great art without a beautiful national life, and the commercial spirit has killed this in England. There can be no great drama without a noble national life and this too has been killed by the commercial spirit of the English." Enthusiastic applause encouraged the lecturer at this vigorous passage, and it was apparent he had won the affectionate curiosity of his audience.

And then Wilde spoke to the North Americans: "You, perhaps, children of a new nation, may be able to achieve here what costs so many pains to achieve in England. Blessed be your lack of ancient institutions, for this is a lack of obstacles; you are not bound by old traditions nor are your critics armed with hypocritical and hollow conventions with which to belabor you. You have not been trampled by starving generations. You are not sentenced to imitate forever a type of beauty whose elements are dead. From you may come the splendor of a new imagination and the wonder of some new liberty. You lack in your cities, as in your literature, that flexibility and grace that lends sensitivity to beauty. Love everything beautiful for the pleasure of loving it. All rest and contentment come from that. The devotion to beauty and the creation of beautiful objects is the best achievement of all civilizations: it makes the life of every man a sacrament, instead of a number in a ledger. Beauty is the only thing that time does not erase. Philosophies die, religious creeds become extinct; but that which is beautiful lives forever, and is the crown of all ages, the sustenance of all peoples and the eternal glory. Wars will become inconsequential when all men love the same things with the same intensity, when they share a common intellectual climate. England is still a powerful sovereign through force of arms; but our renaissance would bestow upon her a sovereignty that would abide after her yellow leopards tire of the clamor of battle and the red rose of her shield is no longer tinged with the blood of battle. And you also, Americans, by enshrining in the heart of this great nation the artistic spirit that sweetens and elevates, will lay up such riches for yourselves that you will think puny by comparison those you now enjoy from the network of rails you have thrown across your land, and from your harbors, which are the refuge of all the ships plying the seas known to man."

These noble and thoughtful words the young English poet of long hair and short trousers spoke in Chickering Hall. But what is there in that gospel to bring down such a storm on its disciples? These are our daily thoughts; this the reverence with which we regard the miracles of art; in us there is no excess, but a poverty of the commercial spirit. What peculiar greatness attaches to those beautiful, but commonplace and self-evident truths that Oscar Wilde is shepherding in strange garb through England and the United States? Can it be that what we take for granted arouses wonder in others? Is this intrepid young man to be scoffed at or admired? He is to be admired! True, either from fear of appearing presumptuous, or because he takes more delight in the pleasure his observation of beautiful things affords him than in the moral strength and transcendental end of beauty, there is little of the profundity or vision that would please a thinker in the lecture we have abstracted. True, there is something childish in preaching such vast reforms attired in a garb whose extravagance adds neither dignity nor grace to the human form and is nothing more than a timid demonstration of hate for ordinary dress.

True, the esthetes err in seeking, with peculiar love, to learn the secret of future spiritual well-being through adoration of the past and the extraordinary of other times. True, the vigorous reformer would pursue the evil to its source, which is the excessive love of physical well-being, rather than the neglect of art, which is a result. True, in our luminous and fragrant lands we hold those truths to be timeless that are now presented to the Anglo-Saxons as startling and bold reforms. Yet, with what sorrow one sees this young man; how attenuated in the children of his land is that fervent cult of the beautiful that comforts the greatest sorrows and is the source of ineffable pleasures. What chagrin he must feel to see his native land worshiping temporal idols, lost forever to the eternal life. What energies are needed to combat the criticism of cartoonists and satirists who live by flattering the taste of a public that dislikes those who confront it with its defects! What courage and determination are needed to defy the fearful anger and corrosive disdain of a cold, hypocritical and calculating people! What praise is too great, despite his long hair and short trousers, for this gallant youth who is trying to transform the dull orange disk that sheds its light on the melancholy English into a sun of gleaming rays that will suffuse the air with gold! Love of art melts the dross from the soul and lifts it up: a beautiful picture, a limpid statue, an ingenious toy, a simple flower in a pretty vase, bring a smile to faces stained

moments before by tears. Beyond that pleasure in possessing something beautiful that strengthens and im-
proves one's spirit is the pleasure in possessing the
beautiful which makes us content with ourselves. To
adorn the home, hang the walls with pictures, enjoy
them, judge their merits and discuss their beauties, are
noble delights which give value to living, diversion to
the intellect, and high employment to the spirit. A new
sap seems to course through the veins when one con-
templates a new work of art. It is like an intimation
of the future. It is like drinking the ideal life in a
goblet of Cellini.

And how brutal that nation that killed Byron! How
foolish a people, as if made of stone, to have scythed
the tender verses from the youthful lips of Keats! The
disdain of the English congeals like the frigid mountain air that freezes the English lakes and rivers. It
flies like an arrow from the cold and bloodless lips. It
delights in wit, which entertains; not genius, which
consumes. It seeks the half-light and is injured by too
much light. It enjoys the elegant poets who make one
smile; not the poetic geniuses who make one meditate
and suffer. It always opposes custom, like an iron
shield, to any spirited voice that disturbs the dream
of its spirit. Against that shield the young esthetes
hurl their darts; with this shield the critics try to
stifle the spirited voices from those burning lips, just
as it sealed Keats' lips even before his death. From
Keats comes that vigorous poetic breath asking music
and spirit for verse, and the ennoblement of life
through the cult of art. The bards of England learned
from Keats that subtle and careful love of form, which

he gave to the simple Greek thoughts. Keats gives birth to that painful struggle of the English poets who fight, as if against an insurmountable force, to awake a love for impalpable beauty and the spiritual intangibles in a public that rejects everything that does not woo, flatter or lull its senses. Where can the poet turn, in that land, but to his inner self? What is he to do, but fold upon his soul like a violet bruised by a horse's hoof? In Keats, the ideas overflow his winged and tuned stanzas, like the waters of a spring sea. His images tumble over each other, like Shakespeare's; only Shakespeare dominates and plays with them, while Keats is carried away at times by his own imagination. An inner fire consumed his body. A worshiper of beauty, he went to his shrine, Rome, to die. May his fervent disciple, whose defiance of the critics gives evidence of majestic integrity and whose verses invite his soul to abandon the market place of virtues and cultivate itself in sad silence, stimulate in his busy and disdainful nation the love of art that is the fount of true happiness and of the comforts that heal the spirit crushed by the sorrows of life!

CHARLES DARWIN

July 1882

Darwin was a grave old man who glowed with
the pride of having seen. His hair fell over his shoulders like a white mantle. His forehead terminated in
the craggy brows of one who has often closed his eyes
to see better. His gaze was benevolent, as it is in those
who live in fruitful communion with Nature, and his
hand, soft and affectionate, was made to care for birds
and plants.

He had created about him a living miniature of the
universe he carried in his spacious mind: here a mound
of moist earth in which to observe insects preparing
the vegetal layer, there a family of plants eloquently
arranged to show the elaboration of a flowering plant
from a plant initially barren of flowers, and beneath
that bell jar, a tiny island of the coral that had revealed to him the master work of the lowliest organism.
Off in a corner of his garden, he kept the group of
voracious plants that subsist on tiny insects, like that
terrifying African plant that spreads its brightly mottled leaves on the ground and suddenly, as a lion grasps

a man, enfolds its prey in the broad, lip-like leaves that crush and drain of blood like the boa, and drop their lifeless victim to the ground once they have satisfied their fatal hunger. In this, as in the power to attract, fascinate, and crush, the shrub, the tree, the lion, and the serpent all go together in human life.

One often came upon him seated beside his crowded, picturesque greenhouse, diligently jotting down notes, or drawing up lists paralleling the habits of humans and quadrupeds in an effort to discover new evidence to add to the dawn of reason in simians in support of his theory that the human species descends from that hairy quadruped with ears and a pointed tail, denizen of the trees, in which he thought to see, in his solitude populated with hypotheses, the origin of man. Or one might find him in his handsome study filled with bones and flowers, and that benign light that illuminates rooms where honest thought takes place. Standing before his book shelves, he would leaf respectfully through the works of his father, a poet of science who studied the loves of plants with fervor and tenderness, and the essays of his grandfather, who burned, as he did, to wring living answers from the mute earth. Gathering together his major works, which are humble in style, faithful in observation, and fanciful in theory, he would set aside space for two, and place the rest side by side on the shelf, starting with the *Origin of Species*. That is the work in which he maintains that living beings are capable of change, adaptation, and improvement, and of transmitting to their offspring their improved existence. From this, drawing analogies down through the scale of living beings, which are all analogous, he concludes that all the animals that populate the earth descend from four or five progenitors, and the myriad, varied plants from four or five others. These primary species, in constant struggle for survival with others of their kind and different species, have developed and improved, producing offspring ever superior to themselves, which, in turn, endow their offspring with new superiority. From this successively improving, unbroken line of creation, the *monera,* which are albuminous mass without form, and *bathybius,* which is living protoplasm, have evolved into magnificent man. This law of creation, which assigns to each being the faculty of overcoming its rivals in the struggle for existence by its powers of adaptation, and of transmitting its adaptations to its offspring, is the now famous law of natural selection, which today inspires the easily dazzled, novelty-seeking theorists, whose eyes travel swiftly but do not penetrate the surface, influences the German philosophers, who consider it infallible and carry it to extremes, and illuminates the hidden recesses of the earth to noble students engaged in the eternal quest for truth with what the exaggerated theory has of basis in faithfully observed facts. Next to the *Origin of Species,* whose appearance caused as great delight and amazement in the thinking world as that of the *Animal Kingdom* of Cuvier, wherein epic and novelesque things are told, or the *History of Development* of Von Baer, whose lightning flashes illuminated the wonders of the shadowy unknown, or the geological works of Sir Charles Lyell, which reconstruct forgotten worlds, Darwin's gentle hand placed *The Descent of Man.* In this work,

he maintains that an intermediary hairy animal must
have existed as a link between the simian and primitive man, a theory which moved large numbers of men,
unprepared to respect the liberty of sovereign thought
and the efforts of a sincere and dedicated investigator,
to unjust anger, which error never arouses in those
who have the strength to overcome it. To be sure, the
similarity between all living beings proves they are
similar; it does not follow that certain beings evolve
from others. To be sure, there is a similarity between
the intelligence of man and other animals, just as
there is a similarity of form; this does not prove that
animals develop spiritually by stages that parallel the
progressive evolution of form. While this thesis will
cause no alarm among those who maintain that the
spirit is an outgrowth of the material being, there is
cause for alarm in thinking that things as beautiful
as the affections, and as sovereign as thoughts, spring,
like flowers, from the flesh, or as exhalations of the
bone, from the perishable body. The human spirit is
horrified and outraged at the suggestion that man's
barbarous sufferings are for nothing, and that he is
the contemptible toy of a magnificent madman, who
amuses himself by lacerating the flesh of his creation
with burning irons that leave wounds no one will ever
heal, and kindling in his thirsting mind, ever a tinder-
box, flames whose impious tongues consume the brain
they lick and scarify.

Nature, moreover, does not reveal a spiritual superiority corresponding to successive stages in the
evolution of form. Anyone who has visited the rivers
of Brazil has seen the manatee cow, as loving as a

human mother, carrying her brood on her back as she swims; he has seen that the American monkey, while further removed from humans in form than the African monkey, is closer to man in intelligence. The tiniest spider constructs a web to catch insects, which it repairs in a twinkling if a thread parts, that resolves the problem of the nonagon in a manner that has not yet been revealed to man. Is it that the science of the soul has gone mad, closing its eyes to the laws of the body that moves, harbors, and enslaves it, and is the science of the body equally mad, denying the laws of the radiant soul, which opens the sky to the minds of men and canopies, guides, and glorifies thought?

Thought can cause the skull to burst. It can cleave the earth with golden warmth, and cover the burning sands of the Sahara with a sea of fresh water. A cold skull benumbs thought for the earth, and the whirling sands of the Sahara can smother the body which harbors the spirit of a hero. Life is twofold. Whoever studies life in simple terms goes astray. Dear reader, please forgive this idle tongue of mine that always turns to serious things!

We were in Darwin's study, and we saw him there putting to one side what the harsh Flourens and Haeckel, who venerates and supplements him, and the respectful Kollicker have said of his works, and filling a space in his book shelves with others of his volumes: *Insectivorous Plants,* which seems a collection of fantastic tales; *The Effects of Cross and Self Fertilization in the Vegetable Kingdom,* which draws from itself the elements of its life; *The Different Forms of Flowers on Plants of the Same Species; The Power of Move-*

ment in Plants, where marvels, tricks, and mysteries are disclosed of trees, shrubs, and algae, which in the season of courtship select a portion of themselves to seek out the desired mate in her remote abode; *The Structure and Distribution of Coral Reefs; The Geological Observations on the Volcanic Islands:* his monograph on the animals of the family *Cirripedia,* filled with revelations and surprises; and his final book, *Formation of Vegetable Mould Through the Action of Worms,* which moves one to gratitude, for the tenderness that is revealed in his ineffable love of the small, and the new grandeur he imparts to science, always a pleasing subject for the mind. He tells in this book how the selfless little worms prepare that portion of the soil from which the vegetables later spring, scented and heavy with fruit, for the shelter and nourishment of living beings.

Scattered among his books was abundant evidence of the high place he held in the world's esteem—diplomas, medals and honors from Prussia and England, titles of honorary membership in the Academies that scoffed at him until recently, and degrees from the universities which may question his theories, but count his innumerable and diverse discoveries, which by their number are like a forest that entraps and bewilders, among the greatest, most honest, and most admirable of human conquests. And what of those two works for which he set aside space on his shelf? Well, did you not know? The genius of that man flowered in America: he gestated in our lands; our marvels bestirred him; our luxuriant forests molded him; he was awakened and brought to his feet by our potent nature. He came

here as a young naturalist with an English expedition
that set sail for the oceans of Africa and America. He
discovered himself in the presence of our nights, which
moved him to respect; he sat on our peaks, amazed by
the surrounding beauty; he showered praise on the
inert Indians that a romantic and avaricious people
scythed in their first flowering; and he seated himself
in the middle of our pampa among our antediluvian
animals. Here, on our shores, he gathered the precious
stones, hard as conch and of fine enamel, that so marvelously imitate elemental plants. Patiently digging
and scraping, he observed how the ocean created the
valleys of Chile, which still abound in marine fossils,
and how the level lands of the pampa were deposited
grain by grain at the primitive mouth of the ancient
Pista River. He studied basaltic lava flows in Santa
Cruz, petrified forests in Chiloe, cetaceous fossils in
Tierra del Fuego, and observed how slowly the land of
America rose in the east, and how Lima on the west
has risen eighty-five feet since men first arrived there.
He noted that all the lands of America, both to the east
and the west, have risen evenly and gradually, and not
by convulsions, or by starts. All these things are told
in his *Geological Observations in Parts of South America* in the simple language, not of the autocrat, but of
the modest student. His other book is a delightful
romance, in which serious things are told in a bright
and airy fashion. The gallantries of the gaucho go coupled with observations on the habits of insects, and the
appearance of horses in the old America with the manner of breaking horses today. He is a scholar on horseback, who dismounts to examine the strings of blue

beads which the Indian girls of the highlands wear on their wrists as bracelets, or to remove the jawbone of the fetid puma whose pelt bears the claw marks of the condor. There is no note of presumptuous arrogance in *The Diary of the Investigations in Geology and Natural History of the Countries Visited by His Majesty's Ship Beagle, under the Command of Captain Fitz Roy, from 1832 to 1836,* nor of the deplorable fancifulness of the impassioned scientist who refuses to admit those natural facts which are in conflict with his theory, exaggerates those which support it, and find facts in his imagination to supplement the real facts when it is to his advantage. The book is not majestic, as it might have been, but it is pleasing. It is not profound, but it is honest. There is no trace of the fanatic who lays violent hands on the universe or importunes it with impatient gestures. There is only the serene observer who rigorously reports what he saw. In matters of the mind, he sees only the surface of things; he does not see deeply into men, and they and their rich world do not greatly arouse his curiosity. As for the affections, he sits down with veneration in the shade of the white-trunked trees deep in the Brazilian jungle, and he wields a branding iron against those who abuse slaves in his sight. But he sees the slaves only as miserable devils. He is a tower of strength who is too little disposed to be charitable toward weaklings. For in addition to having been born in England, which makes men proud, for it is like entering the world in the cradle of Liberty, Darwin was a contented youth with a fresh, eager spirit who knew nothing of that science of forgiveness that comes with a long or a hard life. Sadness makes the soul old and wise before its time.

Whether traveling with his pack horses, or camped in a rude hut, he surveyed the land, buried his hand beneath the bark of trees, lowered himself into deep caves, scaled flowering mountains, and collected insects, bones, leaves, seeds, sands, shells, potsherds, and flowers; he compared the teeth of the new horse of the fertile pampa with the gigantic jaws, capable of girdling trees, of the monster horse of the primitive pampa, which became extinct, perhaps from hunger among the suddenly withered trees on which it fed, perhaps from thirst beside the great, dry bed of the dying river. He coupled facts, drew comparisons, and made an index of all the animals whose remains he was able to find in the various layers of the earth; he noted how the native races of animals prospered and grew, and how those brought in from other lands weakened and degenerated; how there are plants that have something of the reptile, minerals that have something of the plant, and reptiles that have something of the bird. He offers piecemeal in this work the things that were later to appear in the *Origin of Species* cast by reflection into a structural unity. He traversed luxuriant America on horseback; he saw valleys that seemed freshly risen from the primeval slime; he saw rivers gliding like the Lethe; he sailed beneath canopies of butterflies, and canopies of thunder; he witnessed a battle between lightning at the mouth of the River Plate; he saw the ocean glow, as if showered with stars, for are not the phosphorescences the Milky Way of the oceans? He saw the velvet night that fills the heart with starlight; he savored coffee in the roadhouses of Brazil, which are our inns; he saw Rosas laugh his terrifying laugh; he crossed damp Patagonia, desolate Tierra del Fuego, arid Chile, and superstitious Peru. One expects the appearance of a gigantic monarch when one enters the Brazilian jungle, and the apprehensive spirit seems to see him approach in a great, green cape, broad as a mountain slope, crowned with pleached saplings, his beard tangled in long vines, clearing a path through the thick cedars with hands as shaggy as the hide of an old bull. All the jungle is a firmament, with garlands of green moss festooning the trees. Playful deer graze together on one side, while on the other, myriad ants form living mounds that are like hummocks, or those mud volcanoes of Tocuyo which Humboldt saw; now, almost from under the traveler's feet, the sly *tucutuco*, of the pointed snout and ribboned tongue, springs on the crawling mound; now one comes upon a clump of cassava trees, whose flour nourishes men, and whose leaves refresh the weary pack horses. The terrible vampire sinks its sharp teeth in the horse's neck and bleeds the beast, which utters a soft whinny, rather than a neigh; the swift hummingbird flits past on transparent wings that glitter and vibrate. There is a clearing in the forest, dripping from a recent rain, and the foliage, kissed by the sun, gives off a steaming vapor that rises like a column of smoke; in the distance the splendid mountain emerges wrapped in a veil of mist. Mangoes and cinnamon trees entwine branches with the useful breadfruit, the *jaca*, which casts a black shade, and the spreading camphor tree. Graceful is the mimosa; elegant, the fern; thick-bodied, the vine.

The eyes of the irritated glowworm burn in the deep of the night with the living fire that noble anger brings to a human face. The base cuckoo, which lays its eggs in the nests of other birds, croaks its song. Another day is born, and one must kneel a-tremble before the solemnity and color of Nature. After Brazil, Darwin saw Buenos Aires. The wild deer would stop beside the path to see him pass, looking at him with gentle, trustful eyes, as ingenuous as children, the brave American deer, that have no fear of the musket's report, but flee aghast when they see that the bullet of the stranger has wounded a tree in their forest.

The trip is like a fairy-tale; this day they warily avoid the Indians; the next night they see the eyes of the wrathful jaguar burning in the night as, irritated by the coming storm, he sharpens his strong claws on the trees; yesterday was a day of breaking horses, hobbling a hind leg to a foreleg, and to these the rebellious, curb-bitted head, and setting them walking, sweating and hobbled, with the saddle on their flank and the rider in the saddle, across the torrid plain from which they return panting and conquered. Lunch is with Rosas, whose campaign tent, like a feudal lord's, is a buffoon's court; dinner is with gauchos, the slender, hot-blooded gauchos, who tell how the tyrant of the pampa, who bends trees, and tames wild ponies by placing his hand on their flanks, orders men stretched like drying hides, hanging hand and foot from four stakes, on which they sometimes die.

Darwin saw the sacred Wailechu tree, from whose threads, which are its winter leaves, the pious Indians hang the bread they carry, the cloth they bought

for the house, or the flute with which they while away
the hours of the journey, because human nature takes
joy in giving, and because that thorny tree, standing
at road's end of a most difficult journey, is a symbol of
health to the Indian. He gives his garments and horses,
expecting in return that his pack horses will never tire,
and that he will never know misfortune; the tree means
so much to him, that if he does not have something to
give, he will draw a thread from his woven poncho
and hang it from a thread of the tree.

And beyond, what a magnificent surprise! Gigantic
rodents, spectators of other worlds; remains of megalo-
saurs; bones of the megathere sloth, a predecessor of
the great American horse. The haunches of those moun-
tainous beasts! What claws, the size of tree trunks!
They would sit at the foot of those gigantic trees, and
clutching the trunk, bring down the branches to their
mouths with the rending sound of a mountainside giving way. The travelers stirred up an ostrich's nest, and
learned to their sorrow that the ostrich attacks without
hesitation whoever touches its nest, whether the enemy
is on foot or on horseback. A jaguar passes with a roar,
trailed by a band of foxes, just as the Bengal tiger is
followed by jackals, for the fox is the jackal of America. Or a herd of the proud cattle of the pampa surprises the traveler with their elegance and alertness,
for the herd is like a crowd of mischievous schoolboys.
There are the peaceful Indians of the highlands, who
glitter like genii of the plain on their horses with silver-
studded trappings, which they guide with strong, invisible wire reins; the sunlight glints from the shiny
stirrup, the jeweled halter, the heavy spur, and the

knife handle. There, also, the eunuchs of the plain, the shepherd dogs that tend the sheep.

The road becomes indistinct, and the land turns sad; the gaucho looks back at the receding pampa like a lover who longs for a last glimpse of his sweetheart. The peaceful *guanacos,* jealous of their females, graze in a herd; when they feel the hour of death approaching, they turn, like the men of Tierra del Fuego, toward the place where all the *guanacos* of their herd before them have gone to die. Suddenly, a shudder runs through the herd, and the *guanacos* flee; bounding after them with a roar comes the fierce puma, the lion of America, who prowls from fiery Ecuador to dank Patagonia, and does not whimper when he feels himself wounded: brave American lion! Beyond, there are dead *guanacos,* with vultures hovering, like the puma's crown, for crumbs from the lion's feast.

The travelers advance silently; the shrubs are thorny; the plants, stunted; stones are dry; the ravenous rodents of the forest slake their thirst with drops of dew. That was how Darwin saw the Patagonian desert.

And how black Tierra del Fuego! Little sun, much water, endless marshlands; everything murky, everything mournful, everything damp and sad. The trees without flowers; the plants, alpine; the mountains, eroded; the valleys, almost fetid; the atmosphere, blackish.

The natives materialize like divinities from the marshes, their hair tangled, their faces streaked with white and red, their backs covered with *guanaco* hides leaving the rest of their brown bodies naked. After

some observation, the man gradually emerges from the
beast. They beat the breasts of their visitors, as if to
let them know they trust them, and bare their own
chests in turn for the visitors to return the salutation.
They have shamans, tribes, and remarkable memories.
They regard murder as a crime that will bring down
the furies of the elements on their bowed heads. They
have heard of the devil, but they say the devil is not
there. They know of love and gratitude, which is to
know a great deal.

From that land the traveler went by ship to Chile
where the hills bear the scars of the quest for gold. No
longer was the industrious Englishman accompanied,
and his great scientific collection borne, by the romantic, dangerous and happy gaucho, radiant and detached as a beautiful Satan, but instead, by the vain
guaso, with his heavy spur, white boots, black or green
puttees, baggy pants, red *chiripa*, and coarse poncho.
They passed the bald mountains, dotted here and there
by clumps of green forest, like emeralds cast among
ashes, crossed the shaky bridges suspended over murky
Maipu, with their treacherous footing of dried hides
and wooden rungs, and the floating islands of Tagua-
tagua, which are great clumps of old roots continually
sprouting new roots, on which the travelers crossed
from shore to shore as though in a comfortable launch.
On the slopes of those bare mountains, the traveler
read Molina, who sang the ways of the animals of the
land, and Azara, whose work is a treasure, and the
good Acosta, who revealed unsuspected things about
the Indies. He made a special trip to see at first hand
the pale miners in their long shirts of dark, uncarded

wool, their tanned leather aprons, their brightly colored sashes, and jaunty red hats; he saw with a start the miserable ore bearers, who are men and seem beasts, even dying monsters, until they drop their huge loads, which weigh upward of 200 pounds, and set off on their return journey laughing and joking, even though they eat meat only once a week.

Now the traveler was leaving Chile, and now he was at the nitrate mines of solitary Iquique; yet swimming before his eyes, like a permanent, radiant vision, were the valley of Quillota, where living is a joy; the green, peaceful *llanos,* which seem morning's natural habitat; the wild bamboo trees, which sway like thoughts in the mind; the snowy Andes, which the soul makes warm and golden, and the setting sun dresses in flame. His mind thus charged, the youth returned to Europe. Not a day without work, and no day's work without return. He turned these memories over in his mind, and in his mind's eye, he could see all the animals of the globe walking side by side. He recollected, more with the disdain of an Englishman than with the insight of a deep thinker, the barbarous natives of Tierra del Fuego, the rude African, the agile Zealander, and the new men of the Pacific isles. Since he does not see man in his compound character, nor thoroughly grasp that it is as important to know whence comes the sentiment that moves him and the reason that guides him, as the ribs of his chest and the layers of his skull, he hit on the thought that there was only a short step separating the Feugian and the simian. Others look desperately toward the sky, their eyes filled with grief's sweet tears. Darwin, with clear eye and inquiring hand, free of the

desire to know where we are going, bent over the earth
with serenity of spirit to discover whence we come.
There is truth in this: nothing should be denied that
has a place in the solemn spiritual world, neither the
noble impatience with life, that is relieved ultimately
by giving of oneself to life; nor the ineffable colloquy
with the eternal, which bestows on the spirit the
strength of the sun and peace of the night; nor the
certainty, real because it provides real joy, that an
afterlife exists in which there will be no ending to the
profound joys, that with a glimmering of the truth, or
the practice of virtue, fill the soul; but when it comes
to the construction of worlds, no better answer can be
had than from the worlds themselves. He saw well, who
saw this, despite his errors, which stemmed from seeing only half the being; who spoke to the dumb stone,
and received an answer; who entered the palaces of
insects, the bowers of plants, the bowels of the earth,
and the workshops of the seas. He has earned his repose where he rests: in Westminster Abbey, beside
heroes.

IV: THE

PATRIOT

Marti's patriotic writings disclose his most intimate side, for he dedicated his life to Cuba. Martí loved his homeland. He loved the special blue of the Cuban sky, her rivers, her animals and plants, and above all, he loved her people, particularly the common people, for the dignity of their ways, the music of their speech, their customs and their dress. There is no hint of chauvinism or the bombast of the politico in Martí's patriotism. It was a pure, deeply-rooted sentiment of sacrifice and devotion. Although his pen and tongue had been its only weapons during the 24 years he worked tirelessly preparing the revolution, Martí shouldered a rifle in the final struggle, and died in battle at the age of 42 fighting on Cuban soil for Cuban independence.

The selections in this section contain some of Martí's finest pages on Cuba and the Cuban cause. They also reveal some aspects of Martí as a man of action, although it is impossible in this volume to touch on his vast political literature, which includes speeches, pamphlets, editorials, tracts, and manifestoes. The following pages contain the essay on Carlos Manuel de Céspedes and Ignacio Agramonte, which is a literary monument to the two great leaders of the unsuccessful revolution of 1868 that inspired Martí's generation of Cuban patriots to continue the fight for independence, successful with the Spanish-American War. Memories of the War *is a conversation with a veteran of the fighting in 1868 in which one sees Martí's deep attachment to the common Cuban that made him a great popular leader. Martí knew that for a revolution to be a civic, as well as military success, the Cuban Negro and the Cuban white man had to fight side by side, with one purpose, with mutual respect, and on an equal footing.* My Race *is one of the best statements of the theme of racial equality that runs through all of Martí's writings on Cuba.*

Plans for the new revolution were completed in 1894, with Martí in a frenzy of activity collecting funds from wealthy Cubans in New York and poor Cuban cigarmakers in Tampa and New Orleans, arranging for the purchase of arms, and reconciling the demands of the two military leaders, Máximo Gómez and Antonio Maceo. On the eve of sailing for eastern Cuba to launch the war, he wrote a moving letter to his old friend, Federico Henríquez and Carvajal, which is reproduced here in translation, explaining why he, a man of peace all his life, was taking up arms.

The final pages of this section contain selections from the diary that Martí kept during the expedition against the Spanish, from the day he and Gómez sailed from Cabo Haitiano, Santo Domingo, to two days before his death during a skirmish with a Spanish force near Dos Ríos, Oriente Province, Cuba, on May 19, 1895.

—J. D. O.

CÉSPEDES AND AGRAMONTE

October 10, 1888

The foreigner, or the pedant, or the opportunist can write these names without trembling, but not the good Cuban. The impetus was Céspedes'; the virtue, Agramonte's. The one was like a volcano, emerging, awesome and imperfect, from the bowels of the earth; the other, like the blue firmament that crowns it. Céspedes' was the passion; Agramonte's, the purification. The one challenged with the authority of a king; the other triumphed with the power of light. History will come, with its judgements and its justice; and after it has nibbled them away, and retouched them to suit its taste, there will still remain the impulse of the one and the dignity of the other, fit subjects for an epic. High-flown words are unnecessary when speaking of great men. Let others, on some other occasion, cast up the balance sheet of their errors, which will never equal their achievements. Today is a day of celebration, and what we want is to see them anew, the one erect, bold and magnificent, dictating with a gesture, as night fades, the creation of a free people; and the other in his grave garments, the welt of the whip still marking his angelic countenance, victorious even in death. Life is still worth living when our eyes have beheld men like these.

One needs to have felt the weight of a people on one's shoulders to measure the strength of a man who, with a gold-headed cane as his only weapon, made up his mind, facing an implacable nation, to wrest from it for freedom its unhappiest possession, as one who should rob a tigress of her last cub. Such a sense of majesty must have flooded his soul at this, that the man may well have been blinded by it. Who does not recall our cradle days? Our backs were striped by the lash, our faces the favorite target of the tyrant's hand. There was no longer patience for further mulctings, nor cheeks for more slaps. The island was in a ferment. Havana was hesitant. Las Villas looked to Occidente. Santiago was undecided. "Lackeys, lackeys," Ignacio Agramonte upbraided Camagüey, heartsick. But in Bayamo the wrath exploded. The lodge there, whose authority was recognized by Manzanillo and Holguín and Jiguaní and Las Tunas, called into secret session the lawyers and landowners of the region, the Maceos and the Figueredos, the Milaneses and the Céspedes, the Palmas and the Estradas, Aguilera, named president because of his position and his kindliness, and a Negro stone-mason, the noble García. On the unhewn stone two hands worked side by side, the white and the black; may God wither the first of these that raises itself against the other. There was no possible doubt; the moment had come to take up arms. Nobody knew how, or with what aid, nor when Havana, from which

Pedro Figueredo had just returned in discouragement, would make up its mind, when in Manzanillo, where Céspedes' was the leading voice, those who saw the gleam in his eye sought him for their guide. The mountains are the summits of the earth, and men like this, of the nations. Possibly Bayamo wanted more time; the council of the lodge had not yet reached a decision; perhaps they were waiting to take it when the unsleeping enemy was at their throat. Is a revolt perchance a piece of lace woven by the light of day until every thread is in place? Unless we burn our bridges behind us, they will never make up their minds! And after a few moments of silence, during which the heroes lowered their heads to conceal their sober tears, that brilliant pleader, that master of men, that restless man of affairs, arose as though transfigured by incredible splendor. Nor was his finest hour that in which he declared his country free, but when he called his slaves together, and held out his arms to them like brothers.

The word spread; the conspirators assembled with their freed slaves and their friends, and lost in admiration of his daring, proclaimed Céspedes their leader in the field of Mabay. Jiguaní and Holguín fell to Mármol; with Céspedes in command, Marcano advanced on Bayamo. Their arms were razor-edged machetes, muzzle-loading rifles, and rusty revolvers, with withe-wrapped guards. They encircled Bayamo, where the Governor hesitated, thinking they had risen in support of his friend Prim. And it was the morning of the 19th, with the sun in all its glory, when the cavalcade of freedom crossed the river in orderly ranks, a river that seemed to have broadened. It was not a battle, but a festival. The most peaceable citizens came to join them, and with them their slaves. The Spanish cavalry came out to meet them; with one machete blow they left its leader beardless, and his terror-stricken men carried him in their arms to the shelter of the barracks. With stones covered in kerosene-soaked cotton for bombs, the Cubans set fire to the roof of the barracks. The garrison surrenders, and with sword in scabbard marches through the streets between the rows of their respectful conquerors. Céspedes has set up the city administration, has ordered with that firmness of his that the necessary loan shall be voluntary and not forced, has divided the administration into four departments, writes to the cities that the Republic of Cuba has just come into being, puts in several Spaniards as members of the city council. He establishes peace among the envious, is magnanimous toward the lukewarm; he confirms his power by the serenity with which he employs it. He is human and conciliatory. He is firm and gentle.

He sees himself as his people, and as he was the first to act, he feels he has natural and personal rights, like those of a father, over his work. In the recesses of his mind he had been present at the divine mystery of the birth of a nation through the will of one man, and he sees himself, not as a mortal liable to error and obedience, but as a sovereign of liberty, transported alive into the heaven of the redeemers. He feels that those who lacked the determination to precede him lack the right to advise him. He looks upon himself as sacrosanct, and never doubts that it is his judgement that should prevail. Perhaps he failed to realize that he was like the tallest tree of the forest, but that without the

forest the tree would not tower aloft. Never again did
he show himself as during those days of complete authority, for men with original powers display them to
the full only when they can exercise them without
hindrance. When the forest began to fall upon him;
when he began to see that revolution is more than raising the standard of paternalistic ideas; when the young
men with apostolic zeal confronted him with the tablets
of the law; when he bowed his head, like a suffering
martyr, before his unexpected collaborators, he was
perhaps as great, given his opinion of himself, as when
he decided, in epic solitude, to guide his unformed
country to freedom by rudimentary methods, as when
in the jubilation of victory he did not avenge the blood
of Cubans spilled by Spain on the Spaniards, but seated
them beside him in the government, displaying the
genius of a statesman. Later his glory was clouded
over; he felt himself stripped of what was his by right
of conquest; he haughtily withdrew that energy they
refused to let him employ, guided by no other considera-
tion than his blind faith in the union he held to be the
fruit of a supernatural alliance between his person and
the Republic. But never, not even in his hut, did he
cease to be the majestic person who feels, and makes
all feel, the dignity of the nation. He stepped down
from the presidency when the country so ordained, and
died firing his last bullets against the enemy with the
hand that had just penned, on a rustic table, verses on
a sublime theme.

Tomorrow, tomorrow we will know whether we
might have achieved liberty sooner by his peremptory
and personal methods than by those of his followers;

whether the courses suggested by patriotism through fear of a Caesar have not placed the country, brought into being by the hero, at the mercy of the generals of an Alexander; whether Céspedes, with his heroic dreams and tragic readings, was not the man, both exquisite and primitive, imitator and creator, self-centered and public-minded, august through natural kindliness and the events, in whom there clashed, as against a cliff, shattering it in the first encounter, the unbridled forces of a new country, and the aspirations which the knowledge of the free world and the passion for the Republic kindled in the devout young people. Meanwhile, blessed be thou, man of marble!

And the man of Camagüey, that diamond with the soul of a kiss? He loved his Amalia madly; but he did not ask her to build a home with him until he returned from his student triumphs in Havana, convinced that those gentlemen still had years to go: "They are good for nothing, nothing!" And a few days after arriving from Camagüey, the chamber of judges visited him, astounded at the moderation and authority of so young a lawyer; as he passed through the streets people whispered: "That's the one," and sensed the presence of a king. But not he, not he, who until the day his wife, with her own hands, made him the blue jacket he wore off to war, did not feel that he was really married.

His modesty made him seem proud; his brow, over which the black hair fitted like a helmet, was silken, white and smooth, as though made for the kiss of glory; he listened more than he spoke, although his was the only eloquence worth prizing, that which comes from the purity of the heart. He blushed when his merits were extolled; his eyes filled with tears when he thought of heroism, or heard of a misfortune, or love kissed his hand: "I am afraid of so much happiness." He read deep books slowly. He was a defending angel, and a child to be caressed. He was slender, finely rather than robustly built, and very agile. But war came, and its first impact tamed his natural pride, and his strength of body was the reflection of his virtue. It was as though where men have their heart, he had a star. His radiance was like that of the heavenly bodies; and his friends, when they recall him, speak of him with unction, as one talks on starry nights, and as though with bared head.

Possibly there is not another man who, to the same degree, submitted his natural authority in hours of tumult to that of his country. Perhaps there is no more beautiful ballad than that of this warrior, who returned from his glories to take his rest, in his house of palm fronds, beside his bride and his son. "Never, Amalia, never will I be a soldier when the war is over. Today it is an honor, tomorrow it will be a crime. I swear it by this child, who was born free. Look, Amalia; here I will hang my rifle, and there, in that corner, where I first kissed my son, my sword." And the hero bent over, with only his wife's eyes for mirror, for her to cut, with the scissors she had used to make him the two suits of drill in which he always looked so immaculate and handsome, his long hair, so he would look well for the celebration of his son's birthday.

And was this the man who, pure and boundless as the forest where he had hidden away the house of his mate, drilled his men to the pace of glory? Was this

the man who harangued his troops with a voice that
was new, and fired their patriotism with his enthusiasm
and prideful gestures? Was this the man who, for sport,
jumped his sorrel, Mambi, so high over a fence that
his body was lost from sight in the treetops? The one
who never allowed anyone to outstrip him in battle,
and when in an encounter he met *El Tigre* face to face,
El Tigre who had never been beaten in hand to hand
fighting, dug his spurs into Mambi so he could not be
stopped, and with his major's sword, and the one that
gleamed in his eyes, rendered *El Tigre*'s machete power-
less? Was this the man who, when the Spaniard profaned his marriage home, went alone, hand at knife,
with only Elpidio Mola, to spy out the camp where they
were holding his love prisoner? Was this the man who,
when a thousand Spaniards were carrying his friend
off to prison, fell upon them with thirty horsemen, and
making his way through the enemy's horse, brought his
friend away? The man who, with only his genius for
military training, organized the cavalry, rebuilt devas-
tated Camagüey, set up shops to manufacture war supplies in the woods, planned and directed victorious
attacks, and put his renown at the service of the prestige of the law, when he was the only one who with
general approbation might have always defied it?

This was the man; the friend of the mulatto Ramón
Agüero; the one who taught his mulatto to read with
the point of his knife for pencil and the tree leaves for
paper; the one who spoke his stern words in decorous
privacy, and seemed to cure like a doctor when he reproved as a general; the one who when he could not
share his sweet potatoes or honey with all his men, be-

cause there was not enough, made *cuba-libre*, mixing
the honey with water, so all the officers could share it,
or gave his sweet potatoes to his horse rather than eat
them himself. This was the man who never humiliated
man, either in himself or in others. But he was never
so great, not even when his enemies profaned his
corpse, as when, on hearing the government criticized
for its slow workings by his officers, eager to see him
master in power as he was in virtue, he got to his feet,
and with a stature they had never seen in him before,
and a voice indignant and proud, said these words: "I
will never tolerate slander of the President of the Republic in my presence!"

These, Cuba, are your true sons!

MEMORIES OF THE WAR

A Conversation with a Soldier

November, 1893

The room breathes freedom. On the desk, piled with letters, proofs of love that are never published, sad testimony of human vanity and self-seeking, greater proofs of abnegation and greatness of soul, there is hardly room for the thin arms of the man who writes. Presiding over it, on the wall molding, stands an unfinished portrait of Páez, the Páez of Las Queseras and of Carabobo in the yellow cloak with frogs of braid, with two scorpions for moustache, a nose sniffing war, wide, far-apart eyes, and coarse, curly hair. Beside it, a portrait of San Martín, the liberator of the three republics to the south, a long neck supporting the powerful jaws, and cheekbones like two lances under his eagle eyes, and the hair smoothed tight to temple, as though by a hand accustomed to obedience. And at San Martín's feet a grenade the Spaniards threw into a Cuban camp during the war, and which Camagüey sent to this office in New York that it might speak with its mouth of bronze, and to be hung about the neck of those who forget. It is thus the cowards, the heedless, the ungrateful should appear before the world, with the grenade hung about their neck! Occupying a place of honor in the office, with the law in his hand, stands a statue of Hidalgo, the liberator of Mexico. There alone, with a glint of winter sun in the room filled with freedom, a Cuban talks with a man of the war. The war is at hand. It will be leashed or unleashed, as the best interests of the country demand!

The feeling of gratitude satisfies. He who sins is forgotten; let him go his way, give him time to recover himself, and leave him the doors wide that he may return without abjection to affection and honor. But for him who served his brothers, who left his crop-full comfort for the danger that purifies, who gave himself wholeheartedly to his country, and to his people the right to look other men in the eye, we feel a love as though he were part of our own self; we cherish his memory, we make a place for him beside us, we open our heart that he may walk in, and cover him with our lacerated heart. We were talking of Agramonte.

"There was courage," said the man of the war, "and how we loved him. Just to see him, with those big eyes and those tight-shut lips, made one want to die for him. Always so clean, always the first up and the last to go to bed. And his wife, how that man loved her. You could tell when he was thinking about her, because he would walk up and down, fast, with his hands behind his back. When he reproved us, he never did it in front of others. He was too much of a man for that. He would take us to a corner of his shack, or beside a tree, far

off, and appeal to our honor, and as he had a gesture
with that big hand of his when he was talking fast,
like sprinkling salt, the men would say when they saw
him talking like that to someone: 'Hm! The Major's
giving him a salting.' That's what we always called
him, the Major. And brave! When he was with the
riflemen of Villas and the cavalry of Camagüey he
thought that Spain didn't exist. And it didn't.

"Was Ignacio Agramonte a good man? I remember
when Rafael Hernández, the captain of the Chinese,
one of those blue-eyed, red-bearded fellows, drew a
knife on a Chinaman one day, I don't know why, because the Chinese were fine patriots; there's not a case
of a Chinaman who ever turned informer; with a Chinaman, even if they capture him, there's no danger: 'no
savvy.' That's all they can get out of him: 'no savvy.'
Rafael Hernández went to see Agramonte to ask to be
relieved of the Chinese. The conversation took place
beside a tree, and the Major's hand went up and down,
as though the salting was a good one. Afterwards we
asked Hernández, curious to know what had happened:

'How did it go? Did the Major relieve you of the
Chinese?'

'Relieve me? If I'd known what was going to hap-
pen to me, I'd never have gone to him. I'll never go
near the man again. If I ever went back, I'd wind up
the father of those Chinks.'

"It was at the Academy that I knew him best, in
Jimaguayú. He was the man who made the Academy,
but the way things have to be done, man by man. It
takes sweat to do a big thing. Men are always slipping
and falling, that's true, but when they see one walking

straight, they keep on walking out of pride. True, you
have to keep them on their toes, for the world gets
drowsy. There never was an Academy like that one.
After the changing of the guard, the bugle sounded
for the officers. A pavilion covered with palm fronds
had been built, with the teacher's table in the middle
and wooden benches around the walls. In came the officers, nearly every one of them naked, one using his
hat as a fig leaf, the other, two tanned *jutia* skins, one
north, one south. Barefooted, or in cowhide sandals.
They had made themselves hats of *yarey*, or of *yuru-
guana*, which is more pliable, or a cap of *cataure;* their
machete belts were twisted vine, or a strip of cowhide. The one who had revolver, knife, and machete
was the lucky exception. And there they spent the two
hours, listening to the book. But the real Academy was
when the Major inspected the company, and said to us,
moving the men around, 'This is how it should be done.'
When we were drilling we were sometimes so hungry
that I have had men faint on me, unable to stand up
from hunger.

"Food? Sometimes it was very good and sometimes
very bad; and I don't want anybody talking to me
about shortage of food, for with a good leader and a
friend, and the satisfaction of fighting the way you
should, a man has enough with a piece of sugar cane
or a mango. The fact of the matter is that after a long
march, or a hard skirmish, or a retreat over the savannah, there's nothing like a piece of fresh cane or a nice
ripe mango. The mango is a great fellow; when they
were in season we ate them every way you can think
of, raw, baked, boiled, fried; the green ones baked,

and the ripe ones fried, which taste like plantains. *Piña de raton* is good roasted, too; once a farmer brought Agramonte a very good one, when we were short of rations; and he got up from a *guasima* log, where he was teaching Ramon Agüero to read, using tree leaves, and went around to each one of us, giving us a taste. One of the city fellows turned up his nose at the *piña*, and the Major opened his eyes wide, the way he did when he wouldn't take 'No' for an answer, and said to him: 'Taste it,' in a tone that was command and pity; and the city fellow tasted it, and said it was good. To be sure, you can't eat more than four or five of them without your tongue starting to bleed. One day a fellow was in bad shape, with pains and stomach ache, from eating too many. 'I'll never touch *piña* again.' 'Yes you will,' I said to him. 'Yes you will. *Piña* is the only thing that's like a woman.' It was a banquet when we sat down to roast jutia, and baked squash and raw *palmito* or cooked with red pepper, and sweet potato with hot chile. And for coffee, we had either 'monkey tail,' which was orange leaves steeped in water, or *cuba-libre*, which was honey water. Only the bees must be native, and not from a Spanish hive, because the Spanish bee stings. Ours is noisy like the Cubans themselves, but it's considerate, and does you no harm. The Spanish bees, when they sting, die, and their guts pull out with the stinger.

"Cartridges? You find a way. Necessity is the mother of invention. You should have seen Guerra, the Venezuelan, when he came with the men from Las Villas, on the way back from Camagüey. He didn't have any cartridges. The men found an old dictionary in an abandoned house. They already had powder; now they had a dictionary; they needed glue to paste the paper; they needed shrapnel. The glue was easy: *jaguey* sap, which they collected in gourds, tapping the tree with their machete, but just a light cut, so the *jaguey* won't take offense; and the devil himself can't unstick that glue.

"Shrapnel? You strip the old houses, and take the iron railings, and there you've got everything you need. When we'd make camp at night, after marching all day, at eleven o'clock, the officers would get together, near the chief's tent, under a tree, with the gourd beside them. The man who had the dictionary was a very reliable fellow; paper's very important in a war, no matter what they say, and he'd bring over his treasure. He would pass out the sheets, as though they were communion wafers, and each officer divided his sheet in four pieces, for four cartridges; there were two chisels, and a sledge hammer we used for an anvil. Some pasted the cartridges, others cut up the nails and the railings, leaving each piece with a sharp point. After a fight the Spaniards would say to us: 'Savages, don't shoot with iron railings.' The easiest thing in the world to make cartridges."

+

At this point in the conversation it was beginning to get dark, but the room had a light like that of day. Nothing more was said about the past, but about the present. What was is the root of what is to be. There was Hidalgo; they hung his head from a hook, but Mexico is free! There was Páez; they once had him in prison, and with one mighty effort he freed himself, cowed and tied up the guard, and went back and liberated his comrades. There was San Martín, who learned his soldiering in Spain, and armed his men of Cuyo, who were simple folk, and with them he drove Spain out of America!

MY RACE

April 1893

The word *racist* has fallen prey to confusion, and its meaning must be clarified. Men have no special rights because they belong to one race or another: the word man defines all rights. The Negro, by being a Negro, is neither superior nor inferior to any other man. The white man who says "my race" is redundant; so is the Negro who says "my race." Everything that divides men, everything that sorts, separates, and categorizes them, is a sin against humanity. What sensible white man prides himself on being white, and what can the Negro think of one who harbors such a conceit, and thinks that being white gives him special privileges? What must the white man think of the Negro who prides himself on his color? Constant harping on racial divisions and the differences between the races in the case of an already divided people impedes the attainment of national and individual well-being, which are to be secured by the greatest possible coming together of the racial elements that form the nation. If it is said that the Negro has no inherent weakness, and no virus that incapacitates him for the fullest realization of his human soul, one speaks the truth, and it must be said and proved, for the injustice of this world is great, as is the ignorance of many who pass for sages, and there are many who still honestly believe that the Negro is incapable of the intelligence and spirit of the white man. If that defense of nature is called racism, well and good, for it responds to the natural fitness of things, and is the voice that wells from the breast of a man moved by the spirit of peace who seeks the welfare of his country. If a Negro asserts that slavery does not in itself demonstrate an inferiority in the enslaved race, since the white Gauls, of blue eyes and golden locks, were sold in chains in the Roman markets, that is good racism, because it is eminently just and helps to jar the ignorant white man out of some of his prejudices. But just racism ends with the Negro's right to maintain and prove that his color does not deprive him of any of the capabilities and rights of the human race.

With what justice can the white racist, who believes his race to be superior, complain of the Negro racist who considers his race specially privileged? How can the Negro racist, who insists on the special character of his race, complain of the white racist? The white man who rates himself superior to the Negro because of his race admits of the idea of race, incites the Negro racist, and gives him grounds for a like position. The Negro who proclaims his race, although it may be his mistaken way of proclaiming the spiritual identity of all races, provokes and justifies the white racist. Peace asks that the universal rights of Nature be recognized;

discriminatory rights, which are contrary to Nature,
are enemies of peace. The white man who isolates himself, isolates the Negro. The Negro who isolates himself moves the white man to isolation.

There is no danger of war between the races in Cuba.
Man means more than white man, mulatto, or black
man. Cuban means more than white man, mulatto, or
black man. The souls of white men and Negroes have
risen together from the battlefields where they fought
and died for Cuba. Alongside every white man there
was always a Negro, equal in loyalty, brotherhood, and
cunning for the daily tasks of war. Negroes, just like
white men, align themselves with the different parties
in which men are grouped along lines of character,
timid and valiant, selfless or grasping. Political parties
are aggregates of preoccupations, hopes, interests, and
personal qualities. The essential element in a party is
to be sought and discovered beneath surface differences: the common motive is the fusion of the funda-
mental in analogous characters, who may differ in view
on incidentals or details. To sum up, similarity of
character is decisive and dominant in the formation of
parties and outweighs the internal bonds that stem
from man's variable color, or antagonisms that differences of pigmentation sometimes arouse. Affinity of
character is stronger in men than affinity of color. The
Negro, relegated to the thankless and unequal employments of the human spirit, could not, and would have
no desire to, join forces against the white man similarly
employed. The Negroes are too tired of an imposed
slavery to enter voluntarily into a slavery of color.
Pompous or self-seeking men will gravitate toward one

party, regardless of their color, and generous, disinterested men will enter the other. Men worthy of the name will show each other loyalty and tenderness, for merit's own sake, and from pride in everything that honors the land in which they were born, black or white. The word racist will drop from the lips of the Negroes who use it today in good faith when they realize that it is the only semblance of a valid argument that sincere, but timorous, men can adduce to deny the Negro his full rights as a man. Both racists are equally at fault: the white racist and the Negro racist. Many white men have already forgotten their color, as have many Negroes. They work together, blacks and whites, for the improvement of their minds, the propagation of virtues, and the triumph of the creative act and charitable spirit.

There will never be a war between the races in Cuba. The Republic cannot take a step backward; and the Republic, from the drafting of the first constitution of independence on October 10, 1868, in Guaimaro, which is the only day of redemption the Negro has known in Cuba, has never spoken of either blacks or whites. The civil rights conceded by the Spanish government now for astutely political reasons, which have long been in practice among the people, will never be taken from the Negro, either by the Spaniard who will maintain them while he breathes Cuban air to continue dividing the Cuban Negro from the Cuban white man, or by the independence, which could not deny in the hour of liberation what the Spaniard conceded in the hour of slavery.

When the independence comes, every individual will be free in the sanctity of the native home. Merit, the tangible, cumulative of culture, and the inexorable play of economic forces will ultimately unite all men. There is much greatness in Cuba, in both Negroes and whites.

LETTER TO
FEDERICO HENRÍQUEZ Y CARVAJAL

March 1895

F riend and Brother:
So great are the responsibilities that devolve upon those men who do not deny their scant powers to the world, and who live to add to the sum of its freedom and decency, that their words are but half-expressed and childlike, nor can a single phrase convey what one would say to a cherished friend with an embrace. This is what happens to me as, standing on the threshold of a great duty, I reply to your generous letter. You did me the greatest good with it, and gave me the one strength great undertakings require, that is to say, the knowledge that a warm-hearted, good man passionately approves them. Rare as mountains are the men who can look down from their heights and feel with the bowels of a nation or of mankind. There is left, after clasping the hand of such a man, that inner cleanliness which should be the reward of winning, in a just cause, the good fight. I deliberately say nothing of the true preoccupation of my spirit,

because you have completely divined it; deeply touched, I am writing you from the silence of a home which, perhaps this very day, for the good of my country, is to be left abandoned. The least I can do, in gratitude for this virtue, inasmuch as in this way I do not shirk but come to grips with duty, is to face death, whether it awaits us on land or sea, in the company of one who, as the result of my efforts, and out of respect for his own, and the passion of the common soul of our lands, leaves his loving and happy home to set foot on our enemy-infested country, with a handful of brave men. I was dying of shame—aside from the conviction that my presence in Cuba at this moment is at least as useful as it could be abroad—at the thought that in the face of such a hazardous undertaking I might become convinced that it was my duty to let him go alone, and that a country might allow itself to be served, without scorn and indifference, by one who preached the need of dying without beginning by risking his own life. Wherever my first duty lies, in Cuba or outside Cuba, there I will be. It may be possible or necessary, as seems the case up to this moment, to do both. Perhaps I can contribute to the basic need of giving our reviving war a character that will carry within it the embryo, without superfluous details, of those principles indispensable to the good name of the Revolution and the security of the Republic. The difficulty of our wars of independence, and the reason for their slow and imperfect accomplishment, has resided more than in the lack of mutual esteem on the part of their initiators and the rivalry inherent in human nature, in their failure to assume a form that should at once encompass

the spirit of redemption and dignity, which, added to
the active sum of motives of a less pure nature, launch
and maintain the war, and the habits and the human
element of the war. The other difficulty which our nations, staid and bookish, have not yet overcome, is that
of viable forms of government, after the emancipation,
which, without leaving the intellectually superior element of the country discontent, shall take into account
—and make possible their natural and growing development—the more numerous and uncultured members
of society whom a government imposed upon them, however good and generous, would lead to anarchy or
tyranny. I called up the war; my responsibility begins
rather than ends with it. For me, country will never
be triumph, but agony and duty. Blood is now at the
boiling point. Now the sacrifice must be given respect,
and a humane and forbearing meaning; the war must
be made feasible and invincible. If I am ordered, though
my soul dies, to remove myself far from those who die
as I would know how to die, I will have the courage for
that, too. The person who thinks of himself does not
love his country; and the ills of nations reside, however subtly they may at times be disguised, in the
barriers or pressures of haste their representatives put
in the way of the natural course of events. From me
you may expect my complete and unvarying submission. I shall arouse the world. But my one desire would
be to stand beside the last tree, the last fighter, and die
in silence. For me, my hour has come. But I can still
serve this unique heart of our republics. The free
Antilles will preserve the independence of our America,
and the dubious and tarnished honor of the English

America, and perhaps may hasten and decide the balance of the world. You see what we are doing, you with your youthful gray hairs—and I, dragging myself along, my heart broken.

What need is there for me to speak to you of Santo Domingo? In what does it differ from Cuba? You are not a Cuban, and where is there a better Cuban than you? And is not Gomez a Cuban? And I, what am I, and who shall assign me a soil? Was not mine the soul, and the pride which enveloped me and throbbed about me, in your voice that unforgettable and virile night at the *Sociedad de Amigos*? All this is that, and part of that. I obey, and would even say that I accept as a superior privilege, and an American law, the happy need to set out, under the protection of Santo Domingo, for the war of liberation of Cuba. Let us do on the surface of the sea, with blood and love, what the fire of the Andean range does in the depths of the sea.

I tear myself away from you, and leave you a warm embrace, and a prayer that my name, whose only worth is that it is today at the service of my country, will be remembered for whatever justice and charity Cuba may receive. Whoever loves her, I fervently acclaim as my brother. I have no other brothers than those who love her.

Farewell, and farewell to my noble and indulgent friends. I owe you the pleasure of your loftiness and purity in this harsh and sordid human universe. Raise your voice high: if I fall, it will be for the independence of your country, too.

Your

José Martí

FROM CABO HAITIANO

TO DOS RIOS

Excerpts from a Diary

1895

April 10. We leave the Cape. At dawn in Inagua. Hoist sail.

    11. Set out at eleven. Skirt (4) Maisi, and see beacon. I on the bridge. Dark by seven-thirty. Activity on board. Captain moved. They lower the boat. Raining hard as we push off. Set course wrong. Conflicting and confused opinion in boat. Another downpour. Rudder lost. We get on course. I take forward oar. Salas rows steadily. Paquito Borrero and the General help in the stern. We strap on our revolvers. Steer toward clearing. Moon comes up red behind a cloud. We land on a rock beach, La Playita [at foot of Cajobabo]. I last to leave boat, bailing out. Jump ashore. Great joy. We overturn the boat, and the jug of water. We drink Malaga. Uphill, through rocks, thorns, mud. We hear a noise, and make ready, near a fence. Skirting, we reach a house. We sleep nearby on the ground.

    12. At 3 we decide to call out. Blas, Gonzalo

and Niña. José Gabriel, wary, goes to call Silvestre. Silvestre ready. Uphill, heavy pack, we set out to look for Mesón, Tacre [Zaguere]. We wait in the woods from 9 till 12. I persuade Silvestre to take us to Imía. We follow the bed of the Tacre. The General decides to send a note to Fernando Leyva, and Silvestre goes. We get into the cave, an old camp, under a crag to the right of the river. We sleep—dry leaves—Marcos shakes down; Silvestre brings me leaves.

13. Abraham Leyva comes, with Silvestre carrying pork meat, sugar cane, sweet potatoes, chicken sent by Niña. Fernando had gone to look for a guide. Abraham, rosary around his neck. Alarm, and we get ready, as Abraham comes striding up. Silvestre follows with his load, 11 o'clock. In the morning we moved alongside the river risen in the night, and the rattling of the stones was like shots. A guide is coming. We eat lunch. Silvestre leaves. José comes at one with his mare. We'll go on with him. Whistles and neighs; we jump up, rifles at the ready, without Abraham. And Blas. From a talk with Blas, Ruenes learned that we had arrived, and sent to find out, to join us. We decide to go to meet Ruenes at Sao del Nejesial. We'll leave in the morning. I gather dry leaves for my bed. We roast sweet potatoes.

14. Set out at 5. Cross the river waist-deep, and recross it—tall *bayas* along the bank. Then, shoes on again, heavy pack, up the steep slope, covered with delicate-leaved *yaya,* Cuban *majagua,* and *cupey,* with starry cone. We see the first *jutía,* curled in a *lechero.* Marcos takes off his shoes, and climbs the tree. He cuts its throat with one machete blow: "It's stunned.

It's dead." We eat wild oranges that José gathers, twisting them off with a stick. "How sweet." Up the slope. Climbing hills makes men brothers. Over the hills we reach Sao del Nejesial: a pretty spot, a clearing in the wood of old palms, mango trees, and oranges. José leaves. Marcos comes with his neckerchief full of coconuts. They put me in with Guerra, and Paquito for guard. I rest in camp. Cesar mends my belt. The first thing was to gather palm fronds, spread them on the ground. Gómez with his machete cuts and brings enough for him and for me. Guerra builds his cabin: four forked sticks, covered on the sides with branches and palm fronds over the top. All of them, some scrape coconuts, Marcos, helped by the General, skins the *jutía*. They wash it in wild orange, and salt it. The pork is doused with orange juice, and the skin of the *jutía*, on the improvised spit over the wood fire. Suddenly men: "Ah, brothers." I leap to readiness. The guerrilla of Ruenes: Felix Ruenes, Galano, Rubio, the ten of them. Gleaming eyes.

Embraces. All carrying rifle, machete, revolver. They came up the big hill. The sick revive. We load up. They wrap the *jutía* in palm fronds. They want to carry our packs for us. I follow with my rifle and my hundred bullets, down hill, down the Tibisial. A guard. Another. We reach the cabin of Tavera, where the guerrilla is camped. In line they wait for us. No two dressed alike, some in undershirt, some in shirt and pants, others, in jacket and unbleached drawers; peaked palm fibre caps; Negroes, mulattoes, two Spaniards— Galano, white.

Ruenes introduces us. The General draws himself

up to speak. I speak. Review, gaiety, kitchen, groups. In the new outpost we talk again. Night falls, wax candles; Lima cooks the *jutía* and roasts plantains, arguing about guards, the General swings my hammock under the entrance to the palm frond cabin of Tavera. We sleep, wrapped in our rubber capes. Ah, before going to sleep José comes, with a candle in his hand and two baskets, one full of fresh meat, the other of honey. And we fall greedily on the honey. Delicious honey, in the comb. And all day long, what light, what air, how full the breast, how light the weary body! I look out of the ranch and see, high on the hill behind, a dove and a star.

16. Each with his offering, sweet potatoes, sausage, *licor de rosa,* plantain broth. At noon, up-hill march, river to thigh, a beautiful and open wood of *pomarrosas,* orange trees, *caimitos.* Through shady openings and mango groves without fruit we reach a palm thicket, with two beautiful mountains in the background. There is the camp. An Indian woman . . . with glowing eyes, surrounded by 7 children, in a ragged black dress, with kerchief tied over her braids, cleans coffee beans. People swing hammocks, cut cane, gather wood for fire, bring cane to the mill to grind syrup for coffee. Earlier, at the first stop, in the house of the mother and her big frightened daughter, the General gave me honey to drink, to show me how it quenches thirst. The correspondence for N.Y. is written, and all that of Baracoa.

17. Morning in camp. A beef was slaughtered yesterday, and by sun-up the cauldrons are bubbling. Domitila, busy and good-natured, with her bright ban-

danna, goes off up the hill and brings a supply of tomatoes, rosemary and oregano. One brings me a sack of *malanga*. Another, a hot bowl of cane syrup with herbs. A sheaf of cane is ground. At the back of the house, the cleared slope with patches of coconut and plantain, cotton and wild tobacco; beyond, along the river, the pasture lots; and in the clearings, oranges, on the round, rolling hills; and the infinite blue overhead with those white clouds . . . behind the night. I put Cicero's *Life* in my pocket where I carry 50 bullets. Write letters.

18. We set out at 9.30. Up the steep slopes we cross the Jojo river six times. We ascend the rugged slope of Pavano, with El Panalito towering above. On the heights there hung from bush to bush, like a thick curtain, a delicate vine with small, lanceolate leaf. Along the slopes, wild coffee. A wood of *pomarrosas*. Around, the valley and beyond the blue mountains and the crest of clouds. On the road to Angel Castro's place —we decide to sleep on the slope. We clear the brush with machete. From trunk to trunk we stretch the hammocks. The beautiful night makes sleep impossible. The cricket chirps, the lizard shrills, and its chorus responds. Even through the darkness one can see that the wood is of *cupey* and *paguá*, low, thorny palm; the fireflies circle slowly about; above the twittering nests, I hear the music of the forest, blended and soft, like delicate violins; the music rises and falls, comes together and breaks off, spreads wing and settles, hovers and soars, always subtle and minimum—a myriad of fluid sound. What wings brush the leaves? What tiny violin, and sections of violins, draws notes and soul

from the leaves? What dance of souls of leaves? We forget about dinner; we eat sausage and chocolate and a slice of roast *chope.* Our clothes dry by the fire.

24. Through the ravine, past Acosta mountain, by the stream of worn pebbles, with its pools of clear water to which the *sinsonte* comes to drink, and its bed of dry leaves, we climb, from sun-up to sun-down, the weary road. One feels danger. Ever since Palenque they have been close on our trail.

25. Day of combat. Straight through the woods we are drawing close, already in the claws of Guantanamo, hostile in the first war, as far as Arroyo Hondo. We lost our way. The thorns lacerated us. The lianas choked and slashed us. We cross a wood of green *jigüeras.* At eleven, heavy gunfire. Steady fire, that re-echoes, answered by concealed and sharp counter-fire. The combat is as though at our very feet; three bullets reach us, hitting the tree trunks. "How beautiful is shooting at a distance," says the pleasant lad from San Antonio, a child. "More beautiful close by," says the old man. Following our route we ascend along a brook. Heavy firing. Magdaleon, sitting up against a tree trunk, carves designs on the *jigüera* he picked. We make lunch on raw eggs, a swallow of honey and chocolate. In a little while information begins to come in from the village. They have seen one dead, and twenty-five wounded. Maceo comes to look for us, and waits nearby; we hurry to Maceo, joyfully. I said in a letter to Carmita: "On the very battle route, the victorious Cubans were waiting for us; they leap from their horses, horses they have taken from the Civil Guard; they embrace and cheer us; they mount us on their

horses, and fasten spurs on us." Why am I not horrified at the pool of blood I saw on the road, or the half-dried blood of a head that is already buried, with the despatch case of one of our riders for a pillow? With the afternoon sun we began our victory march on our way back to camp.

At 12 midnight they had set out, through rivers, canebrakes and thickets, to rescue us; they had just arrived nearby, when the Spaniards fell on them; without food they fought for 2 hours, and appeased their victory hunger with hardtack; then they set out on an 8 league march, first in the bright, clear afternoon, then under arches of thorns in the dark night. The long column marched single file. We see them, mounted and on foot, on the rolling hills. They enter the cane field, and each soldier comes out of it carrying a cane. (We cross the wide railroad track, and hear the evening whistle of the sugar mills; finally we see the plain, the electric lights.) "Column halt, there's a wounded man behind." A man comes up, dragging his wounded leg, and Gómez mounts him behind him on his horse. Another wounded, refuses: "No, friend, I am not dead," and with the bullet in his shoulder keeps on marching. Poor, tired feet! They sit beside the road, rifle at hand, and smile at us, glorious. An occasional groan is heard, but more laughs, and the talk is happy. "Make way," and up rides mighty Cartagena, Lieutenant Colonel, who won his bars in the big war, with a lighted torch of pine, thrust like a lance in his leather stirrup. And more torches at intervals . . . fire the dry trees, which snap and crackle, and thrust heavenward their lance of flame and a pinnacle of smoke. The river sings to us. We

wait for the stragglers. The last drink, and to sleep.
Hammocks, cooking pots, the camp sleeps; leaning
against a tall tree, I will soon go to sleep, alongside
machete and revolver, with my rain cape for a pillow.
At the moment I am looking in my knapsack for med-
icine for the wounded. Affectionate the stars, at 3 in
the morning. At 5, wide awake, Colt strapped on, machete at belt, spur on sandal, and to horse!

26. Form ranks at sun-up. Sleepily, to horse.
Men limping, not yet rested. We hardly ate last night.
We fall out, about ten, and rest along both sides of the
road. From a poor cabin they send "General Matias"
a present of a chicken and honey. In the afternoon
and evening I write to New York, to Antonio Maceo
who is close by and does not know of our coming; and
the letter to Manuel Fuentes of *The World,* which I
finished in pencil at dawn. At times yesterday I looked
over the calm and happy camp; the bugle calls; they
bring bunches of bananas on their shoulder; the cattle
they have seized low, and they slaughter them; Vic-
toriano Garzón, the wise Negro, with moustache and
chin whiskers, and burning eyes, tells me, humble and
fervent, from his hammock, about his successful attack on Ramón de las Yaguas; his talk is confused and
intense, his soul kindly, and his authority natural; he
truly pampers his white aides, Mariano Sánchez and
Rafael Portuondo; and if they err in a point of discipline, he rights the mistake. Lean of flesh, gentle of
smile, blue shirt and black pants, he looks after his soldiers, man by man. José Maceo, towering, walks his
tall body along; his hands are still scarred from the
scratches of the pines and underbrush, when the ex-

pedition pursued from Costa Rica split up, and Flor was killed, and Antonio carried two with him, and José was finally left alone, fallen under his load, dying of cold among the damp pines, his feet swollen and cut; and he came through, and has conquered.

28. Arise to work. Fall in at 9, and Gómez, forthright and concise, harangues. I talk, to the sun. And of the work. That this strength may be joined to the united spirit to organize, to order the vigorous and magnanimous war; to open communications with the North, and a service of ammunition; to stifle any attempt to upset the war with promises. I write the circular to the leaders to punish with the penalty for treason any such attempt; the circular to the landowners; the note of Gómez to the farmers; letters to possible friends; letters to get the mail and ammunition service under way; letters for the appointment with Brooks; a note to the English government, via the consul in Guantanamo, including José Maceo's report on the accidental death from a stray shot of a sailor aboard the sloop *Honor* which was carrying the expedition from Fortune Island.

2. On toward Jaragüeta. In the sugar plantations. Through the broad, deserted cane fields of Sabanilla. Rafael Portuondo goes to the house to fetch the 5 head of cattle; they are brought in yoked together; poor people, in the rain. We reach Leonor, and giving up the idea of eating so late, had gone to our hammocks with bread and cheese when the correspondent of *The Herald*, George Eugene Bryson, arrives with Zefi's cavalry. Work with him until 3 in the morning.

5. Maceo had told us to join him in Bocucy,

which we will not be able to reach by 12, the hour he
had set. A messenger left last night to tell him to wait
for us in his camp. We set out, the whole force. Suddenly, a group of horsemen. Maceo, on a bright bay,
in a suit of gray drill, silver trimmed saddle, finely
made and star-studded. He had come to look for us,
because his men were on march to the nearby sugar
plantation; Maspón leaves for Mejorana to tell them to
prepare lunch for a hundred. The plantation receives
us like a festival; the delight and admiration of servants and workers is evident; the owner, a red-faced
old man, with side-burns, panama hat, and small feet,
brings out vermouth, cigars, rum, *malvasia.* "Kill three,
five, ten, fourteen chickens." A woman in open-necked
dress and house slippers comes to offer us green brandy
with herbs in it. Another brings pure rum. Crowds of
people come and go. Castro Palomino, Maceo's aide,
lively and talkative, keeps on the move. Maceo and G.
talk in a low voice, near me; in a little while they call
me over to the entrance of the house: Maceo has a
different idea about the government: a committee of
generals commanding forces, as its representatives,
and a General Secretariat; an organized country, that
is to say, with all its branches to create and back the
Army, as the Secretariat of the Army. We go into a
room to talk. I can't get the straight of what Maceo
is driving at: "But are you staying with me or going
with Gómez?" And he talks to me, interrupting my
words, as though I were the visible symbol of the legalistic government, and its representative. I see that
he is offended—"I like you less," he says, "than I did"
—because of being put under Flor in directing the

expedition and disbursing funds. He insists on deposing me before the representatives meeting to elect a government. He doesn't want each head of operations to send his own representative in proportion to his strength; he will send four for Oriente: "In fifteen days they will be with you, and they will be men Dr. Martí won't be able to wrap around his finger." At the lavish, leisurely meal of chicken and roast pig the matter comes up again; it wounds and revolts me. I realize that I must refute the charge being made against me, of defender of the city's hostile restrictions on the military. I sharply stand up for: a free Army—and the nation, as nation represented with full dignity. I do not conceal my annoyance at this indiscreet and awkward conversation there at table, all because of Maceo's haste to set out. Night is falling over Cuba, and he has to travel six hours. His troops are nearby, but he does not take us to see them; the brigades raised in Oriente—Rabí, de Jiguaní, Busto, Cuba, those of José which we brought. Quick leave-taking, on horseback. "You're going that way," and we go on, with a disgruntled escort, night falling, without orderlies, who had remained with José, not sure of our way, to a shed on the road, where we do not unsaddle. They go for the orderlies; we keep on to another muddy cabin, outside the camp, open to attack. G. sends to José's camp for meat; the orderlies bring it. And thus, as though rejected, and with sad thoughts, we sleep.

7. We leave Jagua, and its old, loyal fighters for freedom, for El Mijial. On the way, Prudencio Bravo, in charge of the wounded, comes out to tell us good-

bye. We saw Nicolás Cedeño's daughter, who talks contentedly, and is going with her 5 children to her farm in Holguin. On the road to Barajague—"there was a lot of fighting here," "all this was in our hands"—we talk about the old war. There along the thickly wooded hillsides, or on the heights and sloping curves of the road, they harried the columns, until finally they left; the road leads to Palma and Holguin. Zefi says that he brought Martínez Campos that way to his first meeting with Maceo. "When it was over the man was as red as a tomato, and so mad he dashed his hat to the ground, and went off to wait for me half a league away." We are coming close to Baraguá. We leave the road for the savannah of Pinalito which drops sharply to Piedras Brook, and beyond it, to the slope of La Risueña, with its red rocky soil, domed like an egg, and in the background pleasant summits of odd shape: a little grove, one height the shape of a saddle, a terrace of hills. We come straight into the Vio savannah, a green expanse surrounded by woods, with palms, and in the open spaces an occasional *cayo*, or a single thorn tree, which makes good firewood. The dark paths go through the green grass, sprinkled here and there with purple or white flowers. To the right, on the crest of the dense sierra, pines. It is raining hard . . . To the sound of bugles we reach the ranch, and the troop of Quintín Banderas drawn up in the rain. Very black, with moustache and chin whiskers, boots, cape and panama hat, Narciso Moncada, the brother of Guillermo, embraces us. Quintín in his sixties, his head sunk between his shoulders, heavy-set, eyes kept lowered and laconic of word, receives us at the door of the cabin; he is burning up with fever, and wraps himself in his hammock, his eye, small and yellowish, seems to peer from the depths, and one must bend over it to see; at the head of his hammock is a drum. Deodato Carvajal is his aide, slender of frame, mind on promotion, capable and neat; his words, seeking elegance, become confused, but there is method and authority in him, and vigilance for his own right and that of others; he tells me Moncada received my letters through him. Narciso Moncada, verbose and powerfully built, full of kindness and ceremony: "As for liquor, I never touch it." His brother is buried—"deeper than a man's height, with plans drawn up by an engineer, and only a few of us know the spot, and if I die, another knows it, and if he dies, another, and the grave will always be safe." And our mother, whom they have treated as though she were the mother of the country? "Dominga Moncada has been in Morro Fortress three times, and all because that General who died sent for her to tell her she had to go to make her sons see reason, and she said to him: 'Look, General, if I saw my sons coming by one road, and I saw you coming by another, I'd call out to them: "Run, sons, this is the Spanish general."'" We enter the cabin on horseback because it is too muddy outside for us to dismount, and there is a stench from the mud and the air because of the many cattle that have died nearby. The low cabin is slung with hammocks. In a corner, on a stove, kettles bubble. They bring us coffee, ginger water, and an infusion of *guanabana* leaves.

9. Good-bye to Banderas, Moncada, Carvajal, to the cabins where people crowd to the door, waving

their caps, "God be with you, brothers." We pass
the grave, without a single man turning his eyes that
way. And in a little while, along the muddy road, we
come out to the savannah, and the mango trees in the
background. This is Baraguá, these the mangoes, those
two trunks with a single top where Martínez Campos
talked with Maceo. For guide we have a *mayaricero*
who was there at the time: "Martínez Campos went
to embrace him, and Maceo stopped him with his arm,
like this. It was then that he dashed his hat to the
ground. And when he told him that García had already
entered, you should have seen the man when Antonio
said to him: 'You want me to introduce you to García?'
García was there, on that hill; the whole hill was nothing but Cubans. And on the other side there was another force, in case they were planning a surprise."
From the plains of the protest, we come out along the
upper edge, by the abandoned cabin, where an arm of
the river can be seen, dry now, with the bed grown
up to grass, and fallen trees covered with vines with
blue and yellow flowers, and after a bend, the sharp
descent. "Ah, Cauto," says Gómez, "such a long time
without seeing you." The high, fertile ravines, gashed
in spots, hang over the river-bed, still narrow, where
the first rains run muddy and turbulent.

The breast swells with fond reverence and overpowering affection at the sight of the vast landscape
of the loved river. We cross it, near a *ceiba* tree, and
after greeting a patriot family, overjoyed to see us,
we enter the open wood, with sweet sun, rain-washed
leaves. As over a carpet go our horses, so thick is the
grass. All is garland and leaf, and through the open-

ings, to the right, the green of the cleared fields is visible on the other bank, sheltered and compact. I see there the *ateje*, with its high, thick top, with plants of the air and *curujeyes;* the *caguairan,* "the hardest wood of Cuba," the thick *jucaro,* the *almacigo,* with its silken bark, the *jagua,* with its broad leaf, the gravid *güira,* the hard *jigue,* with its black heart for walking canes, and bark for tanning, the *jubaban,* with light foliage, whose leaves, layer on layer, "turn tobacco to satin," the mahogany with its rough bark, the *quebracho* with striped trunk, and the *yamagua,* which stanches bleeding . . . Here as everywhere I am touched by the affection with which we are received, and the unity of soul which will not be allowed to coalesce, and which will not be recognized, and which will be overridden, harming, at least with the harm of delay, the Revolution in the impulse of its first year. The spirit I sowed, is that which has borne fruit, and that of the Island, and with it, and guiding ourselves by it, we will soon triumph, and with a better victory and for a better peace. I foresee that, for a time at least, the force of the Revolution will be divorced from the spirit, deprived of the charm and pleasure and the power of victory of this natural association, it will be robbed of the benefit of this conjunction between the activity of these forces of revolution and the spirit which informs them. One detail: All the troops since my entry in the camp have called me President, in spite of my public rebuff, and at each camp I come to the respect surges up, and a certain warm enthusiasm of general affection, and evidence of the pleasure of the people in my presence and simplicity. And when

one approached me today, "President," and I smiled:
"Don't call Martí President; call him General; he's
here as a General; don't you call him President."
"Who's going to restrain the people's impulse, General?" Miró asked him; "this comes from the heart
of all." "Never mind, he's not President yet; he's the
Delegate." I said nothing, but I could see the embarrassment and chagrin of all, and in some a kind of resentment.

10. From Altagracia to La Travesia. There as
we arrive I suddenly see the Cauto once more, now full,
its wide bed in the hollow of the ravines on either side.
And there came to my mind, at the sight of such beauty,
the thought of man's low, fierce passions. As we approached, Pablo was roping a heifer, black, with budding horns, and holding her against a tree, shortening
the rope with turns around the trunk. The horses,
heads high, snorted; their eyes gleamed. Captain
Pacheco, slight of body, firm and guarded of word,
underlaid with dignity and ability, arrives: "I have
not come to seek anything but to serve the country,"
but he talks incessantly, and saying only half, one of
those who do and do not, and of those who doing less
generally get more than the one who does more, "but
he has come only to serve the country." "There are my
leggings," his bare calves; his pants to the knee, boots
of cowhide, a yellow and purple *yarey*. Bellito arrives,
Colonel Bellito of Jiguaní, who had remained there
because he was sick. He impresses me as loyal, clear
eyed for attack, brave in deed and word. He likes to
talk his confused jargon from which, in words he makes
up, one must unravel his thought. "The Revolution died

because of that infamous act of rejecting its leader."
"This fills the people with sorrow." "From that time
the Revolution began to lose ground." "They were the
ones who set us the example—they, the members of
the Chamber"—when Gómez bitterly berates the up-
risings of García and his cohort of advisers: Belisario
Peralta, the Venezuelan Barreto, Bravo y Senties, Fon-
seca, Limbano Sánchez and later Collado. Bello talks
striding up and down, like a man on the watch for the
enemy, or who spies him, or falls upon him, or hurls
himself upon him. "No, sir, nobody should talk to us
likė that, for the man hasn't been born from whom
I will take it." "I have suffered as much for my country as the best general." He stands up to Gómez, and
upbraids him because the officers allowed cattle bearing
a pass made out to Rabí to be sent to Jiguaní. "Whoever they are; and besides this is the order of the
Chief, and we have to obey his orders." "I know this
is wrong, and that no cattle should be allowed through,
but the subordinate has to obey his superior." And
when Gómez says: "They've certainly got you in a
state over this matter of the president. Martí will not
be president as long as I am alive," and goes on, "because I don't know what it is that happens to presidents, but once they are in power, they're no good,
except Juárez, up to a point, and Washington." Handsome, excited, he gets up, takes two or three turns,
and the machete jangles at his side. "That depends on
the will of the people," he mutters, his elbows on the
table where I was sitting with Pacheco, "because we
went into the Revolution to be men, and not for anyone
to offend us in our dignity as men." Between showers,

pots of coffee, and talk about Holguin and Jiguaní, night comes.

15. Night rain, mud, bath in the Contramaestre; the caress of running water, the silk of the water. In the afternoon, a messenger: Masó is in Sabana, looking for us. They bring a supply wagon captured in La Ratonera. They empty it at the door; Bellito divides it up; there's cloth, which Bellito measures out by arm-lengths, so much for the escort, so much for Pacheco, the captain of the convoy, and Bellito's men, so much for the General Staff; candles, a length of goods for Rosalio's wife, onions, garlic, and potatoes and olives for Valentín.

17. Gómez sets out with forty horsemen to harry the supply train of Bayamo. I remain writing with the help of Garriga and Feria, who copy the *General Instructions* for commanders and officers, with twelve men, under Lieutenant Chacón, with three pickets at the three roads; and beside me, Graciano Pérez. Rosalio, on his pony, with mud to the knees, affectionately brings me lunch in his knapsack. "I'd give my life for you." From Santiago, which they recently left, come the brothers Chacón, one of whom captured the string of horses day before yesterday, and his brother, fair, pedantic, comical, and José Cabrera, the shoemaker of Jiguaní, stuttering and frank, and Duane, black, young, and as though . . . in shirt, pants and a wide belt and . . . Avalos, timid, and Rafael Vázques, and Desiderio Soler, 16 years old, whom Chacón treats like a son. There is another son here, Ezequiel Morales, 18 years old, whose father was killed in the wars. And those who come tell me

about Rosa Moreno, the country widow, who sent her only son Melesio, of 16, to Rabí: "Your father died there; I can't go any more; you go." They roast plantains, and pound dried beef soft with a stone in the mortar for the recent arrivals. The flood waters of the Contramaestre are very roiled, and Valentín brings me a pitcher of boiled water, sweetened with *higo* leaves.

Two days after the above final entry, José Marti was killed in a cavalry skirmish near Dos Rios on the morning of May 19, 1895.